THREE JOURNEYS

BYRON ROGERS

Three Journeys

Gomer

Published in 2011 by
Gomer Press, Llandysul, Ceredigion, SA44 4JL

ISBN 978 1 84851 201 6

A CIP record for this title is available from the British Library.
© Copyright text: Byron Rogers, 2011

Byron Rogers asserts his moral right under the
Copyright, Designs and Patents Act, 1988
to be identified as author of this work.

This book is published with the financial support of the
Welsh Books Council.

Printed and bound in Wales at
Gomer Press, Llandysul, Ceredigion

This book is dedicated to the Two Great Sawyers of Carmarthen.

The first, described only as 'a wretch' by William Spurrell in his history of the town, in 1804, on the night after the hanging of an old man for stealing a mare, sawed down the gibbet which had stood on a hill grimly overlooking Carmarthen, and made a bedstead out of it.

The second is someone I knew, who, again by night, sawed down its most famous landmark, the Old Oak, in protest at what council planners and 'developers' had done to our town.

ACKNOWLEDGEMENTS

Some of these essays appear for the first time. Some, in earlier versions, apperared in *The Spectator, SAGA Magazine, The Sunday Telegraph* and its colour magazine, or were broadcast by the BBC; these I have taken the fatal opportunity to rewrite. I am also grateful to Academi for awarding me the bursary that allowed me to complete *Three Journeys*.

CONTENTS

page

Inroduction   xi

Prologue   xiii

Part One: *Y Fro*

1	First Journey	3
2	*These Were my People*	19
3	The Minister	25
4	The Last Squires	27
5	The Hangman	31
6	The Liars	41
7	The Devil Walks	43
8	The Wizard	46
9	*And this is what my people got up to*	54
10	The Lane	61

Part Two: The Town

11	Second Journey	69
12	A guided tour of a small Welsh town	80
13	Portrait Gallery (1)	84
14	J.F. Jones, Museum Curator (and Dynamiter)	88
15	The True Queen of England	98
16	The Last Cavalry Charge	106
17	A day out. Aberystwyth	113
18	Portrait Gallery (2)	120
19	Crime in Carmarthen	127

CONTENTS (*continued*)

page

Part Three: Exile and the Past

20	Third Journey	133
21	Griffs	144
22	Welsh in Exile	153
23	A Historical Gazeteer	169
24	Close Encounters of the Third Kind	187
25	Holiday Home.	198
26	Some day my Prince will come	204

Epilogue   210

INTRODUCTION

The structure of this book turns on three journeys, which together are my own experience of growing up in, and leaving, Wales. The first is into the old unchanged Welsh-speaking countryside of which my family, and, briefly, myself were part. It is based on the stories I was told, or which I later found out for myself, so you will meet the characters, the way of life, and the superstitions of a society that had changed little, and is now going or has gone. Like the rest of the book, it is thus part reminiscence, part gazeteer, part portrait gallery.

The second journey is into the old English-speaking garrison town to which we moved when I was a boy, where I was brought up, and to which I will always return. Such towns in Wales have always fascinated me, partly because of their colonial, that is to say English, origins, but chiefly because these, improbably, became traditions their inhabitants preserved. Here you will meet those I myself met, whose sayings and doings I have recorded, because they were, and are, the wittiest, and the strangest, people I have ever known. You may find some of this so hard to believe I feel obliged to give you the sort of guarantee old Gulliver gave his readers: 'I could perhaps like others have astonished thee with strange improbable Tales ; but I rather chose to relate plain Matter of Fact in the simplest Manner and Style ; because my principal Design was to inform, and not to amuse thee.'

The third journey is into exile, itself part of the Welsh experience, and into that increasing, even obsessive, interest in the past which exile prompts, a past which is only a fingernail away.

A note to English readers. To some of you, in particular that literary editor of the *Sunday Telegraph* who once told me, 'Who do you think's interested in Wales?', we are a source of puzzlement and irritation, our language and our traditions, about which you know nothing, an enormous whimsy, much like the toys of childhood which should have been put away long ago. So think of this as a letter from your first, and last, colony. This was what in your time it was like to be part of another country.

PROLOGUE

Edinburgh, 2007

'R'wy'n falch iawn i fod yma heno, yn yr hen ddinas Gymreig.' I am very pleased to be here tonight in this old Welsh city. And to be speaking in the language that was once spoken here. But then you know all this, don't you?

You know that Edinburgh was the Welsh city of Caer Eidyn. Eidyn's fort. Eidyn's borough. You know that the oldest surviving poem in these islands was composed here, probably on Castle Rock, around the year 600. *Hwn yw y Gododdin, Aneirin a'i cant.* 'This is the Gododdin. Aneirin sang it.' You call this a Scottish poem, you even include it in your anthologies, but it was composed in the Welsh language. For here lived the Men of the North, *Gwŷr y Gogledd.* Terrifying as the prospect may seem to some of you, we, the Welsh, are the nearest thing the Scottish Lowlands have to a native population. We are your past.

In the seventh century a man could have walked from Edinburgh to Cornwall, and spoken nothing but Welsh the whole way. Now I drive North through ruins. Past *Elmet,* the kingdom of Leeds. Past *Rheged*, the kingdom of Carlisle. Through *Ystrad Clud,* the valley of the Clud, which you call Strathclyde, an independent Welsh kingdom that lasted for 600 years, with its centre at *Glasgau,* the Blue Hollow you call Glasgow. Six hundred years. And finally the kingdom of the Votadini, the *Gododdin*, its centre here in Edinburgh.

I have come to the capital of *Mynyddog Mwynfawr* who ruled from Castle Rock, and sent his golden youth south, a cavalry army in their red plumes and chain mail, to attack the English at Catterick. *Catraeth. Gwŷr a aeth Gatraeth.* Men went to Catterick.

For this they trained rigorously for a year. On mead. They were on the booze for a whole year, and the fact that they actually managed to find Catterick is one of the triumphs of the human spirit. It was also the greatest military disaster in a history that has never been short of great military disasters. Only one man, Aneirin, survived to come home, to sing his 1250 line epic of linked elegies.

What did we leave you? Not much. We never had much. You could always tell which castles the Welsh built, an archaeologist told me: you never found anything in them. But we left our place names to puzzle you. Melrose. *Moelrhos,* the bare headland. Lanark. *Llanerch,* the clearing. Ecclefechan. *Eglwys Fechan,* the little church. Peebles. *Pebyll,* the encampment. Mysterious little fossils on road signs, from a time before time. Your time.

So it is good to be asked back to the lost lands, and in the old way. *Er aur a meirch mawr, a medd feddwaint.* 'For gold and great stallions, and the prospect of getting drunk.' Which, more or less, is why I too have come, though the great stallion may well become a Ford Mondeo, 40,000 miles, one careful lady owner.

Like Aneirin, I have come home.

Acceptance speech for the
James Tait Black Memorial Prize

part one

Y FRO

Take smoke-dried goats' flesh, desiccate completely, and reduce to as fine a powder as you can. Lay some of this on live coals in a fireproof utensil and put in a commode. Sit on top.

A treatment recommended by the Physicians of Myddfai,
the famous country doctors, for haemorrhoids.

1   THE FIRST JOURNEY

i

Birdsong. And footsteps. Then, suddenly, the sound of a car braking.
A man's voice: 'You lost?'

Narrator: A car has stopped, its driver clearly intrigued, for he
has seen something he may not have seen before, a man at the
beginning of the 21st century *walking* in a small lane in West
Wales. Once he would have met all his neighbours in that
lane, where now nobody walks. And there is something else,
something even more startling. The voice from the car is an
English voice.

'I said, are you lost?'

'No.'

But the man is trying to be helpful, so the walker adds, almost
apologetically,

'I have been here before.'

In a film the violins would cut in at that moment, bringing
the first faint stirrings of menace. For he has been here before,
sometimes it is as though he has never been away. When he can't
sleep he walks that lane, he knows every bend, every gate in it,
and the lane is full of people. Just 50 yards away is the house
where his father was born, 300 yards away the house where he
was born. When she died, his mother's funeral cortege in less
than three minutes passed houses where she herself was born,
got married and gave birth.

This is his *bro*. His *heimat*. There is no equivalent in the
English language for something that inspires this intense
feeling, this fascination.

(*Quietly*)

'I am from here.'

The birdsong starts up again, and this time swells.

Narrator: It is such a lovely little lane. Wild flowers are growing on
its banks. Primroses, celandine, violets, even some wood sorrel,
small, delicate, pale mauve flowers. We called it *Yr Heol Fach*.
   I left it 60 years ago.

ii

Sound of traffic, a lot of traffic, all of it travelling at high speed.

Narrator: Stand with me here for a moment. We have moved, what
is it, a mile and a half, and we are in the graveyard of the chapel
called Cana, on the old A40 between the town of Carmarthen
and Bancyfelin village, a lost eddy of tarmac now. For there is a
new road, a dual carriageway which sweeps by.

The sound of traffic is overwhelming.

   The hamlet in which the chapel stands is called Pass-by, and the
world does as it is told. Nobody stops in Pass-by.

   But see these graves.

The traffic sound stops abruptly, as if switched off.

   I know those who lie here, the farmers (under pillars of alabaster
which look like huge chess pawns), the farm labourers under
black polished granite, the gilt letters fading: the lady called
Alsace, born amid the headlines of the First World War; the
lorry-driver dying in poverty whose employers gave him a small
inscribed vase, and to whose death bed, aged four, I was taken. I
even know the great flying ace, buried across the road, his grave
bristling with medals.

   And here are those I know best of all.

Brenda: My name is Brenda, first cousin to Byron, and the only
one of the family to remember our grandparents in
anything other than their extreme old age. Philip Rogers,
smallholder and farm servant, as his father was before
him, and his father before that. Landless men working
the land. When he died in 1958, aged 94, our grandfather
had not owned a square yard of property.

But this was a cultivated man, a poet in the Welsh language. He could read English, but was never heard to talk in it: he had no need to, in this community.

Byron: What was his job?

Brenda: Well, he would take stallions around in the mating season and he would walk beside the big stallion and sometimes rode a little pony.

Byron laughs.

Brenda: I know, the imagination goes mad, doesn't it?

Byron: Basically, he was a farm servant?

Brenda: Not in the time I knew him. He had been working on a farm when he was very young but then he went on to do this, working with horses.

Byron: But this was a very intelligent man.

Brenda: Well he was, but he'd had no education. With an education he could have probably been a very cultivated person.

Byron: Yet this was a man who could actually talk in *cynghanedd*.
          I remember the story about him in the Fox and Hounds in Bancyfelin, when he was heard to come out with the line, '*Rhech o rhych dyn yn dweud bod cachu ar gychwyn.*' *Fel 'na.* Like that – bang!

Brenda: Oh yes, but he had probably been rehearsing it in private for some time.

Byron: These people who lie here in Cana, they were all Welsh speaking, theirs was an entirely Welsh-speaking world.

Brenda: Well that area of Carmarthenshire was. Few people spoke English 60 years ago.

Byron: You know, I never heard Dadcu speak in English.

Brenda: Oh he could speak in English very well when he wanted to. But he didn't want to. He certainly had enough English to read the deaths columns in the *Western Mail.* And the older he got the more and more interest he took in those.

Byron: When I tell people, especially English people, this, they're startled to hear that a working man was a skilled poet.

The don who interviewed me for a scholarship at Oxford, he was still talking about it when we met not long ago. He called him a hedge poet, which I didn't like.

Brenda: It was not all that uncommon for people to create *englynion* and compete in eisteddfodau and use what talent they had. It was part of their lives.

Byron: But it's amazing that culture should have been *such* a part of their lives.

Brenda: They had a lot of pleasure from it.

Byron: Yes, but it startled George Borrow when he walked in Wales and encountered the *gwerin*, the cultured working class. Has all that gone?

Brenda: (*Vaguely.*) Yes, people do other things. They take their entertainment now, they don't contribute to it.

Narrator: All those who lie here, except when bureaucracy intruded on them, lived in a Welsh-speaking world. As I did. Until I left *yr Heol Fach* I didn't have a single word of English. Yet this is the language in which I am writing this, and from which I now make a living. Had we stayed here my life would have been very different, but we moved.

Where did we go? Abroad? No. Some English city? No, not even that. But we might just as well have done. We moved all of five miles, up the road to the town of Carmarthen, and into another culture, an English-speaking one.

Then at 18 I left for England, where, after a middle-class English education, I have spent most of my working life. Nothing unusual here. It is a road many Welshmen have taken. The Village. The Town. The Exile. *Y fro. Y dref. Yr alltudiaeth.* Each of these a different world, and those who take that road are different men in whichever world they happen to be. So when I told that Englishman I was not lost that was not the whole truth.

I have been lost for most of my adult life. And this is where the mystery starts. I can come back here, to *yr Heol Fach*, and within minutes take on the accent, the language, and the folklore of a place I left a long, long time ago. And sometimes these seem so vivid they make the rest of my life remote. And faded.

So how has this come about? I was not even five when I left. Listen...

iii

The sound of marching feet. VE, ceasfire announcement:

'The prime minister has made the historic statement of the end of the war in Europe.'

Narrator: It is 1945, and the Bancyfelin Home Guard, stood down for a year, is holding its own Victory Parade. It is marching in the lane, past the house called Cowin Villa.

Had you been there, and looked closely, you would have seen something odd. They are all in full kit, only one of the sergeants is without his bayonet. That man is my father. And I am watching very guiltily from behind a curtain, for I am three years old and I know exactly where that bayonet is. It is in the garden where I buried it. I did this because I was very fond of my father and thought that without his bayonet he would be obliged to stay at home.

For weeks I have been questioned, just as at the same time, far to the East, German generals are being questioned about their own war crimes. Like them I have stuck doggedly to my version of events, in my case that I saw a cat called Mickey making off with it, Micky Pussy Ken, the imaginary playmate I blame for all forms of bad behaviour. My parents will find the bayonet in the autumn, rusted through, Excalibur among the potatoes.

This is the house where I was born. Once, like Jerusalem in the old maps, it stood at the centre of the whole world.

iv

Spencer: I was his best friend. My name is Spencer Evans, Major Spencer Evans, Royal Corps of Signals (retired). When we were small, living very close to each other, we could not pronounce each other's names, so to me he was Beimo, to him I was Bempy. Beimo and Bempy. We hadn't met in 60 years, but, when a friend got him to ring me after reading one of his books, I picked up the phone and heard, 'This is Byron Rogers', I found myself saying, 'Hello, Beimo.'

      I lived just up the road in a cottage called, for some reason, Umberton, pulled down years ago so that not even a trace of it survives. Still Cowin Villa, the house where you were born, stands. Just...'

Narrator: The house is amazing. It is like that house in fairy tales which the prince finds, surrounded by brambles already higher than a man. Last year they reached the gate, blocking entry. Now the house has begun to disappear.

      Across the lane is the new face of rural Wales, a line of five bungalows, each one the size of a jumbo jet. The people who live in them do not know who owns the house, people who in my childhood would have known everything about him, even what his great aunt got up to with the insurance man in his Austin 7. He is thought to be a Lottery winner, who bought it at auction, along with two others, but has never visited any of them again. Its neighbours do not even know its name now. This is a house that has dropped out of place and time.

      Yet it is so sturdily built it is just as it was when we left. A few slates, and a coat of paint to the lintels and the door my father, a carpenter, made, that is all it needs *for the house to spring to life again*. But that moment may never come.

Byron: How much do you remember, Spencer?
Spencer: I remember we were frightened a lot of the time.

Byron: *Ti'n cofio Hen Fenyw Craig y Nos?* Do you remember the
            Old Woman of the Crag of Night?

Spencer: Jesus, I was scared stiff of her, the name was enough. And
            that really was the name of her house, wasn't it? Even the
            English wouldn't buy a house with a name like that. If it's
            still there it's probably called Valley View. Why were we
            so frightened of her?

Byron: God knows. All I remember is that she hid from her
            husband under a bridge once. All night she was there,
            for he was even more terrifying than she was. It was ages
            before my mother could get me to cross that bridge again.

Spencer: Did she have a name?

A third voice, a woman's voice.

            'Her name was Mrs Colegate.'

Pause. The woman's voice continues:

            'All of us children were frightened of Mrs Colegate. We
            wouldn't look at her twice. My name is Mai Thomas, Mai
            Danyfforest. We lived in the farm next to Cowin Villa.

            And then there was Mrs Durbridge, she lived at Craig
            y Nos after her. Remember Mrs Durbridge?'

Byron: No.

Mai: Bless her, she spent more time on the road than she was in
            the house. She'd climb the hill to Llangynog Post Office
            to get her husband George's pension. Then she'd come
            back with this to Craig y Nos, zig-zagging all the way for
            she wouldn't walk just one side of the road, and George
            would count out just enough to get him some tobacco. So
            she'd climb the hill again to the same post office for this.
            Then she'd walk to our farm and say, 'George is asking for
            six penn'orth of potatoes', and Dad would give her a nice
            little sack of potatoes. Then back to George, and he'd give
            her enough to buy a loaf of bread so she'd walk the main
            road to the bakery at Pass-by. Zig-zagging all the way.

Byron: She was lucky she survived.

Mai: Oh no, Mrs Durbridge, she went like the Irish Mail.

V

Narrator: It was a world of poverty. Not that anyone noticed, they were all poor together. Neighbours looked after each other: when they killed a pig, portions of meat were shared out; when they cut the hay a horse was lent. Few had regular jobs and nobody, apart from the farmers, owned anything. So twice a year landlords, usually tradesmen from the towns, turned up to collect the rent. The man who owned my grandfather's small holding was a Mr Hodges from Swansea. Nothing was known about him except that, like the seasons, he came and went.

For people materialised in this world, a bit like Dr Who. A Mr Ware turned up, again from Swansea, to take over the little wayside pub called the Wern. A one-legged man and a widower, he later married a local girl. Then one day the bus stopped, and a woman got out. Not dead and not divorced, the first Mrs Ware had come to call on her bigamous husband.

But one man straddled the little world and the larger, unreal, one outside it. Lord Kylsant, six foot five inches in height and a shipping multimillionaire, owned just about everything, from the smallholdings here to Harland and Wolff and the White Star Line. He divided his time between his estate at Coombe and his town houses in Carmarthen and London. They called him 'the Lord of the Seven Seas.'

This was a man so rich and powerful that when his eldest daughter married the heir to the Earl of Coventry he had the Great Western Railway stopped all day so carriages could use the level crossing at Sarnau. *'Mae e'n meddwl bod spindl y greadigaeth yn tarddu o'i din e,'* said an old man. He thinks the spindle of creation spurts out of his backside. But they liked him, even in his fall, which was tremendous...

From dawn to dewy eve he fell, a summer's day.

When he emerged from gaol after a 12-month sentence for fudging a company prospectus, 40 local men tied ropes to his car and pulled it up the hill to Coombe.

All the people.

vi

Byron: Do you remember the wells, Spencer?
Spencer: God, the wells. I was frightened of them too, when I was
             very small, in case I fell in. Later it was a daily chore,
             getting the water.
Byron: The stones, and the coolness, and your face far below you
             in the clear water as you peered in. But my father did this
             once and saw an adder below him in the well at Plas-pant.
             Remember Mari Plas-pant?'
Spencer: Yes, the old lady who sold butter. She said to me once,
             'You get me water, and I'll remember you in my will
             when I go.' But when she did she hadn't.
Byron: She believed in the fairies. Think of that, you and I, we
             are old enough to remember someone who believed in
             fairies. My father told me she put milk out for them every
             night. I told a reporter from the *Carmarthen Journal* that,
             but when the story appeared in the paper it had become
             'She put milk out for the ferries…' A lot of people used
             to put milk out for the ferries. But, d'you know, I have
             just been round asking people where their wells were. If
             you remember, every house had one. And nobody knew
             they'd ever had a well.
Spencer: Good God, you make us sound a hundred years old.

vii

Narrator: One generation, that's all it takes, and we are back in a
             world of wells. Two, and we are in a world of horses.

My grandfather Philip Rogers, who led shire stallions, those
behemoths of uncertain temper from farm to farm, used to sleep
above them, their farting as efficient a source of heat as a Roman
hypocaust. When he went on the booze, which was often, he
would leave his watch in the stable, where no one, except him,
dared go. Phil *y March*. Phil the Stallion.

Before that he was a farm labourer. This was how it had always been in my family, anything beyond four generations disappearing into unrecorded time. But then for these, apart from the few names in the family Bible, all time was unrecorded. With one exception. There was a moment when my grandfather stands blinking in the daylight, caught in a bureaucratic trawl. It is the 1881 Census, and he is 17, working as a farm servant near Whitland, *Landless men working the land.* When he died he left £100.

Having once been offered a smallholding to buy on terms he could just have afforded, he said, smugly, '*Mae Duw wedi dweud taw dyn bach 'rwy' fod.*' God has said I am to be a little man. He was a remarkable human being.

viii

Brenda: But bone idle. In the 1930s I'd come for my school holidays to the smallholding called Blaenffynnon...

Narrator: To the cold parlour, and the quiet with the clock ticking, and the bell jar with the stuffed buzzard crushing the life out of the stuffed rabbit. And the large folk painting of the black stallion my uncle Trefor said had the biggest balls he had ever seen. And the small Landseer oils. The Stag at Bay. The Monarch of the Glen. All of them bought in long forgotten country-house sales. Welsh squires had a talent for ruin, and our grandmother had a talent for profiting from that in country-house sales.

Brenda: The parlour was the best room and Granny took a lot of pride in it. It had a concrete floor, a very shiny concrete floor, which every six months or so she'd wash, and I was not allowed to walk on it. Then she'd go out and in the hedgerows pick foxglove leaves, and, making a bundle of these in her hands, would use it to make patterns in the floor with a ring round it, and this would stay for quite some time.

Byron: I've never heard of anyone else doing that. We're going back to a time before carpets, before linoleum, before rushes even. Good God, we're almost back in the caves.

Brenda: Then she'd say, 'Oh look, it's snowing. We'll make pancakes today.' She'd put the snow into the batter. On TV the other day I heard one of those chefs recommending you put ice into your batter. But she was doing it 70 years ago, using a knowledge that had been passed on. She was busy all the time, making bread, butter, elderflower wine.

Byron: But what was our grandfather doing all this time? I mean, he was partly disabled, wasn't he?

Brenda: At the age of 12 he was using a chaff cutter which they had to cut up straw for the animals. You pushed this along a channel to the knives, and he got his four fingers chopped off. It was bound up and when the doctor eventually came all he had left was a thumb and four stumps on his right hand.

Byron: So what did he do all day long?

Brenda: Well, he took the *Western Mail*, he spent a lot of his time reading the paper.

Byron: Did he work?

Brenda: He did bits and pieces, he'd bring hay in from the shed ready for the feeding, he'd take the cows to water, he'd occasionally clean the cowshed out.

Byron: Who was doing all this the rest of the time?

Brenda: My grandmother, she did everything. She'd collect the eggs and kill the chickens, taking them, the odd rabbit and the butter to market, and with the proceeds every Saturday she'd buy a joint of silverside. Never pork. Never lamb. That'd be Sunday lunch. Monday it'd be warmed up, and the vegetables too. Also the gravy which by then you could have eaten with a knife and fork. But there were some who didn't even have a Sunday joint.

Our grandfather, he'd sit there by the fire, writing his poems with a pencil held in the wreckage of his right hand. The poems went into a little notebook he kept, along with details of the eggs, the butter, and the chickens, so when our grandmother came back from market he'd know how much money to expect every week. And every week she'd outwit him. There he was, with his sharp old brain, and she'd run rings round him. You know, he even counted the plums on the plum trees, but when I was small my uncles would lower me down from an upstairs window so I could steal them.

Byron: What did they do for entertainment?

Brenda: Well, people would call, and they'd have a chat about what was going on locally. I remember this farmer calling with a box of bloaters, and my grandmother'd just made some elderflower wine. The two men finished off the wine, and he staggered off into the night. Next morning you could tell the route he'd taken from the bloaters dropped in the fields.

Byron: So that was their entertainment, people calling?

Brenda: Yes, it was their socialising with the local people.

ix

Narrator: People like their closest neighbour, Tom Davies, alias Twm Tŷ-newydd, the name of his house, alias Twm *Mamgu*, for he had been brought up by his Mamgu, his grandmother, alias Twm Champion, for in his long-ago youth he had been a jockey, and won races; also, for some reason nobody now knows, Twm Barrels, though he had certainly emptied enough of those. All his life, into the 1960s, this man wore the breeches and puttees of the First World War yeoman cavalry, in which, briefly, he had served.

A claw of a man stepping like mist out of bushes that didn't even move to record his passing, a line of silver trout dangling from a hazel branch. Poacher. Drunk. 'A Character', as my father would say…grimly.

In the tiny house called Tŷ Newydd he and his wife Marged

brought up a large family, largely on the proceeds of her fortune-telling. It was thought she had gypsy blood, her old mother Ruth smoked a pipe, and so the rich farmers called for advice on the future. And on harvests, which were the future.

Mai: I remember coming back one night from a Christmas party at Bancyfelin chapel. Now old Tom would drink like a fish and he'd cycle home from the Fox and Hounds, and what we saw was him in a ditch, the cycle on top on him, and these legs against the moon, still pedalling in the air.

Narrator: All his children were given grand names, one, born during the Great War, was to be called Protheroe Beynon Howell Davies after Twm's colonel in the yeomanry. Only Twm overstayed his leave, and from gaol the telegram came. 'Hold the Christening.' The War ended, and the child, now three, was still without a name. *Babi ni*. Our Baby.

One day Twm met my uncle Tom in the lane. 'And what are you doing in school, little boy?' He spoke as grandly as a squire.

'History, Mr Davies.'

'And what in history?'

'Robert the Bruce of Scotland, Mr Davies.'

That weekend there was a christening in Bancyfelin. Robert Bruce Howell Davies.

Bruce inherited his father's position as rural drunk. One night of rain in Carmarthen, my father, waiting to make a phone-call, saw him reeling down the street. Coming up the other way was the town drunk, Donald Duck, also reeling. For a moment the two paused and stared at each other.

'*Cer gartre'r mochyn meddw*,' said Donald. Go home, you drunken pig.

Bruce drew himself up to his full height of five feet six, and looked at him mildly. '*Sdim parch 'da'ti at y ddynoliaeth?*' Have you no respect for humanity? Heroes passing in the night.

On the village war memorial, after the names of the squire's son, killed in the Boer War, and the long roll-call of the Trenches, there is just one name from the Second World War. James Howell Davies. Jim, Bruce's brother, Twm's son. My father met him with rifle and pack in Carmarthen station. 'There's a waugh in Euwghop, boys, and I'm in it.' He could not say his 'r'. But Jim never came home from Dunkirk.

All this I know because I was told.

Before television, before radio for the most part, they told tales, most of them about their neighbours. Who had killed a snake, or hollowed out a swede and put a candle in it to frighten passers-by at night. They knew everything about everyone. And now I am calling on bungalows where some do not even know the names of their neighbours. What happened?

Mai: The English came.

John: Well there's me . . .

I am the man who asked you in the lane if you were lost. My name is John Hooton. Since 1997 I have lived in Blaenffynnon where your father was born. We bought it from some English people, I can't remember their names. We came from Chesham in Buckinghamshire, which is at the end of the Tube line, having looked for 15 months for somewhere like this to retire to. Finally we found a photograph is an estate agent's window in Carmarthen. My wife and I, we bought it in September, and we moved in the month after.

We don't farm. We have six-and-a-half acres, much less than your grandfather, and I keep some sheep to keep the grass down. Our neighbours? The chap in Tŷ Newydd, he's English. Bronyglyn, they're English. But there's a Welsh lady still at Manordeilo.

Narrator: The curious thing is that the Welsh are in the huge new bungalows. It is the English who have moved into, and converted, the old smallholdings. Even Tŷ Newydd has a conservatory now. But men like John Hooton are fascinated by what life was like in the houses they now occupy, and they look for this in old photographs, they consult old maps. They do not do this in the bungalows, Bungalows have no past.

Hooton: The longer you live in a house, the more you realise how short is your tenure. What did I do before I came? I was in the computer industry. And before that I flew fighter jets off aircraft carriers.

X

The scream of engines. This thins and becomes the sound of traffic, through which you hear the putter of a petrol aero engine.

Narrator: He too was a fighter pilot, this man at whose grave I am standing in Cana. Ira Jones DSO, MC, DFC and bar. MM. He came out of the society we have been describing, 'of parents whose ancestors tilled the soil', as he wrote, to become one of the aces of the Great War. 'I have been in 28 aeroplane crashes, the machine somersaulting on the ground on each occasion, and only once have I been hurt. This was when I was a passenger and broke an arm...'

He was five foot four, weighed nine stone, and had a stammer, as any man might at a time when the average life expectancy of a pilot was six weeks. Every day he saw his friends fall out of their planes, or crash in flames, the British War Office, unlike its German counterpart, having refused to issue its pilots with parachutes. Remember that. Which was why, to the disapproval of the authorities, Ira Jones began to kill those Germans who had successfully baled out and were dangling from their parachutes. It was a world where nothing they had ever been taught applied. They recovered the body of one German pilot and placed it in a hangar, dressed in pyjamas and a dinner jacket, then toasted it in champagne. These are not things Errol Flynn or David Niven ever did.

There was one last moment. He took off in his plane on November 11, 1918, and, diving through the clouds, saw something amazing, huge masses of men beneath him leaving the trenches.

'As the clock neared 11am, we flew closer to the retreating mass, and as soon as the hour had passed we flew over them. *They took no notice of us...*' The Germans were walking home, and it was all over.

So Achilles lies in Cana graveyard now. But there is one thing he never did mention, something that in this chapel society would have been talked about in whispers. He was born illegitimate, that stigma of the old world, and such a common feature of it.

EPILOGUE

It is an autumn morning in 1999, and my cousins and I have travelled, one from Canada, to stand at the small earth grave beside that of my grandparents. And we are there because we have clubbed together to buy a small memorial stone for someone whom only one of us knew. His name was Evan Griffiths, an itinerant farm labourer, who died before most of us were even born.

Brenda: He was my grandmother's illegitimate son, the child of her youth. And we are here because of a story we were told, that when he called on his mother he whistled from the lane to see whether our grandfather was at home. It is a story we could not forget.

Narrator: I wrote this poem.

You whistled from the lane
Outside your mother's house,
You, her shame, asking
To be let in
To family and home.
I hear your nails upon the window pane.

No need to whistle now.
You lie beside her,
She under marble, you,
Still discreet in death,
Your earth grave level with the earth.
And no one knows your secret except us.

You, the man outside,
Unmarried, drunk,
A hired hand on farms,
Your name not written
In the fading Bible ink.
And we are here to give you back your name.
We, the relatives you never knew, have come,
After 70 years, to ask you in.

Narrator: These were my people.

2 THESE WERE MY PEOPLE . . .

It began as a series of articles for the *Sunday Express*, written to show what had become the Agricultural Revolution of the late 20th century. So there was the organic farmer who made cheese, the grain baron with his £210,000 annual fertiliser and fungicide bill, the farmer like an air traffic controller staring at computers that monitored the 3,000 animals in his Pig City. And then there was Selwyn.

I found him through my cousin Gareth, a farmer himself. I had asked if he knew someone who still did things in the old way, though the startling irony is that the old way is the farming methods of just 40 years ago. Forty years, that was all, yet I felt I had stepped back in social and economic history, not to the open fields of the Middle Ages, but to a time I myself remembered. It was a day of memories.

Selwyn could remember when the old squire sold up and his father bought the farm. That was in 1930. He remembered when the tractors came in the 1940s, after the War, for nothing was the same afterwards. But the coming of electricity in the 1960s he remembered ruefully, for he had just bought a new tilly lamp, the ironmonger assuring him, 'These are going to get expensive.' He rummaged in a crowded cupboard and produced the lamp still in its original box. 'Never used,' said Selwyn Davies. Like an old preacher, he spoke in a mixture of Welsh and English, dropping from one to the other for emphasis.

Below the house, Carmarthenshire opened like a huge fan, for most of Carmarthenshire was below his 117-acre hill farm. 'Clean, healthy area,' said Mr Davies. 'No hooligans round here.' Not too many people either.

It is lonely up here in the shadow of the Black Mountain, and, though the old communal spirit had gone (he remembered how, when he was a young man, the farmers got together to cut each other's hay), people still kept an eye on each other. If a day passed when his neighbours had not heard him cursing his dogs they usually called round, he said.

He was 68 years old, a lean, small man with the sort of thick moustache once worn by senior officers in the British Army. He wore a flat cap, indoors and out, also two pullovers, one under the other, and was unmarried ('Why? Nobody ever asked me, that's why'). He told me he farmed as his father had done before him, though with a quarter more of the fertilisers which his father always maintained were the invention of the Devil on a wet afternoon. He was going to keep things like that.

At the approach to his yard there were two Marina vans, both broken down long before, one on its roof. There was a third Marina van in the yard, and when anything went wrong with that he repaired it with parts taken from the other two, for like all hill farmers, he threw nothing away.

Look, stand here a moment. The small, untidy yard; the wrecked pieces of machinery; the puppies and the ducks and the chickens running everywhere; the stream running through the wood; the sheets of corrugated iron put up whenever a gap appeared in a hedge; the plum tree in blossom. Whatever its profit and loss there was one thing that distinguished this from all other farms I had visited: in its disorder and its beauty it was a place where a child could play.

'A balloon came down in that field,' said Selwyn Davies. 'And the man, a Mr Cameron, he had two children with him. I'd never seen a balloon before, *Duw* it was big. But the two children, they seemed in their element here. Mr Cameron sent me a bottle of whisky later.'

He had 29 calves and cows, 407 sheep (a hundred more than his father), 25 chickens, five geese, five ducks and three dogs. He also had a 15-hand Arab stallion, though he did not ride, but there was a horse here in his father's time, so there was a horse here in his.

He was not cut off from the outside world, he was perfectly aware of the changes that had come in the farms beyond his fields. 'I've seen these intensive sheds on television, that's not natural. I could build one here, have all the sheep indoors from Christmas until they lamb. I could increase the fertilisers on the land, but what would be the point? The farm supports me, it could support a family quite easily. I am satisfied with things as they are: this is a better and a healthier way.'

We walked his fields and he took a wry delight in pointing out the remains of what he described as 'crazes'. There was a bit of a plough left after a Ministry of Agriculture craze when a Ministry tractor driver toppled over on a slope they had warned him not to plough. 'Then there was a craze to grow rye. We had a whole field full of rye, but the cows got in and started feeding on it. They swelled up like balloons. Don't grow rye now.'

In almost every field there was a piece of abandoned machinery. An old horse mower. Another plough, this on its side. An old rake. 'I wonder how that got down here, I'm sure it was up there the other day.'

The family was virtually self-sufficient in his father's time. They had milk from their cows, which his mother made into butter; they had home-cured bacon and free-range eggs. Much of this self-sufficiency had gone (his mother, he said, would be shocked at his buying milk), but some remained. His water came from his own well; the fuel he burned was from his own trees. Vegetables came from his own garden.

'I've had beans from that garden 27 inches long. The man who sold me the seeds boasted they'd grow to 18 inches. The next time I saw him I told him that at 27 inches they didn't fit into the saucepan. "But you have to cut them, Mr Davies," he said.'

Day followed day. He fed the sheep, then the cows, then he cleaned out the sheds. He cleared ditches, he cut trees, and stopped when it got dark. Beyond the farm things changed. When hill farms became vacant, it was mostly the English who bought them. On Carmarthen market, Dutch people sold farmhouse cheese; on Brecon market, people he thought could be Gurkhas sold butter. But not here.

We sat having tea in a spectacularly untidy room. 'The maid left,' said Selwyn Davies, who had never employed a maid in his life.

The sequel was quite extraordinary. The article duly appeared, and Selwyn himself appeared, only in his case on the front of the *Sunday Express Magazine,* the first time in years that there had been a cover photograph of someone not a beautiful young woman, a film star or a model. This horrified the then owner of the paper, whose whole world had been rocked at the sight of an elderly gentleman holding a lamb in the crook of his arm. There were many memos and much recrimination. But that was just the beginning.

Strange women, caught by his humour or his bright blue eyes, wrote wistfully to Selwyn Davies, auctioneers stopped in mid-gabble to make their little jokes whenever he appeared in their marts. After a while all this stopped, but the other letters and the phone-calls did not stop. For there had been another photograph.

In this he was shown leaning against his old Fordson tractor which stood at the bottom of the field where it had last broken down, so long ago even he could not remember when. The tractor was bright with rust, ivy reaching up into its innards. But because of that one small photograph men trawled through the Davieses in the West Wales directory, and, believe me, that way madness lies for I had not given his address. Others wrote to me, their letters shimmering with excitement, and all had one thing in common: they wanted Selwyn's Fordson. Some wanted to restore it, others to enter it for a vintage ploughing championship. Some just wanted it.

Selwyn, who had seen the years pass, seen the rain fall on it, and the snow, at first thought he was the victim of some complicated practical joke, but then wondered whether he should contact Christie's. He asked me for my advice, and I advised him to hang on to the Fordson. Like Tutankhamun, he owed it to the future.

ANOTHER FARMER

I came on the story in, of all things, the *Los Angeles Times*. It was in an article written by the then Mrs Salman Rushdie when she and her novelist husband, the object of the fatwa proclaimed by the late Ayatollah Khomeini, were being shepherded from house to safe house by Special Branch policemen. The two at one point had, with their minders, ended up in west Wales. From Edward II on, a lot of people on the run in Britain have ended up in west Wales.

I read the article with great interest for this was not a west Wales I recognised. Mrs Rushdie wrote about slate tombstones, slate walls, even whole houses made of slate; she also saw ravens nodding politely on the roads. Lovely details, all of them, which would have endeared the landscape to Edgar Allan Poe, except that, growing up in that landscape, I had seen none of them.

Still, given the tension she was under, I too might have seen such things. Mrs Rushdie was not allowed out much and so turned to cooking, clearly a new, even exotic, activity for her. 'One day I cooked a swede ... it seemed to take forever.' The rest of the time she read the local weekly papers, and it was in one of these, the *Brecon-Radnor Express*, that she came on the story.

> A farmer who staggered into a neighbour's house half-naked, covered in blue dye, with his hands and testicles bound with rubber bands, has been cleared of the charges that he planted a hoax bomb and wasted police time.

His defence was that he had been attacked by the IRA.

'Stephen...' No, it would be unfair to give his real name. 'Stephen X said he had crossed two fences with his hands tied behind his back and his testicles bound in a rubber band...' And then the masterpiece. '...but Detective Inspector D.A. Davies of Ammanford had tried to do the same and failed to do so...' Had tried to do the same...that was the bit that fascinated me.

But put yourself in her place for a moment. There she was, a woman from California, who must already have felt she had stepped back 500 years with the bloodthreats of religious fanatics hanging over her. And then, with her sense of reality flickering, she opened the *Brecon-Radnor Express*. But me, I was among my own people.

A month earlier I had come on a news-story in *The Cardigan and Tivyside Advertiser* about a Crymych man who had threatened to blow up the first policeman he saw and to shoot his neighbours because he was unable to afford a sex-change operation. An unknown sub, thanking God that he had lived long enough for the opportunity, gave it the headline 'Man Made Threats After Sex-Op Hopes Dashed'.

The man, described by his defence counsel, as being 'not of high intellect, and nicknamed Space', had apparently been often seen around Crymych dressed in women's clothes. But, having found he could not afford £3,000, apparently the going rate for a castration in west Wales, he had got drunk and phoned the Carmarthen police, challenging them to a shoot-out. Failing that, he announced he would start shooting his neighbours.

The police promptly sent their SWAT team to Crymych where they found there could be no shoot-out. Not only did the man not have a gun licence, he did not have a gun. His client, said counsel helpfully, had felt like committing suicide, but hoped the police might shoot him instead.

The chairman of the bench found it 'an unusual case'.

3 THE MINISTER

KILSBY JONES, LLANDOVERY, PREACHER

For ten years I had passed the chapel without a glance. They are so self-effacing, the little chapels squeezed like an afterthought into the villages of Middle England, as they had to be when parson leant on the squire and squire refused worshippers access to his quarry. That is why these are the only buildings not of stone, their frontages thin toothpicks of brick in a street. What made me stop finally was a sentence I read in a volume of 19th-century reminiscences about a Welshman who preached here. 'Had he not feared God he would have been terrible, for he feared no man.'

His name was James Jones, he himself added the Kilsby, the name of the Northampton village where he ministered from 1840 to 1849. Kilsby Jones. The village is a mile from Rugby. Once it would have been on a main road, now the road signs hustle you past and on to the A5 and the M1. The road past the chapel has also been twitched aside, so this stands among modern houses now in its own little lay-by of dissent. It is like a house itself, in size that is, but once inside there is that old smell familiar to Welshmen of my generation, a smell compounded of pine, damp and windows that are never opened. No impediments of human craftsmanship here, no carving, no sculpted graves, just a bleak room cleared for action, and, like the bridge of a starship, the pulpit where a man stood between heaven and earth.

I have sat on bishops' thrones, on judges' chairs, and once, on a quiet afternoon, on the Throne of England in Buckingham Palace, where I then worked, but not one of them gave me the feeling of power that is in the pulpit of this small Nonconformist chapel where in the 1840s he stood, the great preacher.

In the 1950s there was a serial on the BBC Wales radio programme *Children's Hour* called 'The Face in the Rock', about a small boy's quest for the hero whose face was that formed in the rock of the mountain above his valley. He seeks for him in the great politician, the poet, the soldier, the preacher, the remarkable thing being that the great preacher was then considered hero material. How odd that seems now.

I heard the last of them, being taken by my father to hear Dr Martin Lloyd Jones in Carmarthen not long after the radio serial, and I can remember people's faces afterwards, their eyes shining, and the way a matron in the gallery, cupping her left breast, lifted this to show a friend opposite the effect the sermon had had on her.

For these were not the sermons of the Church in Wales, rattled off in ten minutes as though delivered by a station announcer, these lasted an hour or more, and those who heard them, like my father, had great chunks by heart. The men who delivered them were as famous as sports stars in our small communities. And where are those great preachers now? We have forgotten their names just as we have forgotten the names of the heroes of the *Gododdin*.

Kilsby Jones was a farmer's son from Llandovery, who had changed his name the way film stars changed their names in the early Hollywood. And there was an an element of show business in the appearance of a man well over six feet in height, with a high forehead, flowing white hair and a trifurcated, a *trifurcated,* beard worn low on his chest. Add to this the seven-foot shepherd's crook he carried, and it is clear that Cecil B. De Mille, without recourse to a props department, might have cast Kilsby Jones in one of his Biblical epics.

Still his contemporaries seem to have coped with all that. What did stun them was that in a sanctimonious age this man mocked hell-fire sermons ('Men saying there were babies in hell not a span long swimming on the backs of devils centuries old'). The religion of Jesus, he said, was a happy one. 'It is music. It is love.' This in the bleak chapels of the mid-19th century.

He appeared in the pulpit in velvet or in a shooting jacket, poking fun at the dark clothes of other preachers whom he called 'sky-pilots', an extraordinary phrase when you remember that there were no pilots for no planes flew in the skies he knew. But then he did not seem part of his time at all. At the height of the Temperance Movement he smoked and drank, and gloried in doing both.

Awarding prizes at his old theological college in Carmarthen, he chose to address the exam failures. 'I was here in this place many years ago, and I never won a prize in my life,' he told them cheerfully. 'And I can speak English by the yard now.' Speaking English in a largely monoglot Wales was important to him, and he encouraged his countrymen to acquire 'the language of beefsteak and plum pudding', even going so far as to publish a grammar in which he wished his readers 'good luck in your efforts to learn, speak and write in the language of the Englishman.'

He was fresh air and life, and men treasured anecdotes about him. At college, accused of having been to the races, he did not deny this but told the authorities that it had been in deference to the precept, 'Prove all things, hold fast to that which is good.' And having found the races bad, he went on, he would not be going again.

Alas, they have forgotten him in his little chapel at Kilsby now, as everywhere they have forgotten the age of the great preachers. The present minister, who has two other chapels in his care, told me he never went beyond 15 minutes in any of his sermons. 'This is the TV generation. People don't read, so sitting and listening is difficult for them...'

But close your eyes and try to see him in the pulpit he occupied for ten years. He was not a good pastor, he said once, because he found he could not like all men equally. He was without humbug and he did not give a damn, this extraordinary, laughing man.

4 THE LAST SQUIRES

For ten years I had sought it, in dusty bookshops in cathedral cities, on stalls in market towns, and in all that time H.M. Vaughan's *The South Wales Squires* seemed just out of reach, for I kept coming on quotations from it in book after book. Yet when at last I found it in a Laugharne bookshop I could hardly believe my eyes. Still in its 1926 orange dust jacket, the book was a first edition.

But that was because it never went into a second, though Vaughan noted, with surprise, that for the rest of his life he was receiving enquiries about it. *The South Wales Squires* was a book which seemed made to be forgotten, being a defence of a much reviled social class that, as the author acknowledged, was disappearing even as he wrote. Only his book never did disappear.

Like John Wycliffe's bones it was carried irresistibly into the folklore of a nation, for in one sense it never went out of print but was swept into just about every social history and memoir written subsequently about rural Wales. Poor Vaughan. He intended a threnody for the squires, a class of which he had been part, and what he produced was a riot of pure comedy.

Even before I got my hands on his book, I had some of its anecdotes by heart, like the one about the 19th-century eccentric Ford Hughes whose one passion was to rent other men's mansions. He rented these two or three at a time, driving to them by carriage and at night, like Dracula, only to return before dawn, again like Dracula, to what Vaughan described as 'a mean house in Union Street, Carmarthen.' Him I would not have been able to forget, for I was brought up in Union Street, Carmarthen.

As a class, the squires had long been strangers in their own country, despite family trees threaded into the mists of Welsh history by accommodating bards. But, whatever their ancestry, they themselves had been left high and dry, fenced off by their deliberate neglect of the Welsh language (a Miss Clara Thomas was an exception, wrote Vaughan, for she had some Welsh 'though she found few occasions for its use'), by their High Tory politics in an increasingly Liberal country, and by their championing of the Church of England when Welsh Nonconformity was at its floodtide. The last of their authority went when the 1887 County Council Act put power into the hands of elected local bodies.

Many had ruined themselves by then, being drawn to London like moths to a light ('Bosworth blind,' wrote R.S. Thomas of those who had followed Henry VII). There were so many of them, their estates so small, and made smaller in each generation, for primogeniture was not so ruthlessly practised as amongst their English counterparts. Kilvert met the last squire of Glanbran, a hackney cab driver in Liverpool. The last of the Pryses of Gogerddan, the heroes of a Welsh war song, was an old lady living alone in a caravan with a single foxhound for company, the last of her family's great packs. One of her ancestors had ended up as a barman in Shanghai, another had decamped with the proceeds of a local flower show.

Their mansions are also ruined now or made into old folks' homes. Lord Kylsant's daughter, formerly the Countess of Coventry, at the end of her life returned to die in Coombe, the house where she was born, and from which she had been married, her father's tenants drawing the bridal car; Coombe had become a Cheshire Home. Once a way of life, of many lives, had turned around such houses, now the Wales of the Squires has gone as though it had never been, historians drawing neat, and cruel, lines under it. 'The gentry betrayed their birthright, behaved like rich bourgeois and denied... the civilisation they boasted they were cherishing,' wrote Saunders Lewis.

So passed the *uchelwyr*, the high men, some with the blood of the princes in them. And only one man mourned their passing, one unlikely champion. Herbert Vaughan of Llangoedmor (1870-1948) seems to have stepped out of one of E.M. Forster's short stories: a lover of Italy, a man of art galleries and foreign hotels; a High Churchman and a Tory so romantic he could hero-worship such unlikely figures as Cardinal York, the last of the Stuarts, and the Young Pretender's neglected wife; a man who considered himself a lifelong invalid, though in his case from constipation ('You have hinsides like hiron,' said an awed public school matron).

Vaughan was a bachelor whose most important relationship was with another man, an American, like him a lover of art and art galleries, whose ashes he brought back to Llangoedmor, and for whom he wore mourning on each anniversary of his death, remembering 'his beautiful hands and feet', though this is in the autobiography he chose not to have published.

Yet this same Vaughan was the man who in *The South Wales Squires* could lovingly chronicle the likes of Colonel John 'Blundy' Howell of Glaspant, whose one response to a joke was 'Haw! Haw! Very superior!' But then, whatever else he was, Vaughan was also a squire, a magistrate and High Sheriff of Cardiganshire, who felt he could write his book only because he had himself just sold up and so had ceased to be a member of that 'little understood and much maligned class.' He added, mysteriously, 'The book brought me next to nothing, for which I am glad.' Guilt towards his class jostled with a sense of duty as the last squire assembled his defence. And the result is not what he intended.

For we see them, not as they saw themselves or Squire Vaughan wanted to see them, but as Herbert Vaughan, late of Florence and the olive groves, saw the likes of Thomas Lloyd of Coedmor, who mentioned affably to a judge that the coachman and the footman on their carriage were both his bastards. Or the likes of the exquisite George Powell of Nanteos, a friend to the poet Swinburne, whose exasperated father, old Squire Powell, gave him a gun and told him not to come back from the park until he had shot something; George shot a bullock.

I am just old enough to have met the last of one of these families. Aged 11, I was invited by our doctor, a man for whom my father worked and who had one of the few television sets in the town, to a Coronation Day party. The adult guests were what passed for middle class in Carmarthen, being doctors or vets, but amongst them I noticed a couple who were triumphantly smashed before the Queen even reached the Abbey. They were both very tall and gaunt, and the grown-ups seemed to be in some awe of them, so I watched them carefully, these gods behind the gods.

The man's name intrigued me, for it was so Welsh and so much at odds with his upper-class English accent. I was told that he was the one surviving member of an old family, though as the great Lord Burleigh remarked, what be an old family but ancient money? The money in this case had run out long before, there was a ruined estate, and I saw the two of them a few times after that in the town, moving slowly and carrying large bags which clinked. They were a bit like ghosts, caricatures of a class at the end of its time.

But in Vaughan's book, as he remembers the Wales, not of his maturity but of his boyhood, it was still a class very much in being. For look, the tables are laid for dinner and beside each plate, each plate, three bottles of claret have been placed; in the kitchen the cook is passing a damp cloth through the insides of the grouse to remove the maggots.

And it is Saturday night in Bryn Myrddin at the foot of Merlin's Hill on the outskirts of Carmarthen, then owned by members of his family. The little Herbert Vaughan does not dare venture beyond its grounds, for it has been market day in the town and the roads are full of drunks on horseback, and when the drunks have fallen off the roads are full of riderless horses making their own way home. But behind the gates of Bryn Myrddin he is safe, for here the old order still stands.

That was well over a hundred years ago, yet he makes it sound like yesterday. It is always just yesterday in his book.

5 THE HANGMAN

It is the 23rd of May, 1876, and Robert Evans of Fern Hill, a farmer from Llangain in Carmarthenshire, or a *gentleman* farmer as he would prefer it (though Fern Hill is a mere 15 acres), is writing to the Home Secretary. Mr Evans, as he acknowledges in his first paragraph, is used to writing such letters, and the Home Secretary, R.A. Cross in Disraeli's Government, must have been used to receiving them, in his case wearily. For the letters are only ever about one thing.

'Sir, I again trouble you upon this subject, which, it will be admitted, is difficult and delicate to deal with. The taking away of human life is, as the law now stands, a painful necessity...'

And Mr Evans is off, advising the Home Secretary yet again on hanging. But not on hanging as a judicial or a moral issue, nothing so abstract: he is advising him on practical details, in particular of the protocol which, as he puts it, for humane reasons needs to be observed on the gallows. Only he is doing so from his own experience, and, a year earlier, has written to the *Times*, claiming to have taken part in almost every execution in Britain over the past quarter of a century. For, unlike the hangmen of his day, he is far from being illiterate. This, for example, is a letter from the famous public executioner Marwood: 'Sir, this is to inform you that I reseaved [sic] a Letter from you without Naim [sic] and Dait [sic] onley [sic] with som [sic] enseables [sic] asking me some [sic] Questions Concerning Som [sic] Matters…' It is not a job that requires educational qualifications.

Yet Mr Evans has never held an official position of any kind, being recruited as their assistant by hangmen, all of whom he knows, and to whom he donates his fee, for the gentleman farmer is also a gentleman hangman. Even so he has conducted the odd execution himself, being also in the habit of writing to the governors of county gaols, letters along the lines of 'Anyone there need hanging?', though of course in his elaborate Victorian prose he does not phrase it quite like that. When he addresses the Home Secretary it is from a position of what he thinks of as regretful expertise.

'The doomed one should be addressed firmly, and as far as can be, cheerfully assured that he will not be hurried into eternity…' And then the details kick in, helpful, horrible details: on the correct tightness of straps, on the last meal ('spare diet is more conducive to a swift death'), and on what he delicately refers to as 'calls of nature'. But on one thing he is most insistent. Mr Evans is an advocate of the short drop of not more than 18 inches, not the long drop, then recently introduced, of 8 to 11 feet which results in an instant dislocation of the neck: he is, whatever he says, intent on strangling his victims. Two years earlier he has had to press down on the shoulders of a young woman on the gallows in Gloucester Gaol, but he does not tell the Home Secretary this.

He ends his letter cheerily, 'As I am now staying in town, I will avail myself of the opportunity of calling for your reply, with which I hope to be favoured. Should you desire further information, I shall be at your service.' Mr Evans, probably between bare-knuckle prize fights, his other great interest, hopes to fit the Home Secretary in. He signs himself Anderson, an alias which, given his growing notoriety (and problems with paying his bills), he has just adopted.

I was given a copy of this letter in 2001 in a Carmarthen pub, exactly a hundred years after his death.

I grew up with stories about Robert Ricketts Evans, for my aunt later kept the post office at Llangain, and my grandfather Philip Rogers had often called at Fern Hill, a Gothic mansion creepy beyond belief behind its metal gates and permanently in shadow from the trees which surround it, a damp, secret place made for the horror stories of M.R. James and for an eternity of dying autumn afternoons.

Latterly it was owned by my old Latin master (for that is the odd thing, the Hangman still pops up in all sorts of contexts), who for years had been wistfully trying to sell it at some enormous price to the American fans of Dylan Thomas. And this is the final bizarre twist. Thomas's aunt and uncle farmed Fern Hill, where in boyhood he came on his summer holidays, and about which he later wrote his most famous poem. In this, Fern Hill is the setting for a vision of childhood and lost innocence,

> And as I was green and carefree, famous among the barns
> About the happy yard and singing as the farm was home,
> In the sun that is young once only...

this in a place that breathes decay, where his uncle and aunt went bankrupt. There is no mention of the Hangman, though Thomas would talk about him to his smart London friends, assuring them that the man had finally hanged himself in Fern Hill, out of remorse, he said. This is not true.

But the story found its way onto the Llangain tourist plaque, one of those pictorial roadside jobs put up by the local tourist board, from which, after much argument, the Hangman's great grandson, a former London policeman who now lives locally, managed to have it removed. 'I mean, he was family after all.' There were other stories. It was said that at Fern Hill he had had a windowless room built for his daughter, the real owner of the farm which had been left her in her mother's will, when, that is, she planned to elope. This too is untrue, at least the windowless room is.

But my grandfather talked of a room, its walls hung (oh dear) with nooses and portraits of famous hangmen, for Evans's friends in the craft visited him there, and this, apparently, was his idea of an interior decoration that would make them feel at home. There was also a small fully-operational gallows, on which guests, plied with drink, were invited to stand, at which point he would pretend to pull the lever attached to the trap door. Laugh, we could have died. My grandfather saw these things, and talked of Evans being driven the four miles to Llansteffan where he would do a dog paddle across the Towy to catch the train en route for the prize fights and the hangings; my grandfather said he was in the habit of pausing in the middle of the river to light a cigarette.

I mentioned some of this in the column I was then writing for the *Sunday Telegraph*, adding, reasonably enough, that Evans would have been none the worse for some urgent medical attention. The letter came a few days later. 'Why shouldn't a hangman have a sense of humour?' asked the writer. He himself had been a hangman, he said, and he had a sense of humour. Albert Pierrepoint's last living assistant had written to ask me to tea. More of him later.

In one of the few photographs to survive of Evans he is shown in old age with a man in a long white beard. This sage, who looks older than the hills, is the even more notorious William Price, G.P., Chartist revolutionary, Victorian nudist, and the first to practise public cremation, then illegal in Britain, at whose own cremation Evans is said to have lit the bonfire. In the photograph the two are seated side by side, Price with a whole foxskin on his head, the brush dangling over one ear. Evans, a tough-looking, clean-shaven man, is more conservative: he is dressed as a cowboy. Like the Titanic and the iceberg, two OAPs, the biggest nutters of their time, had come together.

And with that you might have expected Evans's life to drift away to be wrecked on the reefs of local myth where finally it would be swamped by exaggeration. The fact that it didn't is due to one thing: the Hangman kept turning up, caught in the trawl of Dylan Thomas's successive, bemused, biographers.

Constantine Fitzgibbon has the story of the windowless room and the daughter who, he said, had gone off with 'a gentleman from Carmarthen', as the result of which the hangman in his wrath had hanged himself 'in his kitchen or as some say in his hall'. A nice touch, that, uncertainty being the ultimate guarantee of a writer's good faith, and it allows Fitzgibbon to throw in one of Thomas's own embellishments, that he had hanged some of his victims in Fern Hill where their ghosts could be heard squeaking and gibbering. John Malcolm Brinnin adds another of these embellishments, that he had hanged himself out of remorse. Paul Ferris, a far more industrious biographer, drawing on information from a later owner of the farm, says that Evans was the assistant hangman at Carmarthen, whose daughter did indeed run off, but with a German called Bloomer. That was all it needed, a German called Bloomer.

It was left to David Thomas to sort out the story. In his two-volumed *Dylan Thomas Remembered* he did not attempt a biography but sought instead, drawing on 140 hours of interviews recorded soon after the poet's death by the radio journalist Colin Edwards, to portray the poet's background, the landscape and the people he knew. The effect is remarkable for, though Dylan Thomas is often off-stage, the details are such that the book tells you more about the man than any biography, and, by extension, about his writing, for this is the raw material out of which that came. And, of course, the Hangman bobs up again.

In a photograph taken of him in elegant middle-age he is shown leaning back in a horse and trap, a languid, moustached man in a bowler hat, only he is not driving the horse and trap: beside his bulky coachman the squire is shown taking the air. But then Evans had married money. A Carmarthen solicitor's son aged 23, he had eloped with a little heiress of just 17, with whom came a considerable estate, including Fern Hill and the Coffee Pot, a grocer's shop in the town, where, by a freakish coincidence his great-grandson Bob, the retired policeman, but then a delivery boy, will meet his own wife Liz, one of the assistants.

The only thing was, the little heiress's estate was entailed on their daughter, so when Mrs Evans died just four years later, it all passed to the child, who at her death became a ward of Chancery,

with the proviso that Evans could enjoy the rents until she was 21.
And that was where the trouble started.

He appears from his diaries, which David Thomas found
in the National Library, to have been very fond of her, but felt
free to indulge his various interests. The child, he would have
argued, was safe in Fern Hill with her governess and three servants,
and afterwards at the boarding school in Southport where he sent
her.

So there was boxing. According to his remarkable 4,000 word
obituary of August 28, 1901 in the *Western Mail*, the sort of space
no newspaper would accord a Prime Minister now, 'There was
now not a prize-fight in the Kingdom that Evans did not attend...'
And there were women, for his obituary goes on, this was a man
'with a most pronounced penchant for the fair sex.' He employed
a housekeeper, got her pregnant, married her and had two more
children by her before she ran off to Llansteffan. So there was a
second housekeeper, by whom he had another child. And then there
were his boasts of his experiences in Victorian London among its
50,000 whores.

These two interests prompted a third, for, with Chancery
understandably starting to take an interest in his daughter's affairs,
Evans developed a passion for litigation. He would sue anyone,
usually his many creditors, just for the sheer hell of it. A friend
entrusted him with the care of a pony which became pregnant by
Evans's stallion, so there was the matter of who owned the foal.
Evans took the man to court, and when he lost the case immediately
bought both pony and foal, remarking that anything that had
cost £1,000 in law and purchase was too valuable an animal to be
worked. He had the animal's shoes removed and until its death it
was allowed to roam his fields, serving no other purpose, according
to his obituarist, than to be shown to friends as the '£1,000 pony.'
Evans claimed to have received so many county court summonses
in his career as a litigant that he could have papered his house
with them, and for exterior decoration bought and installed two
fully operational cannon at his front door. This apparently was
something you could do in Victorian Britain, a time when the

Crawshay family, ironmasters in Merthyr, had cannons put in front of their house to deter social visits from their workforce.

But not even these diversions would account for a 4,000 word obituary. This, starting with the gleeful news that Evans had 'at last "shot his bolt" – as he himself would have expressed it…' was the result of the fourth of his little interests. Fascinated by litigation and also by the various forms of self-publicising celebrity which in another age would have made him a natural for *Big Brother,* it was perhaps inevitable that he was drawn to hanging and to hangmen, just as his contemporaries Dickens and Hardy were.

According to Matthew Spicer, who has compiled a register of the 130 British hangmen from 1800 on, these men at the start of 19th century were nonentities, usually criminals or debtors, who, because hanging was in public, wore masks. The irony was that in the 1860s when hanging became private, being carried out inside gaols, hangmen became public figures. Marwood, Calcraft and Berry were household names, and, at a time when the only other public figures were either politicians or generals or, curiously enough, writers, they were, with prize fighters, the only working-class heroes. When Berry turned up in Carmarthen in 1888 to carry out a hanging, the first for 50 years in the county gaol and one for which Evans had unsuccesfully applied, crowds met him at the station to escort him through the streets, and he played up to his role. When he entered the condemned cell, the *Carmarthen Journal* reported, 'Mr Berry, unostentatiously dressed in a plain suit of dark clothing, *and wearing a red Turkish fez…*' The italics are mine, for it must have been bad enough contemplating one's last minutes without sharing these with some clown strayed from a carnival.

But then a black humour had never been far from the job and its strange practitioners, as I was to find when I met Syd Dearnley. His old master Pierrepoint kept a pub called *Help the Poor Struggler* and is said to have had this sign on his counter, 'No Hanging Around the Bar'. Dearnley himself when he came to write his own memoirs called them *The Hangman's Tail.* Robert Evans would have been at home in their company.

His own weakness was practical joking. When someone he knew well died, he called on the family to pay his last respects and asked as a special favour if he could be left alone with his old friend. In the silence that followed the family, waiting downstairs, heard some strange shuffling sounds, but it was only after Evans had gone, with more expressions of sympathy, that they found he had taken the stiffened corpse and propped it up in a corner so this was the first thing they saw when they came into the room. As his *Western Mail* obituarist observed, 'the horrified feelings of the household, when they discovered the empty coffin, and the new position taken up by its occupant, can be better imagined than described.'

Remarkably, given his interest in the subject, Evans always maintained that he did not believe in the taking of life, but, according to Matthew Spicer, this again is typical. 'If you read their memoirs you will find these all end the same way, even Pierrepoint's. They hang 500 people and then in retirement say they don't believe in capital punishment.'

Evans loved animals and children, one of whom in the recorded interviews remembered his own delight as a boy in calling at Fern Hill. 'He was bringing us sweets, apples and anything, and he had a son, and very often he wanted us to come into the garden and have a little play on the way home, and the little boy playing with us. He liked children, and children liked him.'

Which is why his daughter's estrangement must have hurt him. By considerable detective work, David Thomas tracked down what really happened. Frances Evans at 16 was taken ill at school and her father, frantically travelling between Fern Hill and Southport, arranged for her to be treated by a doctor called Blumberg, a Hungarian refugee who had founded a seaside convalescent children's home in the town. Despite the 15 years between them she and the doctor fell in love and some of his poems to her survive,

> We walked upon the velvet lawn,
> Amid the shade of oak and lime;
> We watched the day's resplendent dawn;
> We talked of love, defying time...

It was a remarkable interlude, given the context in which it took place. At 21, having come into her property, she eloped with him. Thereafter she refused to see her father except in the presence of her solicitor, a Carmarthen man called Barker whose diary records that, when they did meet, Frances and her father argued over money. Anything she did give him, she insisted, was to go towards paying off his by then considerable debts. Frances did not return to Fern Hill until 1901, when she came back to take over the arrangements for her father's burial in Llangynog church. He died, according to David Thomas, a poor man, leaving instead, as the *Western Mail* put it, 'the reminiscences of a career which, for remarkable incidents and wealth of originality in various phases, stands alone...'

But Liz Evans, his great-grandson's wife, says, 'He was just spoilt and very lazy. From the age of five he had been brought up by his grandparents and for the rest of his life he just went and did his own thing.' All Mrs Evans and her husband were left were some photographs of the Hangman and a small chair. When that happens in Wales the myths and the creepy glamour get brushed aside like cobwebs by Welsh matrons, whose unshakeable perspectives are things they share with the god-kings of the East.

And so it was, having accepted Syd Dearnley's invitation, I found myself having tea in a small terraced house in Mansfield, which, I suppose, gives me another sort of perspective; I must be the first to write on Evans who has actually met a hangman. Syd Dearnley, a former coalminer, was a strange human being, and what made the occasion even more strange was that Mrs Dearnley was making scones. His tales got more and more horribly funny, my eyes widened and widened (I had long before run out of speech), and the scones kept coming.

A good-looking bouncy man in his late sixties, he would have been the life and soul on any OAP seaside excursion, or, with his pipe and cardigan and slippers, anybody's grandfather. Except, that is, for his mementoes, a noose and a miniature guillotine he had made, and the odd little detail he threw in from time to time, like the fact that the Home Office paid its hangmen half their fee on the following morning after, half of it a fortnight later, this to ensure they did not gossip. In his case the fee was three guineas, later raised to five, plus third-class railfare, though Pierrepoint travelled first. He had applied for the job, he said, because as a lifelong devotee of detective fiction he hoped to meet criminals; he had not bargained on the fact that he would only meet them for eight seconds, which was the most extraordinary thing he told me, that being the time between the hangman's entering the condemned cell and the actual execution in a room next door. 'Though me and Albert, we did get one down to seven.'

And then there were the stories. There was the training course at Pentonville in 1948, when for a week he, and three other applicants, spent a week *doing long division sums*. 'What for? For the length of drop of course. You divided 1,000 by the man's weight. Otherwise you take his head off.' The rest of the time was taken up by exercises in pinioning, and in turns on the lever ('Push forward, just as in a signal box'). One of the others was an ice-cream salesman in Birmingham until news of his other job leaked out, sales fell, and his boss called him in. 'Harry, ice cream and hanging, they don't mix, boy.'

Like Evans, Dearnley was fascinated by the mechanics of the procedure, and when he retired bought the old gallows from Cambridge Gaol. It came in a Pickfords van. 'I put it up in our cellar, I was keeping a post office then. I got a shop model from John Collier's, put that on it, and fitted two green spotlights which you switched on at the cellar door. People would call round, and we'd have a few drinks down there, and it all went well until my wife got taken ill and her cousin came to keep house for me.

'I was stamping pensions when I saw this car drive down the road and a bloke get out and walk up my path. I thought no more about it until a few minutes later he came running out of the door and up the road, which was odd as he'd come by car. Apparently he'd called to read the electricity meters, the cousin didn't know where these were, and he said to leave it to him, that they were probably down the cellar...Odd thing, for ten years after that nobody came to read our meters. It were all estimates, got a bit expensive, that.'

In between the stories there were the practical jokes, the wobbly rubber hand he extended when we met ('Shake'), the safety razor stuck in one of the old round plugs ('Know where I can get this fixed?'). He lent me the memoir he was writing, and I must have kept this a long time, for a short reminder came by post ('If you don't want to find yourself dangling from one of your apple trees'). Another time he sent me a table of weights and drops, a sort of hangman's ready reckoner.

When we last spoke, a month before his death, he told me the last gallows in Britain had been dismantled. 'You know, the one they'd kept at Wandsworth for blokes with a mind to run off with the Queen'; it sounds barely credible, but at that stage, long after it had been abandoned for murder, it was still a capital offence to commit adultery with the Queen. The gallows, Dearnley told me, had been reassembled at the Prison Officers' Museum, where he urged me to go and see it. He himself, he said, had been twice.

Yes, I knew Robert Evans. Almost a hundred years after his death I felt I had met him.

6 THE LIARS

My father was one of an old, and, according to D.J. Williams in *The Old Farmhouse*, honoured part of Welsh society: he was a liar. And in middle age he came on someone he must have waited all his life to meet, someone bookish and arrogant and pleased with himself. He met me as a teenager.

He told me about the king cockle first. About three miles out from the cockle beds at Llansteffan, near where we lived, there was this king cockle, three feet across. All cockle beds had one, said my father, but they were never seen by men for they were yards down in the primordial mud of the estuary, only every so often, like the Kraken, each king cockle rose, and headed out to sea. When he did this all the little cockles followed, thereby emptying the beds until the king cockle took it into his head, or in what passes for a head with cockles, to return, at which point the beds filled again.

I went to the University of Oxford, believing this story, and talked about it to those I met there so that now, somewhere in Britain and the United States, there are elderly men, retired judges, doctors, civil servants, who believe in the king cockle.

There was also, my father said, a patient at Carmarthen Mental Hospital, an establishment so vast it was an alternative town on its hill, a patient who, like the king cockle, also occasionally headed out to sea. I remember seeing him, a small man in a striped bathing costume like that worn by Captain Webb, swimming on and on until his head was a dot far out among the breakers at the bar.

That man, said my father, had the digestive system of a python. He would pass a motion once a month, going into labour for this, and the end product would be the size and consistency of a brick. My father must have sensed some disbelief on my part, for at this point he administered the coup de grâce. A man from *The Lancet*, he said, had come all the way from London to photograph it. Ah, *The Lancet*, the written word. The old liars knew the weak points of their audience.

If you have ever driven along the A40 from Llandeilo to Llandovery, then you will know the huge stone in a lay-by just after the Llangadog turn. It is a perfect cube, which is its most extraordinary feature, about ten feet square. Known as the Great Stone, it reeks of ancient mystery, for what giant builders left it there in unrecorded time?

'No, it was Haydn and me,' said my father. 'We were moving some stones on the back of a lorry, and that one was just a bit heavy so we left it there. We must go back and move it one day.'

But then he knew his audience. My father was talking to someone who in one year, aged 17, had won three State Scholarships. He was talking to the most gullible fool who ever came down a turnpike.

7 THE DEVIL WALKS

March, 1712. The great judge Sir John Powell, having heard evidence from the clergy at the last witchcraft trial held in England that the accused, an elderly woman called Jane Wenham, could fly, something she confirmed in court, said wearily, 'There be no law against flying.' The judiciary can be blunt when confronted by the supernatural.

March, 1991. Mr Justice Douglas Brown, having heard evidence at Rochdale from more expert witnesses, social workers this time, that 16 children had been taken from their parents on the grounds that they had been subjected to Satanic abuse, said just as wearily that it was highly unlikely this had occurred as Satanism usually involved people of high intelligence, 'a description which cannot be attributed to the people of the area we are talking about.' In other words, you need a degree to talk to the Devil.

This would have been of interest to Jane Wenham, who was not a graduate, but claimed to have enjoyed many chats with him in the shape of a cat. But it was of even more interest to me as I am probably the last person living to have been mistaken for the Devil.

I was staying with my mother who then lived in the village of Llangadog, and, having no car at the time, was obliged to rely for transport on a friend called Lynn Hughes. This night we had had a few drinks in local pubs and when these closed he suggested we call on someone we both knew who ran a small hotel in the back of beyond, in the foothills of the Black Mountain, near where the present Prince of Wales now has a foothold on his Principality. It must have been close on midnight but with the confidence of the half-cut we did this, and, remarkably, the man opened up, and even more remarkably opened up a bottle of whiskey as well.

Most of this had gone when the row broke out. It was the sort of small-hours row which usually seems to involve facts. I had been going on, and probably on, about the battle of Agincourt, as one does, when Hughes said casually that it was common knowledge that it was not the long bow that had won Agincourt, but the short bow, used at close range. One thing led to another, and I stormed out.

All very dramatic, except that, among the dripping laurels, it was then I remembered I had no car. Still there was no going back now so I set off down the drive, muttering to myself, and fell into a hedge. That was when I realised I had no moon either. Or stars. Or lights anywhere in the whole landscape. When I got out of my hedge, I found I could not see the hand I was holding in front of my face.

I had never known darkness like it, but, still, I was on a road and set off in the general direction of home, stamping my heels to reassure myself I was still on tarmac. I was wearing a pair of ex-cavalry Wellington leather boots I had bought at an Army surplus store, the heels of which had been fitted, not with steel tips, but with complete small horseshoes, so the stamping, and the reassurance, were remarkable. I was in the hedge again once, but it didn't matter; I was encased in indignation, like an astronaut in an alien and meaningless world.

Which was why I took no notice of the splash. I had heard it some way off in the darkness, but thought no more about it until, drawing level with the spot, I suddenly heard a voice, a quavering voice speaking in Welsh, so low down it seemed to be that of a goblin and to come out of the earth itself. '*Pwy sy'na?*' Who's there?

Had I been less preoccupied I should have been off like a shot, for this was the Black Mountain where you expect to meet goblins. After all, one local man had married one, and their upwardly mobile sons, having had a head's start, all became doctors. As it was, I merely snapped, 'What business is it of yours?' The conversation which followed was in Welsh.

'For the love of God tell me.' That stopped me in my tracks, for the English on the whole tend not to appeal to the Deity. 'Where are you going?'

It was at that point that I realised that the man, if he was a man, was terrified, and I heard myself telling him my name and destination. And suddenly there was a hand, followed by an arm that wrapped itself round my knees. I was frightened then, for how tall was the creature?

'Oh thanks be to God, thank God.'

I put my hand down and there was a mass of wet hair and a head that seemed to be the right size. I bent and there was a coat, also wet, very wet, and as I pulled him to his feet, for he seemed to be a man, everything about him, in the middle of Wales, felt as though he had just come out of the sea.

The words tumbled out of him, between shudders. He had been coming home, he said, when in the darkness he had heard footsteps and, peering into the darkness, had seen sparks coming towards him. Of course, the heels and the reassurance. But he, he had had no doubts: the Devil was out, and he had done what any reasonable man would have done in the circumstances. He had dived into the nearest ditch, into which, for it had been raining for days, the Mountain had drained.

We stood there, our arms round each, neither of us, it must be said, entirely sober, for I kept getting whiffs of his breath. Slowly his trembling subsided. We moved apart, shook hands, and that was it. It had been such a brief, and strange encounter, I had not even thought to ask his name, or where he was going. I had not even seen his face, it was that dark, so I had no idea of how old he was. I sensed he was smaller than I was, and quite thin, but when I made enquiries the next morning I could find out nothing about him.

All I know is that in my lifetime, in a world of satellites and the Internet, it was still possible to meet a man who believed that the Devil walked. Oh yes, and one other thing. Thanks to Mr Justice Brown, I know that my lost friend of the small hours had been a man of high intelligence. Most probably a judge by now.

8 THE WIZARD

A man tinkering with his car beside the A482 main road in the village of Pumsaint gave directions. He knew the small farm of Pantcoy in the hills, he said; he knew the people who lived there. The only thing was, in 2002 he seemed to know less about them than he did about a man who had died there in 1839.

But in the village of Caeo amongst those hills they knew his grave. 'Come with me, I'll show it to you,' said a man in the pub. We stood in the village street. 'That's it, by the church wall, the last one in that row of three. But you'll have to go in on your own. I went to see it one Halloween, and I haven't been right since.'

It is a small slate gravestone on which is written in English, 'In memory of Henry Jones, Pantcoy, who died August 6, 1805, aged 66. Also...' And there it was, the name I was looking for. 'Also of his son John Harries, Surgeon, who died May 11th, 1839, aged 54.' The discrepancy in the surnames was the first mystery, but 'John Harries, Surgeon', that was to be expected. They could not have described him as anything else on consecrated Christian ground.

If you look him up in the *Dictionary of Welsh Biography* you will find a job description accorded to no one else with the one exception of his son Henry, with whom he is sometimes confused, 'Astrologer, medicine man, and conjuror.' Astrologer, medicine man, and conjuror? Not in Transylvania, but in the hills of North Carmarthenshire? But John Harries was more than that. 'The man was a genuine full-blown wizard,' said the Rev. Dr Patrick Thomas, once vicar of Brechfa. In the churchyard at Caeo was the owner of the Book With The Seven Locks.

And I saw a strong angel proclaiming with a loud voice, Who is worthy to open the book, and to loose the seals thereof?

In the archives of the National Library of Wales in Aberystwyth there is a photograph of a dark, heavy-lidded man, a high cravat at his throat, the costume of the early Victorians. His hands clasped, the man stares dreamily out of his frame. The catalogue description reads simply, 'Dr John Harries, a year before his death, taken at his home by M.D. Bourne of New York. On glass.' I had heard of this, but had not believed what I had been told. *This photograph should simply not exist.*

For we are going back to the origins of photography, to a time before Julia Margaret Cameron, who photographed Tennyson, before Matthew Grady, who photographed the American Civil War, before Fox Talbot even. We are going back to a time when, to have his picture taken, a man had to sit motionless for up to a quarter of an hour in the controlled setting of a studio. Yet this picture, it is said, was taken by an American photographer who for this one purpose had travelled to a small farm in one of the remotest parts of Wales, to meet... what? And where?

Pantcoy, Cwrt y Cadno. The Court of the Fox. The Court of the Fox is not on any map, it is just a meeting place of lanes in the hills and to find it you will need to ask directions, as I did, but not of the young or the new English settlers. You will need to go to the old and the Welsh-speaking, to whom the knowledge was passed down. 'It's another world up there,' a man in Carmarthen had told me. At night you are startled to see a light, any light, in the landscape.

Yet in Roman times this would have been the last glimpse men would have had of this world, before as slaves they were herded underground to work until they died in the dripping galleries of the Imperial gold mine at Dolaucothi. You feel anything can happen here.

And it was in this area that once a year John Harries, cowled and carrying his Book With The Seven Locks, was said to climb the hills to a stone. When he did this the skies would darken over Caeo, and thunder would roll as he opened the Book. It was a time when in London the men who finally passed the Reform Act were debating the opening of the franchise, but far away in west Wales one man was opening Hell. 'I conjure thee, thou great and potent Prince...'

'When I was headmistress at Caeo school, an old gentleman turned up who offered to show me and the children John Harries's stone,' said Esme Jones. 'I'd always known him as Mr Jones, but he

47

now told me that he was John Harries's direct descendant, but that the family had changed their name out of shame and because of the Methodists. He took us up into the hills and there was a stone, the size of a single bed. His ancestor, he said, had derived some power from it, but after his death local people had tried to cut into it to see what was there. And sure enough the stone was broken.

'I don't think I'd be able to find my way there again.'

His spells survive, also in the National Library of Wales, where it is thought no one has repeated them, possibly on the grounds on which the Keeper of Egyptian Antiquities at the British Museum refused someone access to the galleries at night, that his request might involve too much broken glass. The man had asked, very politely, if he might raise the dead.

I called at Pantcoy, a neat smallholding set back in the hillside, which for 12 years had been rented by Tim Davies, a retired headmaster, from the Royal Society for the Protection of Birds. 'Yes, I must admit I do feel a certain aura here, but it doesn't concern me much. I am coming to the end of my days and I don't worry about the future. But people call on us, they still seem to want to know about the Doctor.'

There are few facts. The first is that Harries was sent to London by his father to study medicine, so he may well have qualified at one of the hospitals at the same time as John Keats. He then came home and began to practise as a doctor, and was said to have been so successful in treating mental illness that a path over the hills trodden by lunatics and their concerned relatives became known as Dr Harries's Path. His methods were startling.

'See that stream beneath us?' said Tim Davies at Pantcoy. 'He would take the lunatics down there, stand them on the bank, then fire a pistol behind their backs, which would so frighten them they usually fell in.'

This may have been his early equivalent of electric shock treatment. Stories like this about his medical prowess are hearsay, but there is one eye-witness account by a Brecon farmer recorded in the *The Carmarthenshire Antiquary*. As a youth, this man had gone to consult Harries with a lad of his own age whose grandfather was very ill.

'We walked across the hills and were there by three, maybe. There was old Harries on the midden with a dung fork, hard at it. "Hello," he says, "you've been a long time coming. Well, I can do nothing for you. The old man's time is come, and he won't last long…"

'We hadn't opened our mouths to him. And he did see us staring. "Have I made a mistake?" he says. "Haven't you come from Brecon, boys, to enquire about old___?" Well, I reckoned myself pretty clever then, and I thought I could see (through) it. But he turned round and caught the smile on my face. "I know what you're thinking. You think I have friends to send on word who's coming, and what is their errand. Maybe, but maybe too I can see for myself and hear for myself at a distance. Maybe. Now shall I tell you what I can see below your left knee? I can see a great white scar."

' "Nothing of the sort," said I, and up with my trousers and down with my stocking. No scar there of course. "Maybe not," he says. "And maybe. Go home, and remember." So we went. And the old man did die in a few weeks.

'Come harvest, I was on the rick, and, the last load up, I slipped and came down on top of the hay-rake, and, as God was pleased, it was there I caught it, and there the scar is now. Ripped to the bone and bleeding, oh dear, oh dear, but thankful it was no worse…I was very respectful of old Harries after that.'

In this account you will note how quickly we have moved out of the world of medicine. Something similar is true of the collection of John Harries's books presented by the family to the National Library of Wales in 1937. These include the first edition of the *Encyclopaedia Britannica*, published in 1771 and worth God knows what today, books in Greek and Latin, and an edition of *An Anatomy of Melancholy*: in other words, the small library of a well-read and intelligent man. But there are other books as well.

There is an edition of the mutterings of the seer Nostradamus, also a manuscript, *John Harries of Cwrt-y-Cadno, His Holograph Book of Incantations, Astronomical Signs and Calculating Bills*. It is a lovely touch, the *Calculating Bills,* but then Harries, whatever else he was, was a businessman. This manuscript is mainly a workshop manual for the raising of spirits, and contains the sentence, 'I conjure thee, thou great and potent Prince', this in English, presumably on the grounds that the Devil could not understand Welsh, which would have endeared Harries to the Methodists. Of *The Book,* that of the Seven Locks, opened once a year, there is no sign.

Yet once its rumoured existence was enough. An unpaid printed medical bill survives among Harries's papers. 'Sir, Unless the unpaid amount is paid to me, on or before a certain date, adverse means will be resorted to, for the recovery...' The suspicion lingers that by that Harries did not mean a bailiff would call, at least not one of this earth.

Harries found things. He told people where stolen rings were, and cows, and, on the odd occasion, bodies. This could have complications as when he told her relatives where a missing girl's body lay, and who had killed her. As a result, for it had been as he said, he was brought before the bench at Llandovery, charged with being an accomplice. It was a very short trial. Harries looked at the magistrates and helpfully offered to tell them the date, to the hour if they liked, when each of them would die, and was acquitted.

The modern world intruded once, in 1839, the year of his death, when his son Henry, like all sons rejoicing in the opportunity to try out new business methods, placed an ad in a magazine. It shows what he considered to be his family's trading concerns. 'NATIVITIES CALCULATED, in which are given the general transactions of the native through life, viz: Description (without seeing the person), temper, disposition, fortunate or unfortunate in their general pursuits: honour, riches, journeys and voyages, success therein, and what places best to travel to (or reside in); whether fortunate in speculations, viz: Lottery dealing in foreign markets, etc. Of children, whether fortune or not, etc, deduced from the influence of the Sun and Moon, with the Planetary Orbs at the time of birth. Also judgement and general issue in sickness...'

There is no reference to demons: Henry is running an astrological agency. The irony is that he, who claimed to foresee so much, had not foreseen what would happened next. The magazine's editor, having accepted the ad and been paid for it, rounded on his advertiser in the next issue.

'We have heard of countless numbers of impostors in every age, who were effective and successful in securing credibility for their enchantments from the populace; but there is some impudence and devilry in Mr Henry Harries's card, far above anything on offer before...' And so on. And on. It was an extraordinary outburst, quite impossible for an editor to make today; his marketing men would see to that.

But the Harrieses never doubted their power. When the Doctor died, having predicted that his would be no natural death, he had, as any sane person would under the circumstances, taken to his bed and was waiting. Unfortunately Pantcoy caught fire, and he fell from a ladder while throwing buckets of water at the flames, falling into his burning house as the roof collapsed.

The burial was even more extraordinary. The bearers, who had initially staggered under the weight of his coffin, said it got lighter and lighter the further away from the house they got, and a herd of cows stampeded as it went by and did not stop running for miles.

Henry the businessman took over, and when he died in 1862 his son John took over. But John had no flair for it, so the long agricultural years, and the quiet, returned to Pantcoy. A Mrs Jenkins of Aberystwyth, who had lived with the family as a child, said she had often opened the great locked Book without ill effects of any kind. But when a stranger called towards the end of the 19th century and said breezily as he was shown it, 'Well, this is the book used to raise evil spirits', a local man, his guide, ran screaming from the house as he made to open it.

So who, or what, was Harries? In *The Carmarthenshire Antiquary* of 1924, Mary Lewis sought to present him in terms of a long tradition. 'From the days of Merlin downward, the Wise Man (*y Dyn Hysbys*) has always been a tradition in rural Wales.' Lefi Gruffudd, general editor of Lolfa Books, who wrote a thesis on the Wise Man, said that in the 1930s one such actually held surgeries in Aberystwyth. 'They offered help when there were no other options.

At one level they were witches, at another they were doctors, and, at a third, detectives. Where Harries may have been different is the atmosphere he conjured up to convey his power. People believed he could do anything.'

'Here was a literate man in a remote area,' said Dr Patrick Thomas. 'Latin and spells and mumbo-jumbo would have made a deep impression on people. When I first came to Brechfa, I can remember watching someone cut down an elder tree, and the old man I was with turned and said, 'He who cuts down an elder tree / A death in his house soon will be...' Sure enough, a few weeks later...'

I sat in the pub at Caeo with the man who had earlier shown me Harries's grave, and asked what had happened to the wizards? As I asked that, I was aware of an irony, for he, sharp-faced and rosy-cheeked, his hair falling to his shoulders, his beard halfway down his chest, would not have needed make-up to appear in the film of *Lord of the Rings;* he was old Gandalf to the life.

'What's happened?' He leant forward, his beard wagging. 'Everything's changed, a man can't *move* for Englishmen here now.'

There is an epilogue. It has nothing to do with the Harrieses, and you will have to imagine what Alfred Hitchcock would have done with the black comedy that followed when Christopher Challener, a retired chef, turned up at Caeo, intent on research into his family tree.

'My father had told me his mother's name was Tremble, and that her family had come from Ireland. But when I traced them on the 1881 Census I found she and some of her brothers and sisters had been born in Wales, in a pub called the Sexton Arms in Caeo, though by the time of the Census they were living in Clapton in London. What was even more puzzling was that there was no mention of a father; at 38, my great-grandmother was a widow with six children.

'Anyway time passed, and, in Wales trying to find a house to retire to, my partner and I were looking at a map when we noticed how close we were to Caeo. When we got there, to this village in the hills, there was no Sexton Arms but there was a pub, and the barman, a young chap, said, yes, there was a house called the Sexton opposite the graveyard. It seemed so small, just two up, two down, I couldn't see how it could ever have housed six children and two adults. Then the barman introduced me to a chap he said was the churchwarden.

'I told him I was looking for my great-grandfather, and when he asked me his name I said "Henry Tremble." The moment I said that everything stopped. He didn't say anything, he just sat there, his eyes bulging, as though all the lights had gone out in his head. I bought him a pint, at which the lights began to come on again. Very slowly he said, "That name is very well known around here." And then he told me the story.'

In 1876 Tremble, the butler at nearby Dolaucothi Mansion, one August morning shot the squire, wounded his daughter, then shot all the dogs. His motive was that his employer had promised him the tenancy of the Dolaucothi Arms, then gone back on his word.

'He told me all this, and now my eyes were bulging. He took me to the church where he unlocked a chest with a huge key. Among the details of the burials we came across something scratched out, across which someone had written, "This space reserved for Tremble", which puzzled me as I thought murderers were buried in jail in quicklime after being hanged.

'The churchwarden couldn't explain this, but he took me to see a woman actually living in the house called Sexton, whose old mother might know. But she was ill so we returned to the pub, it was about nine o'clock at night by now. Then suddenly this woman appeared in the doorway, beckoning. She had told her mother the name, and the old lady had insisted on getting up just to see me.

'She didn't ask me in, I remember that. Well, what would you do, faced with the great-grandson of a murderer? She peered out at me, the door between us, as she told me what had happened *after* the murder.'

Tremble had fled to his house, the Sexton Arms, where, besieged by the police, he finally shot himself and was buried in the churchyard. Only a few days later, such was people's revulsion, he was dug up and, arrangements having been made, was taken by night to a quietly dug grave in the next county, in the churchyard of Llandulas in Breconshire. From this three months later, as local people got to know who, and what, he was, he was dug up again, his coffin driven a second time through the night, then dumped at dawn at the church gate in Caeo. That was the end of his travels, and he lies there now in an unmarked grave.

Challener, having heard all this, drove away. But the President of the Immortals, in the phrase of Thomas Hardy who would have loved this story, had not yet done with him. On a May night, 125 years after these events, a Dyfed-Powys police squad car near Llandovery stopped a car which was going so slowly it had aroused their suspicions. On being questioned, the driver Challener said this was because an hour earlier he had found out that his great-grandfather was a murderer. Which cleared everything up wonderfully.

9 *And this is what my people got up to*

ANOTHER WALES

It looks like an academic work. *Secret Sins* by Dr Russell Davies of Aberystwyth, a social historian, is published by the University of Wales Press, and footnotes occupy a quarter of its text. It is just that I have never seen an academic work with a title like that, and certainly not one which has this for a foreword: 'In view of some of the disturbing nature of some of the evidence which is contained in this book, it is probably sensible to begin with the statement that I was born and raised in the county of Carmarthenshire. The people we will encounter in this book, saints and sinners, are my people.'

And here they come. One or two you will have heard of, like the visionary who saw the Devil in a hedge at Newcastle Emlyn, and, what was much worse, heard him *laugh*. But in a wink of an eye he is gone, shouldered aside by a merry rout of drunks, whores and wizards, not one of whom you will ever have come on in any history book. These are the people of what seems like a parallel Wales in the 50 years between 1870 and 1920.

There she goes, Rose Barnes, who looked into the future with such success, she was charged during the First World War with 'making statements likely to interfere with the success of His Majesty's Forces'. And Sarah Williams of Manordeilo, who claimed that a Fred Rodley had 'slid down my chimney and seduced me.' And Daniel Jones, shoemaker of Carmarthen, so rarely out of court that, in an age which lauded Gladstone as its Grand Old Man, became known as the town's 'Grand Old Drunkard'. On his last appearance, when the workhouse let him out for an afternoon, he was 74: it was his 97th time in court.

Here too are the members and officers of the Ammanford Conservative Club, swearing blind that their club had been formed 'to promote the interests of the Conservative Party'. At which the whole court, it was reported, burst into laughter, for everyone there knew that the club had been formed so its members could drink on Sundays. Bleakly the police revealed that £86 6s 10d had been spent at the bar, 17s 6d on books and newspapers.

A prostitute, arrested in Carmarthen, was so drunk she had to be taken to the police station in a wheelbarrow, unlike a Mrs Bowen of Llanelli who attended so conscientiously to the cast of the Buffalo Bill Wild West Show this had to be postponed.

And here come Daniel Rees and Evan Jones, farmworkers of St Clears, who in 1905 called on a neighbouring farm, hoping to attract the attention of its servant girls, when in the time-honoured way they threw sand and gravel at the windows. When this didn't work they threw, first cockles, then bricks, and broke all the glass.

But, leading them all, is a man who, on an April morning in 1907, stood begging on Carmarthen Bridge. '(He) was looking about him and taking stock of the passers-by while he bore on his manly chest a board which stated that he had lost his sight in a colliery explosion,' recorded a journalist from the *Carmarthen Weekly Recorder*.

'Feeling convinced there must have been a mistake, I asked the man how he could see so well after a total loss of sight. He could not read, evidently, and he asked in an agitated state what the board said. On it being read to him, he said, "Here's a pretty mess, I've taken out some other chap's board. *I'm really deaf and dumb!*"'

All the Immortals...

For this was the time of the Great Religious Revival, when men saw the Holy Ghost in flames over the pine pews, a chapel a week was opening, and the Welsh were being told they were the Elect of God, a minister in Llanelli reminding his flock that if any impurity existed it had sneaked in from England.

Russell Davies's research started respectably enough. Initially this had been into late Victorian Carmarthenshire politics, but a time came when he moved into new source material often neglected by historians, contemporary local newspapers. And that was it really. Afternoons were long in the National Library of Wales, and he found his attention straying from the reports of Parliamentary elections to police courts, to readers' letters, and to columns, one in particular.

This had appeared in the *Carmarthenshire Weekly Reporter* under the pen name *Alethia*, which was startling in itself, for it was a reminder of the sort of learning you could then encounter in weekly newspapers in small Welsh towns. *Alethia* was the Greek for Truth, and the column came in with the motto, 'Come with me and I will show you truth...' So Russell Davies did, and was.

Picture the enormous quiet of a research library, broken only by the odd cough, the shuffling of paper and the whispered conversation at the main desk. And, in the middle of all this, a man being drawn into bedlam, into a world of booze and brothels, with all its place-names already familiar, only he had known nothing of any of this.

It is a great mystery why *Secret Sins* has never made the big screen, for just think what a film it would make, as a young scholar is confronted by the possibility that once the grandparents of his neighbours, the quiet pigeon fancier in his back garden and the lady who wore a hat with cherries on it to chapel, had been part of a world not far removed from the Wild West, perhaps not quite one of six guns and gartered fishnet, but still a world of terrifying violence and of great comedy, the existence of which had never been recognised.

'There is a wonderful line in the diary of the great preacher, Howell Harris: "I was tempted to smile yesterday, but fortunately I suppressed the urge",' said Dr Davies. 'The Methodists genuinely believed that in Wales they had a society which, if properly directed, could be made one hundred per cent pure. For that they were prepared to suppress the humour, the music, the fun of Merry Wales, and even to deny that its traditions had ever existed.

'But what I hadn't known was that they had failed even in their heyday.'

Central to this push for purity was the claim, or outrageous humbug, that Wales was the Land of the White Gloves, an unique place free of all crime, it being the custom to present a judge with a pair of white gloves when no one on a criminal charge appeared before him at an assize. This has been a claim accepted by responsible Welsh historians.

But now Russell Davies began to encounter the open scepticism of judges. 'Gentlemen, I would willingly congratulate you on the non-existence of crime if it did not exist,' a judge was reported as telling local magistrates, 'but as I believe it does exist, though by some means it is not brought before me, my congratulations must assume a modified form.'

He found magistrates dismissing some cases out of hand, as when in 1901 the Llanelli bench dismissed the case of a woman charged with concealing a birth on a farm where pigs had subsequently eaten the body. He read about a population so contemptuous of the police that when in Tumble in 1906 the village policeman arrested two men his house was attacked by a crowd of 200 who threw 75 lbs of stones (for someone must have weighed them) through his windows. The men were released.

The humbug extended to poetry, where there was the idyllic evocation of family values in the countryside when rural Carmarthenshire had one of the highest illegitimacy rates in Britain. As for the little lime-washed cottages with roses climbing the walls, so lovingly depicted, there was this song composed by, of all people, a county councillor:

> The cottage homes of Gwalia,
> How dreadfully they smell,
> With phthisis in the thatched roof
> And sewage in the well.

But what is so extraordinary is how, until very recently, so many eminent Welsh people were prepared to conspire in the confection of a national myth. A graduate woman student at Aberystwyth 30 years ago was advised not to research mediaeval Welsh poetry as this could be bad for her soul, for in academic circles it was already well known what she would find. The Methodists, and the scholars who attended their chapels, had concealed the existence of the most erotic poetry written in any language. Yet that too was there in the National Library, not the odd poem or two, but a whole tradition of such verse.

This only tumbled into the light of day in 1991, when David Johnston, an English scholar, brought out his *Mediaeval Welsh Erotic Poetry*. And even then Dr Johnston had to form his own publishing house to bring out the book himself. He is now Dafydd Johnston, the professor of Welsh at Swansea; at the time, coming from outside the traditions of Welsh scholarship, he was stunned at the Stalinist conspiracy that had been required to keep this verse secret. But Stalin had the whole apparatus of his secret police at his disposal, this just had the willing complicity of Welsh scholars. In the collected edition of the great Welsh poet Dafydd ap Gwilym, his editor Tom Parry had ignored poems like the one in which, mocking the convention by which a poet sends a messenger, often a bird, to his love, Dafydd had sent his genitalia.

The irony was that while all this seemed part of a parallel Welsh world, it was written with great formal skill, as though Grinling Gibbons had carved a lavatory seat. Not only that, it was not just a lost literature, it was a lost language in that the words used to describe physical detail had themselves been erased in the discreet centuries that followed. In his translation (for oh dear, he translated the stuff into English as well), Dr Johnston had to rely on gynaecological guesswork.

'But the shock was that these poets, a woman amongst them (who wrote a poem to her vagina), were treating such matters without neurosis or guilt, so in my modest way I was presenting a new Welsh national character,' said Dr Johnston. 'Thirty years ago my head of department would probably not have allowed me to publish.'

Thirty years ago, as Russell Davies acknowledges, he would not have had his own book published by an university press. 'I don't think they'd even have believed me, that alongside the high Victorian morality there were these other aspects to life in Wales. But what I have found so welcome is that ordinary people have said, "Yes, that's how my father said it was." Nobody has taken against it.'

Yet this was the nation that was hit by the high tide of the Religious Revival of 1904, when preachers conjured up such descriptions of Hell, and induced such ecstasy in their congregations, some men were quite literally made mad. An old professor of French I knew in my youth in Carmarthen told me of the sermon he had heard in his, when the preacher described a damned soul, after thousands, millions, of years in darkness, coming back to the gates of Hell where he saw that the second hand on the great clock, *the second hand,* had not moved. In one year alone, 1905, 16 people were confined in the Lunatic Asylum at Carmarthen because of their religious delusions. A collier from Llanarthne jumped into the river Towy, from which he bellowed to interested passers-by that his sins were unpardonable. He was dragged out, and he too ended up in the Asylum, which, on its opening in 1865 claimed that 40 per cent of its patients would be cured. Five years later this claim was seven per cent.

The Asylum, a vast Gothic building on a hill above the town became virtually a town itself, with its own farm, tailors, butchers, laundry, and was one of the sights of Carmarthen, work excursions from nearby industrial Llanelli ending up there so trippers, after a day on the beer, could laugh through the gates at the inmates. The first railway package tour of Wales in 1852, starting at Bristol 'for a run on the rails and a few days among the furnaces of South Wales', ended in a visit to the Briton Ferry Lunatic Asylum so those who had taken up the offer could attend the Lunatics' Ball. Here they might have met the Reverend Benjamin Jones who attributed his insanity to preaching and drinking, a possibly unique moment when the two were associated, and it is a pointer to the stress of existing in the two parallel worlds of Wales.

But nowhere is this nether world mentioned. A coachman in Llangynnwr, near Carmarthen, committed suicide when his employer bought a car. Soldiers home on leave from the First World War killed themselves, as did mothers worried about their sons on the Western Front. Yet the deacons at Bancyfelin chapel sent telegrams to every local boy serving in the Trenches to instruct them that they were on no account 'to touch rum'. And the poets wrote steadily on about thatched cottages in the West, their inhabitants sustained by religious faith and their own innate purity. No mention of their poverty.

No mention either of what a mart day in Carmarthen really looked like, which a correspondent in the town's *Weekly Reporter* compared to Matabeleland for barbarism, cows being driven through the streets. 'St Peter's Church stands on an island surrounded by a green sea, ankle-deep in foul smelling manure.' It was at times still like that in my youth in the 1950s, but in its Victorian heyday it must have been like Dodge City when the cattle drives of the Old West hit town.

Carmarthen then had a higher murder rate than Dodge, and more pubs too. There was such a tradition of treating the electorate to free booze that in 1898 a Parliamentary candidate, a rich man, resigned before the election on the grounds that he could not afford the campaign. The Grand Old Drunkard, then at his peak, was merely the first among equals.

'In newspapers you get the colour and the life,' said Russell Davies. 'Some of my colleagues had misgivings, they said such a source was bound to be biased, but any misgivings I had were swept aside when I found they gave me a worm's eye upwards. Here were stories that historians had either filed away or just forgotten.'

People still believed in fairies who, it was said, regularly attended markets at Milford Haven and Laugharne. His family contested one man's will because it was believed he was bewitched when he wrote it. Farmers accepted advice from the Agricultural Department at Aberystwyth University in its beginnings because they believed its lecturers were wizards.

So they swirled around Russell Davies, this remarkable cast from the Wales his research had conjured up. And now they, and the preachers, are gone. The chapels are closing at a rate of one a week, which in Victorian times were being built at the rate of one a week, converted now into lingerie factories, strip-clubs, recording studios, bingo halls.

We have heard the chimes at midnight, Master Shallow.

10 THE LANE

A church, that is your first landmark. It is two miles from St Clears on the dual carriageway of the A40 to Carmarthen, on a T-junction where a signpost points to the villages of Llanybri and Llansteffan, a Victorian church, an off-the-peg job, not a thing of beauty: architectural historians, and motorists, would not give it a second glance. But for us it is a starting point for our walk in the lane. We are not going far, four miles at most, it is just that in those four miles we will move through a thousand years, know horror and wonder, and end up in the Bayeux Tapestry. And it is such a little lane.

But pause a moment and look over the graveyard wall, at one grave in particular. On September 23, 1994, there died, aged 80, Miss Alsace Lorraine Owen, though a startled monumental mason spelt her first name as 'Alscace'. Never mind, take 80 from 1994 and what do you get? A newspaper headline from the start of the Great War: Alsace Lorraine, the disputed provinces of France, a matter for generals, but in west Wales a matter for the Registrar.

The week I first noticed that name I read in the *Carmarthen Journal* of the death a few miles away of Miss Ivy Dardanella Evans, and spent a morning tracing her niece. 'They liked names like that in our family, they liked the sound of them,' said Mrs Glenda Thomas. 'When my second son was born my mother registered the birth and, before we knew anything about it, she had 'Timoshenko' put on the certificate, after the Russian general. We never called him that, so it was a bit of a shock when the doctor came round three years later to immunise a Timoshenko Thomas. We'd forgotten this was our Randall.'

We are in the lane now, going past the first farm on the left, Penyrheol. My mother was born there in 1917, and it was here, two years later, that my uncle Jack returned on leave from the British Army of Occupation in the Rhineland. But see that farm just beyond it? The Gate Farm, Y Gât as they called it, was then being farmed by a man called Jones, who, dressed all in black, drove his horse and trap standing up, his eyes, according to my uncle Jack, like coals. I grew up with the story of Mr Jones.

It was midnight when his wife hammered on my grandfather's door. Jones (Welsh farmers' wives called their husbands by their surnames), she said, had got his cut-throat razor and she was terrified as to what he might do. She was in a state of great distress, also of fear, and they did not like to question her further.

There was a high harvest moon when my grandfather set off down the lane, taking my uncle Jack with him. They had no light, it was a time before torches, and in 1919 there would have been no light anywhere in the landscape, but the moon was bright. My grandfather Caleb Davies was a tough nut, a mountain fighter in the Rhondda in his early days, but what he remembered most in later years was his own terror as they turned into the farmyard, for, though she never admitted this, Jones was thought to have tried to murder his own wife. Put yourself in the place of the two men: moonlight, a dog barking, a horse snickering uneasily, and shadows, out of which at any moment there might explode a maniac with a long razor. The house was locked, so they crept round the side, trying each of the windows in turn until finally they found one that opened. The sound, said my grandfather, was deafening.

'What did you do?' I was ten, and it was the first time I had spoken since he began the story.

'What did I do? I pushed Jack in through the window before he knew what was going on.' My grandfather laughed. He always laughed at that point, whenever I got him to tell the story, and this always filled me partly with irritation, partly, it must be said, with relief.

So now one of them was in the house, crashing through the furniture as he rushed to open the back door, and, if he stopped, there was just the loud tick of the clock. There was no sign of Jones in any of the downstairs rooms so there was nothing for it but to try the stairs, and this was the worst part. The stairs were narrow and without carpet so their feet clattered on the boards, and, there being room for only one, Jack the serving soldier was again made to go first. Between the pushing, the whispered arguments and the clattering, they did not hear the groans at first. These came from a room at the top of the stairs, the one with its door ajar.

The first thing my grandfather saw was corn, sheaves of it on the floor. The Government had got farmers to grow this during the War, something the small dairy farmers of west Wales were not used to, given the rain, so Jones must have brought some indoors to dry. And then my grandfather saw him.

'He was in the moonlight on his hands and knees, he looked like a beast of the field.' When he spoke English, my grandfather's language was studded with the phrases of the Authorised Version. If she was there my mother would try to stop him at that point so the narrative was often interrupted, resumed when she had gone. 'I knelt beside him and I said, "Jones, Jones, what have you done?" But though he was still alive, he was beyond talking. His puddings were hanging out of him.'

The farmer, using the razor, had performed a version of hara-kiri, two sweeps across, one up, according to my grandfather, looking round to see where my mother was, but it was what he himself did next that fascinated me.

'Do? What could I do, except gather his puddings up in my hands and push them back in? Terrible job, but according to the doctor the best thing I could have done, it kept them warm, see. Not that it helped him, he'd gone long before the doctor came.'

Half a mile on the lane forks into two. Of these one leads to the old manor house of Treventy, below which, in a little wood on the edge of the marsh leading down to the River Taf, the Middle Ages await us. The wood hides the little ruined church of Llanfihangel Abercywyn, St Michael's on the mouth of the Cywyn, no more than a stream, where it enters the Taf. This, according to tradition, was where the pilgrims taking the sea route to St David's Cathedral came in from the storms to make a landfall. I was born near this stream, in a house with the English name of Cowin Villa.

'You've no idea who called the other day. Molly Parkin,' said Farmer Thomas at Treventy. Mrs Parkin writes novels, one of which starts, uncompromisingly, with the words 'Lick it,' he said. 'She could probably do with a pilgrimage, that one,' said Farmer Thomas.

The three graves under a huge yew in the abandoned churchyard are a mystery, being older by some 600 years than the farmers' graves lying higgledy-piggledy around them. But then they are older than any of the graves you have seen in any churchyard, for they are from a time when all those who could afford a stone of any kind got buried inside the church. Those under the yew were at the mercy of the wind and rain, and it is a small miracle they have survived.

For another grouping of two, with a small grave between them, probably that of a child, are so broken it is impossible to make out anything about them, though the stones suggest they were cut at the same time as the other three. But it is these that are the mystery, for someone in the centuries has looked after them, cutting back the undergrowth, so they are more or less intact.

Again I grew up with this story. I was told they were pilgrims who were struck down here by the Black Death, one man burying his two companions, then lying down in a third grave he had dug to await his own end. 'I saw them passing in the lane,' said my grandmother, always a bit hazy on history, 'only I didn't see them come back.'

All three graves are coffin-shaped and almost flush with the ground, each with a stone at head and foot, but the carving on each is different. One has a latticed pattern under a figure with crossed arms; this has been taken to suggest that the man was a glazier. But the graves, according to the Commission on Ancient Monuments, are late 12th or early 13th century, so where would a glazier in the late 12th and early 13th century have practised his craft when the only window glass, and that rare, was small and opaque? The church at Llanfihangel Abercywyn was still unglazed in the late 17th century, 500 years later.

Another grave has a rope running the length of the coffin-stone, so this has been taken to be that of a ropemaker. The third shows a man in a short tunic, his feet bare, a sword in his belt, presumably a soldier. A glazier, a ropemaker and a soldier: are these the oldest graves of working men in Britain?

But the carvings may be some kind of forgotten religious symbolism, for the tradition that these were the graves of pilgrims seems to be old. In 1837 a Mr Kempe, writing in the *Gentlemen's Magazine,* made reference to the story ('I cordially invite the opinion of some of your intelligent readers on the subject'). And in nearby St Clears an intelligent reader heeded the call. Only he went further, and two years later in a letter to the same magazine described how he had dug down into one of the graves. You could do such things in 1839, in the quiet places, without reference to the Home Secretary.

Four feet down the writer, who described himself as a 'gentleman', found bones he thought were either those of a woman or a youth, but it was something else he found that puzzled him. Around the bones were half a dozen scallop shells arranged in a pattern, and he confessed himself 'extremely puzzled to account for the appearance of these marine productions in such a locality.'

He had clearly not read Raleigh's lines, 'Give me my scallop shell of quiet / My staff of faith to lean upon.' The scallop shell was the traditional emblem of the pilgrim.

It is so quiet here, it is as though we are at the end of the world. There is no noise of traffic, nothing except the cry of a curlew in the marshes, across which, less than half a mile away, is the only other sign of humanity in the landscape, the farm buildings and another small ruined church, that of Llandeilo Abercywyn, the church this time of St Teilo at the mouth of the Cywyn.

So there are two churches facing each other across the creeks and the mud, though it will take you some 20 minutes to drive by road from one to the other. There is a signpost to Llandeilo Abercywyn, from which you might expect a village, but the lane drops away suddenly and, again, there is just a farm and a church at the edge of the marsh. But why the two churches, and why here, where now roads end?

They still hold services once a year at Llanfihangel, but those at the church of St Teilo have stopped, though only in living memory, the last officiant being a local vicar who was usually accompanied by the farmer, a man called Harris, and his dog. The prayer was always the same, 'Merciful Lord, may blessings be found, for Harris Llandeilo, myself, and the hound.'

My cousin Gareth some years back thought of buying Llandeilo Abercywyn, but was dissuaded by his wife who said she wasn't going to spend her days 'down there among all those crows.' But she might just as well have said that she had no wish to move into the Bayeux Tapestry, in which in one scene the future King Harold is shown whooping it up with some of his pals in his house at Bosham. The needlewomen have done a transverse section so you can see that the whooping is taking place in an upstairs room above a vaulted chamber. There is a line of outside steps.

Now, as we stand in the yard at Llandeilo Abercywyn, look around you. See that large stone house? It may not look old, not with the render on it, but now look again. See that depth of walling? See the line of outside steps leading to an upstairs room? This building with its vaulted chambers and spiral stone stairs, once a house, then a barn, now a house again, was standing before castles were built, and it stands now. There is an intact first floor hall, which to a man of the 11th century would have been the last word in architectural design, at the end of a lane in Wales.

And it is such a little lane.

part two

THE TOWN

In the picture a soldier, so far as I can make out, is grasping his member and about to ravish a woman, though ravish is too strong a word. The woman is pulling up her dress to be of some help, and the soldier is clearly an early proponent of safe sex.

'The bloke is in full chain mail,' said a local builder. 'Makes you proud to come from Carmarthen, that does.'

Elsewhere one citizen is mugging another, and a man is absent-mindedly groping a woman's bottom.

The council in 1997 put the picture up in the square to remind Wales's oldest continually inhabited town of its lost values.

11 THE SECOND JOURNEY

i

Narrator: When I was a very small boy, my parents emigrated. I remember this as though it were yesterday, the men unloading our furniture, the odd curtain twitching as, like unseen headhunters, our new neighbours watched, probably muttering to long-suffering husbands in cold front rooms, 'Haven't seen a three-piece yet'. Some broke cover and made an excuse to walk by, smiling vaguely at my mother who smiled back, in her case nervously.

But the children were everywhere, crowding round to see my toys, more children than I had ever seen in one place. And then the sudden bewilderment as I realised we did not have a single syllable of speech in common. I stared at them. They stared at me. They seemed friendly enough, these children, only they jabbered like some tribe crowding round a helicopter in a forest clearing. The little moment will never occur again on the British mainland for television has come, but this is a time before television, and in my case a time before comics and radio. It is 1947, and I am about to pass into history. I am five years old and a monoglot Welsh speaker.

Still I have seen my first film, which, being in English, has made me even more nervous. This starred Old Mother Riley and it made me cry, for all the grown-ups, for no reason I could make out, started fighting, which, as a result, is what I expect our neighbours in this new world to do at any moment. My parents and I, we have moved five miles from the countryside to the old garrison town of Carmarthen.

And it is the beginning of the rest of my life.

Geraint: My name is Geraint Morgan, I'm a retired university lecturer. Byron and I were at school together. We've been in contact now for something like...Good God, yes it is...60 years.

Narrator: And it was with him that I saw something that, more than any other event, brought home to me the nature of my upbringing in Carmarthen. It was the summer of 2003, and we were going to the National Eisteddfod for the first time.

ii

Geraint: Actually we were going on to Carmarthen, and I was just thinking it was going to be a long journey. You were banging on about, what was it?

Byron: Mathrafal, and Meifod, where they were holding the Eisteddfod, the old places of the Princes of Powys...

Geraint: Yeah, whatever. You were telling me off for knowing more about the 17th-century philosopher Thomas Hobbes than I do about the Welsh past. And then we breasted that hill, and there it was, something quite amazing. Below us was the Eisteddfod field, and what struck me was how big it was, all those tents...

Byron: They made me think of that line in a mediaeval Welsh poem, about the green tents of Llywelyn, which is our one pictorial glimpse of a Welsh prince in his pomp.

Geraint: Yes, it was like an army encampment. I was startled, so startled I stopped the car. At that moment we were both very moved, and I couldn't understand why. Until, that is, we went onto the field and I found myself among people speaking Welsh, which I no longer can, and speaking it in a wholly unselfconscious way. And everything was so well organised. That was when I realised that this was something to do with me, something I had forgotten.

Byron: And it had nothing to do with Mother England. This was us, ourselves alone, but why should it have startled us?

Geraint: Because you and I, we are colonial characters.

Narrator: The town of Carmarthen, like every old Welsh town, was an English settlement. Conquest, Religion, Commerce: it was their way. Military domination, religious control, economic subjugation, in that order. The Castle. The Church. The Town. In the 12th century the blueprint for their Empire had already been established. In Carmarthen.

The inhabitants of the towns were the first English colonials, drawn by what has always drawn colonials, the prospect of lording it over the native population. Only they could live in the town. Only they could hold markets within 15 miles of it.

And some were still there. The Maliphants of nearby Kidwelly, one of whom was in school with me, are the Malefaunts who were there before the defeat of Llywelyn, peering nervously over the walls at the woods.

But time passed, and eventually the Welsh of the woods got into the English towns. And got on. It was all to do with getting on. Morgan Kidwelly, the earliest Welsh surnames being the names of the towns men came from, was Richard the Third's Attorney General. *Richard III*'s Attorney General? What a hell of a job that must have been, but our ancestors were adaptable men. They even inherited the old colonial prejudices.

They did not speak Welsh in our town, or, if they did, kept quiet about it. I could speak Welsh. It was just that, to survive in the playgrounds of Carmarthen, I kept quiet about it.

Geraint: It was the way we had been brought up. Our parents, who could speak Welsh, talked English at home, for English was the language of getting on, and in particular of education. Whatever they intended, we were brought up to believe that the Welsh were an inferior people. And it was a belief underwritten by our time at the Queen Elizabeth Grammar School.

Byron: Remember the way we called the Welsh-speaking Welsh of the countryside 'boskins'? Not a word you will find in any dictionary. It survives only in such 18th-century archaisms as 'bosky wood'. For they were the people of the woods, *pobol y goedwig*. And we, whatever we were (we were a bit hazy on this), we were superior to them.

71

Geraint: My full name is Geraint Rhys Morgan. I think of myself as Welsh, my children have Welsh names, but my view of Wales has always been a filtered view. The English gave me a lovely pair of spectacles to view the people amongst whom I'd been brought up. And then suddenly that day in 2003 there was no need for abstraction. Here was a culture, a major culture. Pura Wallia, that phrase you use. I went to university in England, and spent all my working life there, so I'd never fully understood my background. And if it's painful to be disinherited from your class, think what it is like to be disinherited from your nation. That day in Meifod, it all caught up with me, I realised what I'd missed.

Byron: It was so sad. What passed for a middle class in Carmarthen, spoke with the most exaggerated English accents. I remember a consultant at the hospital talking about Queen Victoria's doctor, 'Darniel Davies, Landyfaelog.' Deliberately mispronouncing place-names. And him from a pub in Llanelli. One of the English girls I brought home, she used to go to the town's poshest grocer just to hear the wives speak, and to mock them as her ancestors must have mocked the Westernised Indians of the Raj.

Narrator: Yet this was a town enmeshed with the Welsh past. Some remarkable men had walked these streets, men like the publisher William Spurrell, who wrote his own history of the town, and compiled his own English-Welsh Dictionary. For this, you must never forget, was the town where 800 years ago in the Priory in the Black Book of Carmarthen an unknown monkish hand wrote out the line

Anoeth byd bet i Arthur

The enigma of the world is the grave of Arthur. And we didn't know any of this.

See that Tesco supermarket, the *archfarchnad*? Somewhere in the foundations of that are the bones of the great 15th-century poet Tudur Aled. See that Crimean War memorial? On it are written the names of the ordinary soldiers who died, the first time such men were commemorated in that, or any other war. And see that chip shop? In a room above that R.S. Thomas's first book was published. Iago Prytherch shuffled out of that chip shop 60 years ago.

But what is so tragic is that men like Spurrell lived their lives in the town, and were part of an educated, articulate, professional middle class. Yet of my class of 30 at the grammar school, only three now live in the town.

Byron: You and I, we were a commodity for export.

Geraint: Like Carlsberg.

Byron: When I went to Oxford, Percy Mott, who kept a sweet shop in Carmarthen, asked me, 'What are you going to study there?' 'English,' I said. 'And what will you become?' 'An Englishman,' I said. *And he nodded.*

For we had seen this happen. Our schoolfellows returned on holiday, newly qualified schoolmasters and doctors, with the most amazingly assembled accents. Some were posh, though one came home from National Service at Catterick a North Countryman. A lot of work went into those. Someone once told Aneurin Bevan that Roy Jenkins was lazy. Bevan said, 'No boy from the Valleys who has cultivated that accent could possibly be lazy.'

Geraint: And then, their parents dead, the schoolmasters and the doctors stopped coming home at all. The boys we went to school with, we rarely saw them again.

Byron: It's changed now. The parents, who were ambitious for their children and keen on them not learning Welsh, have been succeeded by those, perhaps even more ambitious, who are even more keen now to see to it that they do. It's all to do with getting on.

You and I, we are a moment of history. We are people for whose generation the tide ran out. We are the end of Empire.

Narrator: It had happened before, for there was another town before the English colonial Carmarthen, the ghostly outline of which, incredibly, can still be seen in the modern street plan of the eastern part of the town.

For there you would have met someone like me around the year 400 in the derelict streets of Roman Carmarthen, Maridunum, the fort by the sea. Such a man, in his sixties, my age, would have seen the town, one of only two in all Wales, being the civitas capital of the Demetae tribe, he would have seen it in the years of its greatest prosperity. For whatever else the Roman Empire was, it was also Debenhams and Tesco and John Lewis all rolled into one, and the biggest off-licence of the old world.

'Come on down,' said the seductive voices. 'Leave your old hill fort on Merlin's Hill. Come down to the baths and the shops, and the wine.' Come down to the Roman amphitheatre capable of seating 5,000 people, which, until the present Tesco, was the biggest structure ever put up in the town.

That man in 400 would in his youth have thought it would all go on forever. And it had slid away in his lifetime, just as my own colonial Carmarthen slid away in mine.

Professor Sir David Williams: My name is David Williams, formerly Vice-chancellor of Cambridge University. David Glyndwr Tudor Williams. My father was…a historian. I was born in the town in 1930.

Byron: When you go back now, does anyone recognise you?

David: Nobody recognises me. I think I get recognised more at Atlanta airport or on the outskirts of Sydney, Australia, than on the streets of Carmarthen.

Byron: Do you find this sad?

David: Yes, it is very sad. But then, while it was a great town to be brought up in, one always assumed one would leave. To be born in Carmarthen was to await exile.

The grammar school had an enormous impact on the town from the late 19th century on, but it was an export agency.

Byron: It was under your father that it became so.

David: Yes, he was the headmaster of the grammar school from 1929 until he died in 1955.

Byron: Did he ever question what he was doing?

David: No, like me he was consciously British, he was very proud of those who went away.

Byron: So it must have surprised you, what happened later, especially with the new status of the Welsh language?

David: Yes, but you must remember I grew up in a very cosmopolitan town. Apart from the overseas troops, like the Americans who came in 1943, we had a German POW camp within Carmarthen; we had Italian POW's billetted on the farms whom you met on walks on Sunday afternoons. All of this provided an atmosphere so different from the town of the 1950s and 1960s, your Carmarthen.

Byron: You make it sound like Casablanca. Do you recognise anything of your town, now so much has been pulled down?

David: I recognise certain buildings I wish had been pulled down, like the County Offices which replaced the castle. I certainly would not like to see the end of Carmarthen market, which I admire and like walking around the stalls.

Byron: Why do you think the council was able to pull down so much? There was so little opposition.

David: I don't know, I wasn't sufficiently involved, but I do remember some houses in Spilman Street being mutilated. But then I'd gone into the RAF when I was just 18, I missed a good deal of these new planning decisions.

Byron: The point is that in the 19th century there would have been people like yourself who would have been living in the town, and taken action or protested.

David: Well, they did protest once in the days of the Rebecca Riots. It was probably their last hurrah.

Byron: So what do you think of the town now? Once you would have known the shopkeepers, most of whom lived above

David: their shops, where now you walk through streets of charity shops and multiples, and know nobody.

David: I was the third child, I did a lot of shopping, the greengrocery in King Street, the grocery in Guildhall Square, the butcher's in Dark Gate, the fishmonger. I look back on it with affection, an undying affection.

Byron: And they've gone one by one: the fishmonger went first, then the butcher, now the ironmongery and the newsagent are going. I think they've ruined our town.

David: I agree, it's not an attractive town any more. The attraction for me used to lie with all these little lanes, so dark and interesting, and now the buildings are all of an anonymous kind. The new shopping area doesn't impress me very much.

Byron: It's a nowhere town, it could be anywhere.

David: That's right.

Byron: The Tywi valley is so beautiful. Carmarthen straddles it and could have been, was, such a wonderful place. It sounds arrogant, but in our time the best and the brightest left, were expected to go.

David: When I won a scholarship to Cambridge, nobody, not even the left-wing councillors my father knew, thought I shouldn't go.

Byron: People didn't think in those terms then; it's only now they're beginning to see, as I see looking back, the cost of all that talent shot away like human cannonballs.

Narrator: But there was one section of the town's inhabitants which never did leave. My Carmarthen was based on change, on getting on. Theirs had never changed. They would have been there when both Chaucer's sons were in the garrison; for fourpence a day (plus expenses) they would have gone with the English king to kill Frenchmen at Agincourt.

They were the Carmarthen Mob, the lowest of the low, packed into the hovels between the castle and the river. Coraclemen, drunks, men who didn't give a toss for anyone. Catch you a salmon for tuppence, lay on a full-scale riot for a few pints. They were there when the Rebecca Rioters came, intent on a protest march. And it was these, swarming out of their hovels, not the daughters of Rebecca, who turned this into a full-scale attack on the workhouse, and were in turn charged by the 4th Light Dragoons.

The coraclemen don't speak Welsh now, but mixed in with their English are terms only mediaeval Welsh scholars would know. Words like *astell orlais* for bulkhead, and *cyflychwr* for that moment of twilight when the tide comes, a time for fishing. Words passed down from father to son.

It is only now that I am meeting such men, for, when I was a boy, to tidy people like my parents they were another species. The first time I talked to one was when the *Times* sent me down to the town where I had been brought up, to meet one of them, William Elias, a man in his nineties, who had been awarded the British Empire Medal, the BEM, for 'services to coracle fishing'. Which made it sound as though the salmon had nominated him.

Dai: My name is Dai Rees. I am a coracleman, perhaps one of the last coraclemen on the river Tywi.

Byron: You say the River Board is thinking of winding up the whole thing, something they've been trying to do for years.

Dai: What they're trying to do, or so they say, is to encourage tourism by introducing a larger number of anglers onto west Wales rivers. The coraclemen get in the way, so, using the pretence of conservation, they want to restrict a craft that was here when the Romans were in Carmarthen. You've got a piece of living history there that nobody wants to conserve or keep. It's a little bit silly really.

Byron: The coraclemen lived in a certain part of the town, didn't they?

Dai: (*suppressing a laugh*) Yes, under old Kidwelly *fach*, little Kidwelly, which is down towards the old station. The old station's gone too. And Kidwelly *fach*, and the quay area where they lived in one-up one-down cottages, hovels really.

Byron: And out of those little hovels used to come the Carmarthen Mob?

Dai: Yes, they called them the Carmarthen Mob. But you've got to remember that in those days they banded together out of necessity, it was a very precarious living. Poverty abounded.

Byron: We're going back now. Around 1830 something like a third to a half of Carmarthen lived off the river.

Dai: That's right. By the fishing, the dredging of sand and gravel, and various other jobs like stevedoring, for Carmarthen was a port then, and these people made a living from the river, but it was a seasonal living. Winter was another story. I remember fishing with old Steve Thomas who told me that one of his relatives who used to take Steve when he was a boy out on the river with him, he'd deliberately fish in the closed season so he'd get caught. He knew they wouldn't do anything to the boy, but he himself could go into Carmarthen gaol, where it was nice and comfy and you had food. That's how hard it was.

Byron: My Carmarthen was the grammar school and getting on and going away. It was a place where we caught trains. Yours was a much older town, where things hadn't changed, where the traditions went back a lot further.

Dai: Yes, through the good works of your parents, let's be fair about it, Byron, you didn't see that part of it. You were sheltered, and led a sheltered life. Yes, they had a lot of hardship, but they had a lot of comradeship as well.

         Policemen were always instructed to go in twos on the quay, never to patrol alone. Because if there was a row, and there were always rows and bickering between the coracle families and the boat families, if somebody else joined in, he was an outsider. And they'd turn on him. So the police were always advised to travel in twos.

It was a very hard life for all the coracle families. My father didn't have a pair of shoes until he was about eight or nine years of age.

Byron: And you're going back to when?

Dai: To the 1920s, that's how hard it was. I can remember old Steve Thomas telling me that he caught a salmon when he was seven years of age. Think of that, he was on the river at seven years of age, fishing with his dad. And when he went home with the salmon at four in the morning, when they'd finished fishing, the big thing was 'Dad told Mam to cook me an egg'. He thought he'd won the pools, those were his words. 'I thought I'd won the pools', he said. That's because he'd boated his first salmon.

It's hard to believe now, and it's not that long ago. That's the thing that strikes you, all of it is not that long ago.

Byron: But your people were Carmarthen in the sense that we were passing through – you were the old way of life. And when a town cuts itself off from its origins, as has happened when the local council bulldozed a four-lane carriageway between the town and the quay, it's sad.

Dai: Yes, I agree, they had a fantastic heritage on that quayside, and it could have been preserved so beautifully. I remember when one roof was removed from a house in Bridge Street, they found a building on three levels, one going back to medieval times. If you go to Nott Square, you can see medieval windows in that pub there. The Council, I don't know... The lunatics are running the asylum, Rogers.

Narrator: For the town is dying. In the late 20th century the council planners pulled down its old alleys, demolished the narrow street which was all that remained of a town gate, and erased the streets that had housed the Carmarthen Mob. An eyesore these might have been, but it was our eyesore; it had a character, an identity, and in its place has come the newly developed centre of the nowhere town. The District and the County Councils have severed its past from Carmarthen.

For the empires are back, it is just they have other names. Like Debenham's. And Morrison's. And Tesco. Tesco, having already built on the medieval Friary, has now moved on to build the biggest, or second biggest, megastore in Wales, this on the outskirts of a town with a population of only 15,000. It is a vast cancer which will suck the life out of the commercial centre of Carmarthen. My town is a trading post now, the cash it generates streaming out of the town.

Something may yet happen. People who in my lifetime objected to nothing became so indignant about the closure of a street to make way for yet another development that the Council, the all-powerful Council, backtracked on its decision. Posters went up in parlour windows and in cars, something no one had ever seen before. A new spirit is abroad, give it time.

Even this late time.

But whatever happens, do not forget the people of Carmarthen. The English rode over them, their squires abandoned them, the councils they elected ignored them. Yet they are still there, part of your past as well as mine.

Smile at us, pay us, pass us, but do not quite forget.

12 A GUIDED TOUR OF A SMALL WELSH TOWN

Dante and Virgil, we paced the streets of Carmarthen. For Virgil, the guide, it was a holiday job: a sixth-form schoolgirl, she had been hired that summer by the council to take visitors on tours of the town. Only I wasn't a visitor: half a century earlier I had been brought up there, but I didn't tell her this. For Dante it was a chance to see his town through the eyes of another generation.

That street, she informed me, had been famous for the number of its printers in the 16th century. She paused, or was it the 18th century? And that organ (we were standing now in the choir of the town's oldest church), it had been built for George II. Or was it George III? Under the gloom of a stained-glass window we peered into a niche in the church wall. That, she said, was an effigy. Or, there was another of those wonderful moments of indecision to which I could have listened all day, perhaps it was a coffin.

We passed through a side chapel from which a 16th-century consistory court handed over a bishop for burning in the town square (one of the charges against him being that he had whistled at seals, but again I didn't mention this), and we stopped at the high eye-level tomb of a man in armour who, she said, had killed some king in a battle. It was at that point that I dropped the pretence. I said I had once climbed that tomb, unaware that nobody had cleaned it for a century or more. A man in a light fawn suit went up; a chimney sweep came down. I wasn't sure how she would take that, but she just nodded. Most of the people on her tours, she said, were from Carmarthen.

In our time it is suddenly a cruel thing to have been brought up in a small town. Each man makes a village out of a city; he knows fewer people there, usually work colleagues and old friends, so he is inured to change. But in a small town he knows exactly what has gone and what is coming; he will have stared in his local paper at reports of a town plan promising a 30 per cent increase in population in ten years, a plan drawn up by men in offices on the orders of some remote Government minister. He will have seen sketches of malls and piazzas drawn by excited architects, who will not have mentioned that there is already a town just like it 20 miles way, with identical malls and piazzas, and another one 20 miles beyond that, so that whatever made each of these places unique is going, and what remains will be just like a hundred others.

If you have any interest at all in local government and its £200,000-a-year chief clerks, then look at what these clerks, and the developers who have their ear, have done to the place where you were born. Once growth, like decay, was a natural process. Now it is being imposed. The result is the Nowhere Town.

You could be anywhere, and may yet, like those inhabitants of small towns in the American mid-West desperate to reassure themselves that where they live is somewhere, put up signs like 'X, ARTICHOKE CAPITAL OF THE WORLD'. For it will soon be a very real fear that a town, which once had a past and a form, will, as an old American lawyer used to say, be just somewhere on the way to somewhere else.

Dante and Virgil, we looked up from the dock of the crown court in Carmarthen at the hard old drunk's face of the Peninsular War general in his portrait above the bench. Then we clattered down the wooden steps to cells which once enclosed the Rebecca Rioters, but where the graffiti was brand new, ranging from a defiant 'Me and Pigs Don't Mix' to a rueful 'Back Agen, Fuck It.' Oooh, said my guide, the spelling.

But her heart was in the right place, whatever her magical mystery tour of the past. Even at her age she felt that in her time a great wrong had been done. Hers was going to be a very short tour, she said. Once it would have included the quay, which was the reason the Romans had built the town in the first place, for this is the oldest continually inhabited town in Wales, building it beside a navigable river. It would also have included the site of a medieval friary on a bluff above it. But the four-lane carriageway torn through the terraced streets had separated the town from the quay forever, and a supermarket of bright red brick had obliterated all traces of the friary. It would be too depressing to show people such things, she said.

You knew where you were in a small town once. You could see where the heartwood ended and the sapwood began, simply by walking out from the oldest church past the rings of pubs and shops, the grand Georgian town houses, the leafy Edwardian villas, to the encircling council houses. By doing this you travelled in time, moving through the confidence of prosperity to the little patches of decay in the back streets, trees growing through what was left of the town wall, with old stables which had become lock-up garages, and a rusting hoist high on a gable wall, the reason for which nobody could explain. Elder and bramble and willow-herb. All towns had such patches of decay once, even the Great City itself, Constantinople: they were part of urban life, and men just stepped over them. For so it had always been until in the 1970s in Britain (not in France or Spain) the terrible tidying began.

The developer Daddy Bigbucks got off the morning train with his coloured maps and sketches, and lunched the councillors and their planning officers until their small heads reeled. Like a Western gunfighter, Daddy Bigbucks always moved on (in one instance, to Spain, out of reach of the police who were anxious to discuss his vision with them). But he left behind him the supermarket and the arcade, the piazza and the fountains (one in Stourbridge is a stand-fast pipe playing mains water over a round blue slab of concrete). And the desolation.

Have you noticed how nobody lives above the shop now? The town centre is a place the drunken young stumble through at night, dropping litter. The young always drop litter. But then how quickly the shopkeepers went, the grocers and the fishmongers, the bakers and the barbers, so you may not even have noticed, or, if you did, you turned away, so convinced were you that a price had to be paid for change, for the multiple stores and the car parks that are now your town centre. And how long will that centre last? Most shopping now gets done in the huge sheds built in water meadows on the town outskirts to house the new grocers and the exhaust fitters. In the town itself discount shops come and discount shops close, and the only steady commercial growth is in second-hand clothing: there are nine charity shops in Carmarthen's small town centre alone.

And we are walking through its streets, as old Leland walked the streets of Hay in the 16th century ('(It) yet hath a market, but the town within the walles is wonderfully decaied. The ruin is ascribed to Owen Glindour'), and Camden after him ('It hath nothing worth taking notice of, but one only Church, large and fair'), and in the 19th century the great Cobbett ('It is now a straggling village; but, to a certainty, it has been a large market town'). Change and decay, change and decay, but nothing like this, nothing since the Book of Genesis, when '... the earth was without form, and void.'

In Carmarthen my guide had taken me up to a high place to look down on the town. 'Look at all the car parks.' A school was razed to the ground to make way for one (at a cost of £5,000 per parking space), so eventually there will be an inner ring of car parks reaching out for each other like a besieging army. 'And look at those roofs.' In the town centre there was roof after flat commercial roof. 'What sort of place is this?'

We stood there, for a moment like one of Dore's engravings in *The Inferno,* Virgil and Dante on the brink of Hell, guide and witness staring down on the eager desolation that is now my town.

13 PORTRAIT GALLERY (1)

But one thing has not changed. These are the voices of small-town Wales, laughing, irreverent, sometimes poignant, often triumphant.

RAYMOND REES, FISHMONGER

'Round here they know nothing about fish, I don't know why I bother really. A woman came in the other day, queued for five minutes, then asked for some sausages. I tried to make a joke of it and said we'd run out of fish sausages. "Pity," she said.

'I sell duck eggs. A woman came in with her daughter, and I heard the daughter ask, what sort of eggs were those. "Fish eggs," said the mother. When it was her turn she asked me, "They are fish eggs, aren't they?" I mean, where d'you start?

'I bought a shark last year, a porbeagle, enormous thing. This woman saw the cutlets I'd put on the slab. "That's nice," she said. "What's that?" "Shark," I said. "Oh," she said, "can I have the head for my little pussy?" Now I'd spent most of the morning trying to stuff the head into our bin. I held it up for her to see, it must have weighed about 20 pounds. "Oh lovely," she said. "Can you wrap it up? I'll call for it later." She never did.

'Cats round here, they get spoiled rotten. "Kipper for me, and some salmon for the cat." This man asked me for some butter once. I said that so far no one had discovered a way of milking fish. I mean, you can't be rude.'

A SHOPPER

My wife, looking at children's clothes in the Carmarthen Woolworths of blessed memory, was addressed by a woman in a state of some distress. 'I came in specially for the mutants, and there's none here. They promised faithfully there'd be mutants, and now they say there won't be any here until next week.'

My wife, taken aback, having heard some very strange stories about the town (mainly from me), murmured consolingly she was sure she'd find some mutants in Carmarthen. It was only later she realised the woman had been talking about the Mutant Ninja Turtles of TV cartoon fame.

THE PHARMACIST

The pharmacist was showing me his collection of Victorian oil paintings, many of which showed cows standing in rivers. 'All my life I have loved beauty,' said John King-Morgan. I had known him since I was a boy, when he played the organ in our chapel. 'I am in my 90th year,' he said. 'Soon I hope to be knocking on the gates of eternity.'

I reminded him that this had been a word once used in the *Carmarthen Journal* to describe hangings ('the condemned one was then launched into eternity'). Just like a rocket, I said. He looked at me gravely. 'They were taking a lot upon themselves,' he said.

And I felt ashamed.

WELSH OFFICIALDOM (1)

A Welshman in office is unlike an Englishman in office. The Englishman is distant, inured to responsibility by centuries of power. The Welshman is not. So he is either officious to the point of lunacy, or, particularly if the two of you are talking in Welsh, so detached that you seem to have strayed into a situation comedy where neither of you has rehearsed his lines. Either way, the surreal materialises beside you, in small town squares and very large council offices.

Lampeter, the summer of 1991. Seeing some garden peas for sale, and failing to find a parking space, I left the car outside the shop, its nearside wheels on the pavement. I was gone, at most, three minutes.

'Where have you been?'

He was an amazingly scruffy policeman, his cap at an angle and some uniform buttons undone; he looked like a Mexican policeman in films, the sort that used to be played by Peter Ustinov. I said I had just popped into a shop to buy some peas. What followed was the most extraordinary conversation I have ever had with another human being.

His eyes bulged, they really did, something I had only encountered before in headmasters. 'Do you usually park your car on the pavement when you feel a need for peas?'

'Well, in London...' I suppose there were worse things I could have said, like whether it was true his wife had taken up bird-watching with the insurance man, but not many. For a moment I thought he was going to have a fit.

'YOU...' His forefinger was stabbing the air. 'YOU ARE NOT IN LONDON NOW.'

So true. So very true.

Welsh officialdom (2)

Llanina, near New Quay, the summer of 1991. The sign was new. It stood at the edge of the beach, so elegant in its varnished pine frame, in its glass and coloured inks, it was clearly a very important sign. I read it over and over for it wasn't immediately clear what it was trying to say. Put up by Welsh Water, the sign appeared to list three levels of marine purity, blue, green and red, the last being a level of contamination in which the Black Death swims quietly beside you in the sea. The sign went on to invoke the EU, as signs once invoked the Trinity, and bristled with bilinguality, for this was the booming new Welsh bureaucracy in which translation is a growth industry, just as treachery was in Wales in the Middle Ages.

And then I saw it, the proud little square at the bottom of the sign. The water at Llanina was as red as the Hell painted by Hieronymus Bosch.

'Fair play, you have to admire them really,' said a woman just down the coast at Llangrannog. 'They put up these beautiful signs just to tell us they're not doing their job properly. They put one up on this beach. Two days it was there, and then someone stole it. On the third day they stole the post as well.'

In New Quay I went to the tourist kiosk, and asked to see the list of EU-approved beaches. It was not a long list, and it was kept under the counter like hard-core porn. I asked the lady in charge, would she swim in Cardigan Bay?

'Good God, no.' She did not seem inclined to say more.

'Why's that?'

She turned to the window facing the sea, and looked out on Cardigan Bay. 'Even from here I've seen...things.'

'What sort of things?'

'Floating things,' she said, nodding darkly, the way innkeepers in Transylvania nod darkly when they warn travellers about the castle on the hill.

'Floating things?'

'Lumps,' she said, where an English civil servant in her position would have relayed bland statistics. 'Let's face it,' she went on, abruptly philosophical, 'from the dawn of time human beings have been leaving waste products.'

My wife and daughter were swimming in Cardigan Bay when I went to the environmental health offices of the local council. A young man, speaking careful English, was wary, 'Can I ask what your interest is in this matter?', the way Welsh officialdom, asked questions in English, has been wary since the Conquest of Wales. I switched to Welsh, and the effect was electric.

'You've only got to look at the blooming tide-marks, man,' said the young man, suddenly not wary at all. 'There's no sewage plant anywhere on the coast between Aberystwyth and Cardigan.

Welsh Water haven't got the time, you know what they're up to now, don't you? We'll be having electric shocks from the water soon.'

It was a time when Welsh Water were trying to take over South Wales Electricity.

Later they announced plans for a new sewage treatment plant on Anglesey. The site had been chosen with some care.

'I had 30 people from the Smithsonian Institute here last week,' said Kathryn Gibson at Aber, where the last Welsh Prince of Wales had his palace on the hill. 'They had stayed at a hotel owned by Welsh Water, and they had come to talk about Welsh history. So they looked across the Straits at Llanfaes, the Friary where the last Princess of Wales was buried, where archaeologists have found the graves, and where Welsh Water intend building a sewage farm.'

And they did.

14 J.F. JONES, MUSEUM CURATOR
(AND DYNAMITER)

It is a wonderful sentence, so wonderful I find myself turning to it again and again, as I do with L.P. Hartley's much misquoted 'The past is a foreign country: they do things differently there', and with John Aubrey's description of the apparition in 1670, which 'being demanded whether a good spirit or a bad, returned no answer, but disappeared with a curious perfume and most melodious twang.' But both these men were literary stylists. The remarkable thing about that other sentence is that it occurs in *Sir Gar*, a collection of historical essays published in 1991 by the Carmarthenshire Antiquarian Society.

It was written by a school contemporary of mine, Brigadier Glynne Jones, an amateur archaeologist, who was not trying to be funny or stylish, he was merely recording his successful location of a medieval chapel. Until then this was lost in the fields outside Kidwelly, where others had tried to find it before him, notably in the 1950s.

'An attempt by the late J.F. Jones (formerly Curator, Carmarthen Museum) to rediscover the site of the chapel building *using dynamite* proved unrewarding.'

Just that. The italics are mine.

But read it again. No sooner has the shock of the dynamite registered than the dying fall of 'proved unrewarding' lifts the sentence, as J.F. Jones might have lifted the chapel, into the heavens of black humour. Those of you who have watched the television programme *Time Team* and seen archaeologists delicately brushing soil from broken masonry will at this point begin to suspect that in living memory there was loose in the town of Carmarthen one of the great comic, and tragic, heroes of our time.

You and I, we are going back 50 years now, to a county museum then housed in two large Georgian properties knocked into one, in Quay Street just off Guildhall Square in Carmarthen, a place where the gentry once had their town houses and now solicitors lurk. But it is when we step inside that the shock kicks in.

The clutter is such, it is as though we have stepped into a large attic, for there is no classification by time or groups of objects; here the centuries jostle each other and compete, so there are oil paintings and swords, penny-farthing bicycles and needlework samplers by meticulous, long dead little girls. As Dylan Thomas said of the old Royal Institution in Swansea, this is a museum that deserves to be in a museum itself. We leave the street, and are in Narnia.

And you are about to see something so amazing that if you have any imaginative sense of the past you will find yourself swept back, not just 50, but 1500 years. For Carmarthen Museum, amidst its bicycles and its samplers, contains the Voteporix Stone, the single most important archaeological find from the sixth century in Britain.

It is a huge gravestone the height and bulk of a rugby second-row forward, and is the one thing, the one physical thing, that authenticates that century's one surviving text. Think of that: out of those one hundred years, one man alone speaks to us. It is just that without the stone the priest Gildas's *The Ruin of Britain* would have been a rant in darkness.

The Roman Empire in Britain has been gone for a century and a half, when out of nowhere there screams a voice, in Latin: Gildas is castigating the British or Welsh warlords who have lurched to their feet in the twilight of what followed, men for whom Arthur might have been a living memory. One of these is Voteporix, the *tyrant* of the Demetae, as Gildas calls him.

Do not read too much into that. To call a man a tyrant is what an educated contemporary would have called anyone who had set himself up as a king without Imperial authorisation, even though there was no Empire. The Demetae were the west Wales tribe occupying parts of Carmarthenshire, Ceredigion and Pembrokeshire, whose Roman civic capital had been Carmarthen. Still Gildas had no doubts as he reviews Voteporix's c.v.: 'the bad son of a good father, a man who has grown grey hair in the service of the devil and who shows no sign of repentance as he draws near his end.'

There is of course no mention of that on the Stone. Curiously, on this Voteporix is celebrated, not as a king, but as a Protector, a member of the Imperial bodyguard, though no Emperor has ruled in Britain since 410. Rome, even in ruin, still cast a long shadow when he was buried.

But the point is that Gildas was suddenly not a voice in darkness. His abuse was underpinned by history when the Stone materialised in 1876, rather like Dr Who's police box, being found (the accounts are vague) as some building work was being done on a small church at Castell Dwyran near where Carmarthenshire and Pembrokeshire meet. And if you think the fact of its finding bizarre after such a long interval, you try to find Castell Dwyran now.

Archaeologists airily refer to the name, but that name is on no signpost, and few local people even know its whereabouts, or that it is a farm in a dingle with a small ruined church in its yard. Nobody knows when or how the Stone got there, but its travels were just beginning. The vicar, Bowen Jones, having found it, imperiously had it moved four years later to become a gatepost outside his own house in the nearby village of Llanfallteg. At this stage nobody knew it was a gravestone, and certainly not a king's gravestone: the Stone was a garden feature.

Still the vicar's action seems to have been in character, for after his death in 1887, one of his sons had this inscription put next to his father's grand grave in Castell Dwyran.

> Here lie the remains of a Classical Ass,
> The accursed of his sons by the name of Jabrass,
> In the earth he is Ammonia and Triphosphate of Calcium,
> On earth a Home Demon and ferocious old ruffian.

Whatever your interest in monumental masonry, you will have seen nothing like this memorial in the dingle. It is still there, but again difficult to find, being very small, unlike the Stone which had become a gatepost.

And such a big gatepost that drunks on their way home from the local pub kept colliding with it in the dark, or so I was told by the present Bishop of St Davids, which was why, for their benefit, it was whitewashed. Only it rains a great deal in west Wales, which was when men eventually noticed the trailing capitals of a Latin inscription in the streaked whitewash, *Memoria Voteporigis Protictoris,* the Monument of Voteporix the Protector, below a cross within a circle that indicated a Christian burial a full half century before the coming of Augustine, who, according to the English, brought Christianity to Britain.

It may have taken people 15 years to notice this, but when they did, the bells began to ring. Suddenly this was no garden feature, this was a historical monument of national significance. And its travels again were beginning. In 1921 the vicar's sister, embarrassed by having a king in her garden, had the Stone moved to the newly opened Carmarthen Museum. Here the black comedy, which had never been far away, really closed in.

The Stone was there when I was growing up in Carmarthen, but not only did I not know what it was, *I did not even know it was there*. But then, as you and I step into the museum of half a century ago, we do not notice it.

For the Voteporix Stone is behind the front door, in the sort of place people would normally stack wet umbrellas. Yet nearby, prominently displayed in a glass case, are 'DYLAN THOMAS'S CUFFLINKS, believed to be the only pair ever owned by the poet.' You are in an extraordinary place run by an extraordinary man.

The curator of Carmarthen Museum from 1949 to 1970, and as such the impressario of his county's past, was J.F. Jones, a middle-aged bachelor and former primary school teacher, whom his long-time girlfriend, but nobody else, called Freddie. Like many of my contemporaries at school, I knew Jones, whose usual reaction to our being in the museum at all was 'What do you want?'

'To be left alone in a place like that is not good for anyone,' said one of the present staff at the museum, which has now moved to the old Bishops' Palace outside Carmarthen, so the Stone has been on its travels yet again. 'It blurs the distinction between what is yours and what is part of the collection. When we were still in Quay Street, and he had retired, we'd sometimes see him on the pavement opposite just standing there in the afternoons, staring across at the museum.'

Jones hated visitors, but in particular he hated schoolboys, though those with an interest in history afforded him some light relief, for then, appealed to for asistance with some project, he could smile his thin smile and be massively, politely, unhelpful. 'Sorry.' Or, 'We have a Library in this town, you know.' He would stare through his pebble lenses as he said this in a strange small voice, which sounded as though he was being strangled as he spoke. Winter and summer, he wore shirts open on a throat in which, as you stared, hypnotised, a small adam's apple was in perpetual motion.

How much history he knew I never did find out, for he never vouchsafed any sort of information. He boasted that he knew where a medieval chapel was in the fields outside Carmarthen, but refused to tell anyone where it was; luckily he must have been out of dynamite at the time. Once, just once, in a good mood for some reason, he showed me an enormous horn-handled penknife. This, he assured me, had belonged to the folk hero, and Tudor squire, Twm Siôn Cati.

There were many curiosities, with many claims made for them, in the tidal wave of objects that had burst through the door in Quay Street, filling the Museum to its roof, so much that only about 15 per cent of them could be put on show at one time. Carmarthen Museum bulged. Much of these contents came from the private collection of George Eyre Evans, a local man and an Unitarian minister who had become an inspector of Ancient Monuments. He was a small man with a white Imperial beard, similar to that worn by Napoleon III, except this was an Emperor dressed in the uniform, shorts and hat, the full kit, of the Boy Scouts, whose county commissioner he was.

Evans was so eccentric that he figures in the memoirs of the famous archaeologist Sir Mortimer Wheeler, who in his time had been exposed to more than his fair share of eccentrics (being challenged to a duel by Augustus John who offered him the choice of weapons, Wheeler, a former artilleryman, chose field guns, and heard no more). Wheeler writes that George Eyre Evans had an aunt who had expressed the wish to be buried in Carmarthen; the only thing was, she had died in Devon. So her nephew and an undertaker went to fetch her in a hearse, only, having come that far, Evans did not see why his return journey should not be an elaborate archaeological detour. Which was how Napoleon III in Scouts uniform, an undertaker, with an old dead lady in the back of a hearse, came to Stonehenge, and Avebury, and were lucky not to be stopped for some motoring offence. But he was a man of scholarship, on whose death his collection in 1940 was handed over to Carmarthenshire County Council. Had it not been for him, there would have been no county museum.

The trouble was, in 1949 the open-necked shirt and the adam's apple came to Quay Street, and two years after his appointment as curator J.F. Jones stopped keeping an acquisitions book. For almost 20 years until his retirement in 1970, there is no record of what was found, or where, or by whom. The museum had become a skip.

But his employer, the County Council, made him keep a visitors' book. 'You were supposed to sign your name in this, which was what one afternoon four of us from school did, only one of us wrote an Irish name in the visitors' book,' said Brigadier Jones. 'The next minute, on the second floor, this man had materialised. "Which of you is Seamus O'Hara?" He seemed to come out of nowhere.' Henry Jones-Davies, the publisher of *Cambria,* signed himself in, aged nine, awarding himself an M.A. and was chased down the street by the Curator shouting, 'You little devil, you'll never be an M.A.' When he graduated from Oxford, Jones-Davies had to fight the temptation not to call with his certificate.

The museum, having been two houses, one given by the shipping magnate Lord Kylsant, had two staircases, one of which the public used, but the other, hidden away in the interior, the curator alone used. You only saw one entrance to this, on the top floor next to the penny farthing, but in front of this Jones had put a pile of books to discourage callers, adding a human skull to the top of the pile. The museum was not short of human skulls. Yet you knew there was some living thing somewhere for occasionally you heard the creaking of hidden stairs, and sometimes visitors saw a soft white hand flutter round a door like a materialisation in a seance. The hand would then switch off the lights, leaving them to the darkness of a late winter afternoon. People from away, visiting Carmarthen Museum, must have felt they had strayed onto the set of a Hammer Horror film production.

We of course knew what to expect, and some of us retaliated. One boy would tiptoe in gym shoes to the top floor, where he would jump up and down, singing the Davy Crockett song. The next moment, there would be a crashing of books in the hidden interior followed by feet on the stairs and a face peering over the skull. But the boy would be gone, and from two floors down would come, 'Kilt him a bar when he was only three'. Jones never caught him, so the exercise must have kept him fit.

What else he did, apart from pounce, we never did find out, though there were rumours of archaeology. 'I know he had two archaeological tools,' said Brigadier Glynne Jones. 'One was a pointed trowel, which was fair enough, but the other was a burglar's jemmy, which he must have got from somewhere. Oh, and the dynamite.'

Where he got that from is a mystery, but there were some very strange characters knocking about Carmarthen in the 1950s. One, known as the Welsh Bandit, had in wartime been part of Churchill's Secret Army, men chosen for their local knowledge, often for their prowess at poaching, who, had the Germans come, would have been expected to wage a lonely guerilla war. Such men, recruited so secretly their very existence did not become public until some 40 years later, had been armed to the teeth, weapons they surrendered with the end of the War. The Bandit did not surrender his. It was only when the police heard reports of someone machine-gunning ducks and lobbing hand grenades at the salmon in the River Tywi, that there was a discreet night-time raid on his house with, according to my father, many vans waiting outside. No charges were brought, and the rest is silence, which was how Jones liked to keep his archaeological adventures.

'Somehow I heard that he was doing a dig in somebody's garden in an old part of the town,' said my cousin Felicity, who went on to marry the Director of the London Museum. 'I was on holiday from Cambridge, so I went round to offer my services. The garden was in the most awful mess, but the old lady who owned it seemed perfectly happy with this. And then he turned up. He didn't turn me down but he said I had to understand the work had to be done in complete secrecy. I was astonished, and, being young and proper, I told him I wasn't having anything to do with something that was being kept from the public. And that was it.'

The past, like the collection, was his and his alone. A Carmarthen man who had given the Museum his father's old dress uniform, a cabinet of Victorian games, and a woman's full Welsh costume, went to see what had happened to them when the Museum moved to the Bishops' Palace. 'The uniform was there, though for some reason all the buttons and badges of rank had gone. But of the cabinet and the Welsh costume there was so sign, not even a mention in the catalogue. And Jones had not given me any sort of receipt. He never did give receipts.'

A friend of mine, hired to do some digging on an university excavation at Coygen Camp, a Roman coastal fort, found a large metal brooch. 'Jones happened to be there that day, seeing what was going on. I knew him slightly so I showed it to him. "Leave it with me, I'll authenticate it for you," he said. He authenticated it all right, I never saw it again. But I was young, when you're young you forget.'

And there was something else. The treasure known as the Carmarthen Brooch, the silver gilt Roman ornament dating from the first century AD, turned up in a gas trench outside a chip shop in Priory Street. Whether a workman found it, or Jones himself saw it glinting in the street lights as he bought his chips, is not clear. But when he sent this away to the National Museum of Wales to be cleaned and authenticated, his reputation was such that they refused to send it back. It has now come back, and is on show in Carmarthen Museum.

For things did disappear there. No one knows if this was the result of the chaos in which he moved or for some darker reason, but what is known is that the Sea Serjeants' glass, the beautifully engraved 18th-century crystal goblets used by a local secret Jacobite society, are now nowhere to be found. The present Museum authorities searched high and low, and in the end gave up, being already bemused by the life-sized female dummies modelling Welsh costume they had inherited, all of which had pubic hair added, drawn in some detail, and by the Stone Age axe with boot blacking all over it. This was because, 4,000 years on, it had been still the work tool of a local cobbler, who used it to smooth out his repairs.

Other things did not disappear, and were an embarrassment. Dylan Thomas's cufflinks are no longer on show, neither is Twm Siôn Cati's penknife, which, it turned out, was not Tudor at all, but 19th century. There had been other wild claims they had been unable to authenticate, like the portrait, once said to have been contemporary, of Griffith Jones, the 18th-century founder of the Sunday School movement. All were put away, as the British Museum put away the bequest of a mayor of Bedford who had collected every sculpture of an erect human penis he could get his hands on from the Ancient

World. He expected these to go on show in their own gallery; instead the authorities quietly put them under lock and key.

As the church authorities at Steynton, near Milford Haven, wished they could have done with a sixth-century Romano-British gravestone. This is to a Gendilius, of whom all that is known, from the ring cross cut into the stone, is that he was given Christian burial. Only he is not alone. When a local man died, aged 84, in 1870, someone must have thought there was a perfectly good tombstone going to waste, one with no family to object after 1300 years, so an obliging monumental mason cut his name, Thomas Harries, beneath that of Gendilius. The most outrageous gravestone in British archaeology is now hidden away behind a pillar in Steynton church. West Wales has often had an odd relationship with its past.

I had one last run-in with J.F. Jones. When I came down from Oxford, I got permission from the editor of the *Carmarthen Journal* to read through its files. These were kept in a dusty room above the paper's offices where, I gathered, they were read by only one other person, Jones, who used them for his weekly column of historical facts. You know the sort of thing, 'April 3, 1220. Llywelyn the Great ransacked the town. April 4, 1771, Geraint Morgan hanged at Pensarn for theft of books.' Jones had been writing this for years.

But the thing I noticed first was that the huge bound broadsheet files were in no sort of order, so the 1820 volume was followed by 1840, 1840 by 1870. I decided to arrange them in sequence, a huge undertaking, given the number of volumes. I had only got so far when I went home, intending to return the next afternoon. When I did, the then editor burst in and, seemingly out of his mind with rage, started shouting and accused me of vandalism. That morning Jones had called as usual and had had a near breakdown at finding 1820 followed by 1821 followed by 1822. Not only had his world been invaded, the order of its chaos had been shaken, and he had gone straight to the editor. None of this is exaggeration, but I was thrown out, physically if required, or so the editor assured me.

I saw Jones once again, this time in London when I was sent by a newspaper to cover a conference of museum curators. He seemed at home, chatting to his peers, though these were men who had never used dynamite or a burglar's jemmy, so he was taken aback when he saw me.

'What are you doing here?'

'I'm covering this for *The Times*.'

'Oh dear.'

But, having said all this about him, there is one thing I have only recently discovered. Jones took photographs of the old Carmarthen as this was being pulled down around his ears by developers and their eager accomplices, the planners on the local council. He is said to have had 11,000 slides in his private archive, of which only a tenth survive as they were stored in a damp garage. But in many cases these provide the only record of the town I knew as a boy and a young man.

And there is something else, a picture that haunts me. It is of the old dynamiter himself in retirement, staring wistfully as Adam and Eve must have stared, in his case across the road in Quay Street at the Museum that was his Eden.

15 THE TRUE QUEEN OF ENGLAND

In 2001 Randolph Thomas, the vicar of St Peter's in Carmarthen, was having some building work done in his church and, as required, had sent the archaeologists in first. St Peter's was Grade One listed, and so old, within the walls of the Roman town, it had a pagan altar in its porch. The archaeologists assured him they would not be long, that they did not anticipate finding anything interesting. And then...

'When I was appointed in 1994, I was told I was being given the plum of the diocese. All I can say is that this plum had a stone in it. It got to the point where, during a clerical conference in Dublin, my mobile rang and there was this American voice. The Discovery TV Channel in the States wanted to come over to do DNA tests on someone buried in my church two centuries ago.'

For the archaeologists had found something interesting, so

interesting that, to quote *The Journal of British Archaeology,* it 'casts doubt on the legitimacy of the (present) Queen.'

'Oh dear,' said the vicar.

It starts with the organ. The organ at St Peter's was always a bit of a mystery, being so very big and grand, too big and grand for a parish church in the west of Wales. Originally intended for Windsor Castle, it had been delivered to Carmarthen in 1796, and the tradition is that it was a personal gift from King George III. The result is that the King's organ points to what follows, for the organ was sinking.

'It had sunk eight inches into the chancel floor,' said the organist, Paul Watkins. 'This, we were told, was because there were so many tombs beneath it. But it was when a lady put her foot through the floor during a midnight mass that we knew we were going to have to do something about it.'

It was decided that a concrete raft was needed to halt the subsidence, which was when the archaeologists came in. A week after the team from Cambria Archaeology started work they found a brick barrel vault in the centre of the chancel, in front of the altar, the most prestigious place for a church burial.

'And that was the first incredible thing,' said the Rev. Thomas. '*There was no historical account of such a vault in any of the church records.* And there was no gravestone. At least if there was a gravestone, it had disappeared when in Victorian times a new floor was laid, just as though someone wanted to hide it.'

For when there is a burial in a vault, the gravestone is built into the chancel floor. You will have seen many ('Below are laid the earthly remains of...'). But there had been a gravestone. As the archaeologists dug on, they found it laid next to the barrel vault, where, of course, the living would not see it.

The inscription read: 'In this vault are deposited the remains of Charlotte Augusta Catherine Dalton, eldest daughter of James Dalton Esq, formerly of this town and of Bangalore in the East Indies. She died on the 2nd day of August, 1832, aged 27 years. Also the remains of Margaret Augusta Dalton, second daughter of Daniel Prytherch Esq of this town and of Abergole in this county, by Caroline his wife, youngest daughter of the above James Dalton. She died on the 24th day of January, 1839, in the Ninth Year of her age.' Remember that name, Dalton. And note there is no reference made to James Dalton's wife, the mother of Charlotte Augusta Catherine and of Caroline.

Now consider those Christian names. Charlotte and Augusta are clearly family names for they occur in two generations, names too grand for a provincial Welsh family, yet oddly familiar to anyone who has read 18th-century history, for they occur in generation after generation in the family tree of Hanoverian royalty. George III's mother was an Augusta, as was one of his daughters; his Queen, and another of their daughters, were both called Charlotte. Caroline was the name of George I's wife.

There is also something else. The gravestone refers to two burials. As the archaeologists peered into the vault they found it contained four coffins.

The scene changes, to your nearest reference library, where you must consult the *Dictionary of National Biography*. In this you will read the following: 'Lightfoot, Hannah (fl. 1768), the beautiful quakeress. (See under George III.)' No dates of birth or death, you will note, and no particulars of her life. It is the briefest entry in the whole of the *DNB*, but then, if you excuse the pun, establishing that she had ever been under George III was the last thing its editors wanted.

The relevant section in the King's life refers to his teenage years, when he was Prince of Wales. 'To this period belongs the scandal about the Prince's attachment to Hannah Lightfoot, the 'fair quaker', daughter or niece of a linen draper, whose shop was in St James's Market.' This is that part of London which was to disappear under Regent Street.

The *DNB* entry resumes. 'It is said that through the intervention of Elizabeth Chudleigh, who became Duchess of Kingston, he persuaded her to leave home, and go through a form of marriage with one Axford, and that he frequently met her afterwards, and it is even pretended that he secretly married her, and had a daughter by her, who became the wife of a man called Dalton...'

A man called Dalton. James Dalton, a doctor from Carmarthen, later in the employ of the East India Company.

But the *DNB* was not yet done. While admitting that George III, as the teenage Prince of Wales, had probably known Hannah Lightfoot, a curious admission on the Dictionary's part, it went on to dismiss the rest of the story on the grounds that it 'rests merely on anonymous letters of a later date.' Only this isn't so, or rather it depends on what you mean by a later date.

George became King in 1760, aged 22. But ten years later, in 1770, when his brother the Duke of Cumberland was cited by a wronged husband, *The Public Advertiser* newspaper was already referring to 'the Letters of an Elder Brother to a Fair Quaker.' In 1776 *The Citizen*, with heavy irony, mentioned 'The History and Adventures of Miss L..htf..t, the Fair Quaker, wherein will be faithfully portrayed some striking picture of female constancy and princely gratitude which terminated in the untimely death of that lady and the su dden death of her disconsolate mother.' In short, the story was already common knowledge.

These are the only known facts. Hannah was born into a Quaker family in 1730 in Wapping, but her father, a shoemaker, died when she was still small, and she was adopted by her mother's brother, the linen draper of St James's Market. Then in 1756 something remarkable happened. She was thrown out of the Quakers on a charge of having been married 'by a priest to Some Person Unknown.' After this, which is even more remarkable, the Quakers made strenuous efforts to find her, only Hannah had vanished.

The 18th-century writer William Combe, later the author of the best-selling Dr Syntax verses, pointed to the effect of this expulsion. 'With such suitable precautions was the intrigue (he is referring to that between George and Hannah) conducted, that if the body of people called Quakers, of which this young lady was a member, had not divulged the fact by the public proceedings of their meeting concerning it... it would in all probability have remained a matter of doubt to this day.'

Only there is another twist. The Quakers referred to Hannah's marriage to 'Some Person Unknown', when it was the fact that in 1753 she had married someone whose name was very much known. Enter Isaac Axford, grocer, of Ludgate Hill near St Pauls.

When Mary Pendered in 1910 wrote her book on Hannah Lightfoot, astonishingly the only one that has ever appeared, she claimed to have made contact with the aged great-great-grandaughter of this Isaac Axford by his second marriage which took place in 1759. There had had to be a second marriage because, in the story handed down in generation after generation of the Axford family, Hannah had been taken away from her groom at the church, being driven off in a travelling coach and never seen again.

The remarkable thing about this is that a similar story, different only in one particular, had already appeared in 1825 in *The Monthly Magazine*. Its correspondent had also made contact with the Axford family, then still in the grocery business on Ludgate Hill, who confirmed that there had been a marriage, but that Hannah had actually lived with her husband for six weeks until the night the coach and four had called. The Axfords had advertised widely as to her whereabouts, but 'after some time obtained the information that she was well provided for.'

Only the story doesn't go away, and it is now that references start to *an actual marriage* between the future King and Hannah Lightfoot. Charles Bradlaugh, later an MP, claimed that after Hannah's death, Queen Charlotte insisted on her own second, and secret, marriage to George III on the grounds that their first had been bigamous. He also claimed that their first-born, the notorious Prinny, later George IV, always short of money, had used this to blackmail his parents.

It gets worse. *The Historical Fragment*, an anonymous publication, stated in 1824 that Caroline, the estranged wife of George IV, had been heard to say that she was neither wife nor Queen. There can be no doubt about the first, for George IV was a bigamist, having made a secret marriage to Mrs Fitzherbert. But the second claim was much more startling. Caroline was not a Queen because when George III married Queen Charlotte he was already married to Hannah Lightfoot, which would have made George IV illegitimate.

The political diarist Charles Greville, discussing the British Royal Family in 1829, wrote, 'Good God, what a set they are...the three kingdoms cannot furnish such a brood, so many and so bad, rogues, blackguards, fools and whores.' They had two hobbies: one was quarrelling amongst themselves, the other was adultery.

George I imposed a life sentence on his wife for adultery, and plotted to have his son, the Prince of Wales, kidnapped and transported to America. He in turn simply wished his son dead, and said so often enough in public. George III leapt at his son's throat, and the generation of which he, George, was part, introduced a new pastime, that of secret marriage. His brother, Cumberland, already paying out 10,000 pounds to the wronged husband, was secretly married in 1770 to a widow called Horton. Two years later another brother, the Duke of Gloucester, admitted that he had been married for six years. Their nephew secretly married Mrs Fitzherbert, but their sister, the Queen of Denmark, pursued a more traditional line, being imprisoned for life when she was caught in adultery with the Prime Minister of Denmark.

The point is, no contemporary would have been that surprised by news of a secret marriage between George III, or the Prince of Wales as he than was, and Hannah Lightfoot. Cassell's late Victorian *History of England,* the most popular history every published (copies still turn up in country house sales), stated categorically that it had taken place at Kew in 1759, adding that documentary evidence survived, though it did not elaborate on what form this took.

Daniel O'Connell, the great Irish politician, said he had once thought of writing a novel about a child of that marriage, a son this time, not a daughter, and of presenting him as a soldier of fortune. Mrs Piozzi, Dr Johnson's friend, wrote that there was such a son in real life. And, in the most bewildering twist of all, speculation targets a man, an 18th-century immigrant to South Africa, mysteriously set up there in great style. His name, oh dear, was George Rex. His (black) descendants survive, and were interviewed by the Welsh documentary film maker Kenneth Griffith, who told me, 'I started by not believing the story, and ended up convinced it was true.' But George Rex?

So did George III marry Hannah Lightfoot? Did this odd, impulsive, not too bright, lonely young man who had been kept in virtual seclusion, rebel once before his destiny closed in on him? As a newly crowned king he seemed to have brooded on this destiny, and on one aspect of it in particular. He confided gloomily to the Duke of Chandos that, unlike him, the Duke was a happy man, for he would never have to take into his arms a woman he had never even seen before. Of course he himself then did, a woman said to have been the plainest in Europe, and had 15 children by her. By all accounts theirs was a long and happy marriage, in the course of which she called him 'Mr King', he called her 'Mrs King', and, unlike those of his prececessors, it was a marriage unruffled by mistresses. Yet before all that, there is that strange little moment of entrusted confidence which shows this was very much on his mind.

Does that suggest he might have known a happiness that had been possible once but would never be his again?

But where the mystery really deepens is around Hannah. Yes, she married Axford, but theirs was a dodgy marriage, one of those conducted for cash in the 18th century, without licence or banns, by the dodgiest vicar of all, Alexander Keith, a man said to have married 100 couples in one day, marrying seducers, fortune hunters, and on one occasion two women so one could evade her debts. Keith was so dodgy he was actually excommunicated by the Archbishop of Canterbury, whereupon he in turn excommunicated the Archbishop. Why should a respectable grocer and a young Quakeress have agreed to have themselves married by such a man, and this in his notorious chapel under what is now Curzon Street in Mayfair? The questions mount, and there are more.

A portrait survives of Hannah, painted by Sir Joshua Reynolds, the most fashionable portraitist of the day. Why should such a man have painted a grocer's wife? The 1817 catalogue of pictures in the great house Knole, near Sevenoaks, says it is of 'Miss (sic) Axford. This is the Fair Quaker noticed by His Majesty when Prince of Wales.' The King was then still alive, though with the fairies. The portrait shows a serious-looking young woman in white, and it is a face more interesting than pretty. Nobody knows how it got to Knole.

But then nobody knows what became of Hannah, who in the late 1750s, despite considerable public interest in her, just disappears. There is no record of any attempt by her, or by any member of her family, to profit from what may, or may not, have happened. Nothing. Everything is so discreet, and so secret. And there the story ends, except that in 2001 a Carmarthen vicar found it necessary to have building repairs done, at which point not just the chancel floor but, metaphorically, the roof fell in on him, bringing with it the late 18th century. The Rev. Randolph Thomas began to learn an awful lot about the late 18th century, only he learned it in a hurry. For then the letters, and the phone-calls, started.

'The Axford family wrote to me,' said the Rev. Randolph Thomas. 'They said they had a copy of the marriage certificate between the King and Hannah Lightfoot, on which one of the witnesses was William Pitt the Elder. They said they also had a copy of Hannah's will in which she signs herself Hannah Regina.

'And then the Dalton Society of America wrote, saying they intended to come over and hold tours of the church.'

It is such a heady mix, a King's organ sinking, the result of which is the discovery of a forgotten vault with four coffins where there should have been just two: it is beyond fiction. But the Carmarthen Connection? Why not? In a time before railways, when the roads were terrible, what better place could there be in which to disappear than a small market town in the far West, one in which most of the people could only speak Welsh? Sir Richard Steele the essayist came here to escape his creditors, and did so. But consider for a moment a man who only wanted some building repairs done, and had history hit him like a tsunami.

And even then history had not done with the Reverend Thomas. 'The Earl of Essex turned up the other day,' he muttered.

'Who?'

'You know, the father of the Earl executed for treason by Queen

Elizabeth I. We knew he had been buried here, but we thought his tomb had been lost. And then we had to take up some floorboards in the vestry, and there he was.'

In the end the Reverend Thomas did what any man would do who did not want the fuss of turning out the Queen of England in her petticoat, that phrase her predecessor and namesake used. He had two feet of concrete put over the Dalton vault. Just as they did to seal off Chernobyl.

And I have an extraordinary admission to make. I haven't made any of this up; I wouldn't have had the imagination.

16 THE LAST CAVALRY CHARGE

MONDAY, JUNE 19, 1843

A street on a hill. A line of late Victorian villas, a large chapel built among the fields after a minister dreamt he had seen the Day of Judgement start up here, himself barrelling up out of his grave like a ballistic missile from its silo. And, at the end of the street, a prompt from a bleak time, what was once the town workhouse. Remember the workhouse: it has its part to play in what happened here.

Not on moorland, not in the water meadows outside some besieged city. Had it done so, this would be a place with a name nobody would forget. But it happened here, in a street in a Welsh town, where the last cavalry charge on the British mainland took place on a Monday afternoon.

You will not find it in the regiment's battle honours. Balaclava, 11 years later, is there, when the regiment rode into the Valley of Death, but that was its second charge. But there is no mention of the first, when the newly formed Fourth Light Dragoons (now long merged with the Queen's Royal Hussars), with sabres drawn, charged up the hill in Waterloo Terrace, Carmarthen on June 19, 1843.

It all came to an end here, something which may have begun with Arthur at Badon, and in recorded history went on to include the Conqueror at Hastings and Cromwell at Naseby. The last charge.

How romantic that sounds to anyone who has never seen cavalry in action, never heard the squealing of the dying horses at Waterloo or seen living men flutter on the braced lances of the British Army at Elandsgaate in the Boer War. But then, ever since the cavalry of the Goths at Adrianople in 378 rode down the heavy Roman infantry, the Legions which for over 400 years had dominated the known world, ever since then the man on horseback had been a figure of romance. And of hatred, something that has given the protest against fox-hunting its peculiar bitterness. But the further he slipped away, the more completely romance closed around the armed rider. Did he charge out of history with the Polish lancers attacking the German tanks, or as some have suggested, with some Italian unit lost in the Russian steppes? It is just that nobody in the little magazines which are obsessed with such things has mentioned this place.

Had there been killing, the name Waterloo Terrace would forever have been associated with massacre, its name notorious as Peterloo, where the yeomen cavalry, the half-trained sons of farmers, rode down the people of Manchester. But these cavalrymen were regulars, there was no killing, for here the sons of farmers were on the other side. And the only people who have ever heard of Waterloo Terrace are those brought up in Carmarthen, people like me.

The background to the last charge is the economy of west Wales in the early 19th century; the flashpoint is its roads. A rural economy turned on roads, for roads led to markets, but who was to pay for the roads? Men had been asking that question ever since wheeled carriages came in any numbers, carts in particular, for these broke up road surfaces, and the parishes that had looked after these could no longer cope. So it would have seemed sound Thatcherite economics that the roads be privatised, with turnpike trusts formed and with gates at which travellers got charged for their use.

But, as is the case with sound Thatcherite economics, speculators came along, paying gatekeepers on a commission basis, their own profits turning on higher charges and neglect. Men like Thomas Bullen, who by the 1830s had extended his activities into west Wales where the condition of the roads became notorious ('nothing but love of glory should tempt a man to pass along them'). It took seven hours to travel the 16 miles from Laugharne to Tenby, which, as Thomas Foster wrote in *The Times,* was like having to pay to use a farm-track.

What made this even more intolerable was the size of the Welsh turnpike trusts, so small a man might have to pay twice in a few hundred yards, and so many that Carmarthen bristled with gates, being virtually in a state of siege. Of these one of the houses, where the gatekeepers lived, survived in its odd octagonal shape into my childhood, converted into a sweet-shop.

The hardest hit of all were the small farmers in the west of the county, obliged to bring in lime for their poor fields. And it was here that the disturbances which became known as the Rebecca Riots broke out in 1839, when the first gate went down at Efail-wen.

The authorities had expected trouble, for special constables had been recruited and were present when out of the night came 300 men armed with shotguns and scythes. Their leader was a sword-wielding giant on a white horse who looked like something out of nightmare, being in a long dress with horse-hair ringlets dangling over a blackened face. The constables, reasonable men, ran for their lives, but, before they did so, one of them heard him addressed as 'Rebecca'.

The society of west Wales was one soaked in the Bible. Every man, even the running constables, would have known Genesis, Chapter 24, verse 60. '*Ac a fendithiasant Rebeccah...*And they blessed Rebecca and said unto her, "Thou art our sister; be thou the mother of thousands of millions, and let thy seed possess the gates of those which hate thee...*ac etifedded dy had borth ei gaseion."*'
It was a society soaked in drama too. Twice on a Sunday these men from the fields sat on hard varnished pews in the hard light (they had no time for stained glass), listening to sermons in which the minister's voice cracked and roared as he made Hellfire roar and the Damned dance. They enjoyed this, just as they enjoyed

the choreography, established from Efail-wen on, at the gates at midnight.

The gatekeeper, wakened by shots, would watch, probably from behind his curtains, as torches flared and a grotesque crone would hobble to the gate. 'Children, something bars my path, I cannot go on.' 'What is it, mother?' And she (or he) would fumble with the lock, at which point all hell would be let loose, the gates axed and burned, and sometimes the keeper's cottage as well.

Things got ugly only when later the riots spread to the industrial areas, and there was the one murder. Until then they had the support of a community sealed off by language, and by Nonconformity, from its English-speaking, Church-going squires. If there was a trial, no jury would convict.

In spite of this there was a strange lull after 1839, that lasted until the winter of 1842 when in Carmarthenshire the gates began to go down again. There seemed to be an organisation now, and the targets had broadened to include grasping vicars and unpopular magistrates: an element of sheer personal dislike had intruded. There would be the terrible bray of long harvest horns to summon the people, the disguises put on, which got madder and madder, with bonnets added, and parasols; and it would be panto time again. Each of these outbreaks had its own personal Rebecca, but was there a master strategist, some overall Rebecca? One name was mentioned, that of a solicitor, Hugh Williams, buried now in St Ishmael's churchyard, near Ferryside (curiously enough, next to his brother, a lieutenant in, of all things, the Brazilian navy). But you have only to look at Northern Ireland in living memory to appreciate that a closed society in rebellion has no need of overall leaders.

And then suddenly it was no longer a matter of lonely country toll gates at midnight. On Monday, June 19, 1843, 300 horsemen in the full light of day, but still in disguise, invaded the old capital of South Wales. Rebecca had hit Carmarthen.

They had assembled at the Plough and Harrow inn three miles outside the town, a crowd estimated at 2,000, women and children included, a gathering not known in these parts since the rising of Owain Glyndŵr. The riders came armed, and what might have happened is anyone's guess, except that something quite remarkable intervened.

Two local magistrates dared confront them, and managed to persuade them to stack their 250 shotguns in a barn. And with that a little army of irregulars became a protest march, with banners calling in the Welsh language for justice, *CYFIAWNDER*. Down the road to the town beneath them they came, and 50 years later a man who had then been 15 said that he had recognised Rebecca as Mike Bowen, a local farmer; Mr Bowen had winked at him. It was to be a day out.

But when they reached the town, there was the problem that confronts all protest marches (and days out), of what to do and where to go. They had a petition which they intended to present to the town's magistrates, but for most of that morning they just rode, and marched, up and down the streets, banners flying, horns blowing, drums beating. Then something happened that changed the character of the day again: the army had become a protest march, but now the protest march became a mob.

Carmarthen then had some 10,000 inhabitants, most of them crammed into slums by the river Tywi, from which a third of the population earned a precarious living as coraclemen, stevedores, seamen. Together they were the Carmarthen Mob in a town as lawless as anything in the American West. Dodge City at the height of the cattle drives had 13 pubs, Carmarthen in 1843 had 130. Out of these the men came tumbling, and they too were men with a grievance.

The workhouse on the hill above Waterloo Terrace was a thing of terror to the rural poor, but to the urban poor it was a terror they lived with, and saw every day, seeing its stark grey walls and its great locked door. Here families came, at the edge of starvation, and were split up: fathers into one courtyard, where each man had to break one-and-a-half tons of stone a day; mothers into another; boys into a third; little girls into a fourth.

A month before that June day, six men had rebelled against this regime and were in Carmarthen County Gaol for refusing to break stone, not that gaol would have been a hardship to them. In July, a reporter from *The Times* was to find its diet far superior to that provided by the workhouse. We know this *because the London paper printed his story*. It did so because the attention of the country was on Carmarthen because of what was about to happen. Rebecca, egged on by the Carmarthen Mob, turned her attention to the workhouse.

But the reaction of the inmates was not at all what she would have expected. Small children gathered around the matron as their deliverers swept in ('Oh, don't kill our poor mistress'), and in the stone-breaking yard men actually remonstrated with them, saying they did not want freedom as it was out of their power 'to better their circumstances'. But freedom they were going to get, whether they wanted it or no, and beds were being thrown out of the window when, at the foot of Waterloo Terrace, bugles sounded the charge.

In response to the magistrates' appeals, the Government had sent the Fourth Light Dragoons: it was what early Victorian governments did at times of civic disturbance. The Dragoons were at Cross Hands, 14 miles away, proceeding at a walk, when news came that Rebecca had, for all effective purposes, taken Carmarthen. Their commanding officer, a Major Parlby, was so startled that he ordered a gallop, only this was a gallop over 14 miles on a hot summer's day. As they swept over Carmarthen Bridge two horses dropped dead from exhaustion.

In Spilman Street, outside the Ivy Bush Hotel, they were met by a magistrate called Morris who told them about the attack on the workhouse, and, being mounted, led them there. Morris then proceeded to go off his rocker, for as sabres were drawn at the foot of Waterloo Terrace, he threw his hat in the air, shouting 'Slash away, slash away', before the Major told him to shut up. Regular officers, unlike magistrates, do not come badly out of the civic disturbances of the early 19th century.

The cavalry crashed into the crowd, watched by a reporter from the *Carmarthen Journal*. 'A scene took place which we can compare to nothing but the flight of the French from the plains of Waterloo. "Save himself who can" was the order of the day. Those who were on horseback immediately galloped away through different lanes, and those on foot cut their way through the hedges and gardens and over fields of corn towards the country, without once looking back to see what would be the fate of their friends inside.'

Yet nobody was killed.

That is the most extraordinary fact about the last charge. The yeoman cavalry crashing into the crowd at St Peter's Fields, Manchester (thereafter mockingly known as 'Peterloo' after the battle) killed eleven people and badly injured over 400, and the wonder, as the historian David Thomson wrote, is that civic disturbance did not become open rebellion. But in Waterloo Terrace, Carmarthen (as the street was later called without a trace of irony; before that it had been Tabernacle Row), the Dragoons used the flats of their sabres, splitting into two squadrons, one surrounding the workhouse, the other chasing the fugitives, so what followed had the outline of something already familiar to most of those running, that of an expertly conducted sheepdog trial.

It might so easily have become a massacre, and on a scale beyond Peterloo. You will not need reminding of what might have happened had the cavalry faced men armed with shotguns inside a defensible position: there would have been a bloodbath and a rewriting of 19th-century social history. But the 250 shotguns were stacked in a barn at Trevaughan. As it was, the *Journal* reported that one man who had hit a Dragoon with a stone got a sword cut on his head, and another had his arm broken when a horse trod on it. And that was it. There were 60 arrests.

But even then, the Government was so startled it poured troops into the town, three regiments of infantry, another of cavalry, as well as 50 men from the newly formed Metropolitan Police in their top hats and belted blue coats. The result was that the workhouse inmates were forced to explore their unwanted freedom even more, for the workhouse was taken over as a temporary barracks.

And with them, a month later, there stepped off the London coach (it would be another nine years before the railway reached Carmarthen), a Mr Thomas Foster, someone who was to have the biggest effect of all. The man from *The Times* had come.

Foster's reports are remarkable because it is one of those rare occasions when a Victorian gentleman interested himself in the rural poor. There was more drama in the urban poor: they were there in mass and the reporter did not have to travel so far to find them. But Foster in west Wales wrote of conditions worse than in any London slum, of cottages he had seen without a single stick of furniture in them. Because of that cavalry charge, rural poverty was suddenly news, and there was a wave of sympathy which would have been unthinkable had there been the bloodbath. Most of the 60 prisoners were released the following year, the maximum sentence on the others being 12 months.

Even more unique was the Government reaction. A commission examined the causes and, on its advice, a Turnpike Bill was rushed through Parliament, county road boards being set up in Wales to take over the trusts and to make uniform the tolls charged. So something good came of what was set in train by the charge that July afternoon.

Waterloo Terrace should be the worthiest of all battle honours.

17 A DAY OUT, ABERYSTWYTH

The shock first. You need to find the town clock tower, not that difficult in Aberystwyth, for it stands in the centre of the town, is brand new, and looks as though it had been assembled by some giant child from scaled-up Lego. But it wasn't a giant child, it was the local council which, preening itself on its achievement, then added this verse from Deuteronomy, chapter 19, 'Thou shalt not remove thy neighbour's landmark, which they of old set in thine inheritance.'

Eh? It was the council itself which removed their neighbour's landmark when they pulled down the old clock tower 50 years ago. I brightened as soon as I saw that: such a body was clearly capable of anything. But the shock, that came later, all of two minutes later.

I was walking away from the clock when I saw the chapel, the grimmest and bleakest of Welsh chapels, with steps and pillars big enough to have interested Samson. I grew up among chapels: in my childhood 60 years ago, I passed every day uncompromising monoliths called Horeb and Babell and Cana, and thought they would outlast me and all human life. But now I went up the steps, *and found myself in a pub.*

The pulpit was still there, the Ten Commandments on the walls on either side of it, but in the pulpit, the pulpit where once a man stood, nodding politely to the Almighty, there was now a life-sized cut-out of Vinnie Jones, footballer turned film heavy. In a Welsh Wesleyan Methodist chapel he was carrying two shotguns.

'What's it like drinking here?' The elderly lady who might have sat in one of the varnished pews, wearing a hat and unwrapping Mintoes, looked at me grimly. 'I'll tell you what it's like, I have to *force* the gin down.'

This in Aberystwyth, where I thought, where we all thought, the old Wales would forever stand at bay, where the land ends and the last building is the blackening granite of the Theological College, the only Presbyterian academy left in all Wales. But I should have known that nothing was ever what it seemed in Aberystwyth.

When I was a student here, wasting my State Scholarship grant in the amusement hall in the basement of the King's Hall, in particular on the rifle booth where they had .22s *with real ammunition,* something I never found before or since, I came on something so amazing I am still not sure whether it was a vision. Among the 'What the Butler Saw' coin machines there was one newer and more expensive than the rest. This cost threepence, not one penny, and there was a sign, I quote from memory, 'See the Naked Hordes Make Love and War. In Full Colour.' It was the Full Colour that did it (the suspenders and the bearded Edwardian interlopers were all in monochrome). I put my threepence in, and for three whole minutes watched in mounting fury a magnified, flood-lit, ants' nest: the things were alive inside the machine. It was a piece of cheek beyond the great Barnum at his most outrageous. But the King's Hall has been demolished and the ants gone.

In travel books, Aberystwyth is described as the most Welsh of all Welsh towns, and it was here that the Welsh Language Society came into being, when in 1963 an university student, stopped by the police for giving a girl a lift on his crossbar, ignored the summons, when this came, because it was in English. This little moment became history when it prompted a nationwide campaign which, 1500 years after people started speaking it (and almost a thousand years before anyone spoke a recognizable English), the Welsh language was given official status. Odd really, even odder when you consider that Aberystwyth in its origins was an *English* town.

It was purpose-built from scratch as an English colonial settlement by Edward I, and built where it is, on a ledge below the hills, so that its location allowed it to be supplied by sea. It is still difficult to get to Aberystwyth by land, but in its beginnings that hinterland was so hostile to its builders and first settlers, it must have seemed as though they were establishing a base on the moon. They built the castle first, building this by the sea but so near the sea that bits of it kept falling in. They then, in the colonial way, tacked on a town, adding walls and gates, only they forgot locks, bolts and bars, so the gates kept swinging open day and night. And then, at the start of the 15th century, along came Owain Glyndŵr, who took the castle.

But, with the long war turning in their favour, the English were back with the biggest cannon then known, a thing called the Messenger, brought by sea. It had been a guerrilla war, but now they had something they understood, a set-piece siege with rules, and everyone who was anyone turned up for the social event of 1407. The prince who would become Henry V was there, the Duke of York, the Earl of Warwick. But the Messenger blew up, Glyndŵr came out of the hills, and the captains and the kings suddenly remembered pressing social engagements elsewhere and sailed away.

There would be other wars. A local squire, to commemorate Waterloo, on a hill above the town built a memorial in the shape of a cannon barrel, thinking to add a statue of Wellington on horseback, but never did, so the cannon barrel looks like the chimney of an abandoned factory. They built themselves a First World War memorial on Castle Hill, commissioning an Italian sculptor who, putting the finishing touches to this, was so overcome by vertigo he had to be lowered by rope. Still it stands, as, miraculously, so does the statue of the Duke of Windsor, then Prince of Wales, in the College grounds. Twice this has been beheaded by students, and twice made whole when the authorities managed to find the head.

Because of its size (there are eight sudents to every 12 townsfolk), the university tends to dominate Aberystwyth. During the Second World War the writer Caradoc Evans, not that enthusiastic about his countrymen, lived there. 'The university students love Caradoc,' wrote Dylan Thomas, 'and pelt him with stones whenever he goes out.' Evans himself wrote in his wartime journal, 'Mary Tycanol tells me that Hitler was in college in Aberystwyth. That much is certain. Miss Arnold corroborates. Oh yes, everyone knows that Hitler was in college in Aberystwyth. He gave special orders that though London be razed Aberystwyth must be saved...' The mother of a friend of mine claimed that before the war she saw Ribbentrop on the Promenade. But then that is the thing about the town: there is the outside world and there is Aberystwyth, two separate entities, though on occasion they can touch.

When the College principal, a man very much of the world, wrote a series of newspaper articles on his friendship with the traitor Guy Burgess, he was made to resign. The elderly scholar, appointed in his place to restore traditional Welsh values, then promptly made the nationals himself when he ordered the College doctor to produce a list of all female undergraduates who had been prescribed the contraceptive pill, at which point the press, and this time the British Medical Association, duly fell from a great height on him.

The social historian Dr Russell Davies, being asked to hold an university seminar, delivered a learned address on 'Sexuality and Sexual Behaviour among the Welsh'. When he had finished a distinguished historian approached him shakily and said that while this had been interesting, very interesting, he hoped his next paper might be a little less... sensational. What would that be on?

'Mental Illness among the Welsh,' said Dr Davies.

Latterly the town has edged into fiction. *The Woman in Back Row* by Herbert Williams, published by Gomer, is the sort of book the tabloids like to describe as steamy. In it, in a seaside town Mr Williams warily calls Glanaber, an older woman seduces a young newspaper reporter. Herbert Williams, once a young newspaper reporter in Aberystwyth, sets the seduction (in some physical detail) in a house in the town's slum quarter.

'Hey, that's where I lived,' said his cousin.

'No, you didn't. Her house has a back yard, your family didn't have a back yard.'

In *Aberyswyth Mon Amour,* (Bloomsbury), followed by *Last Tango in Aberystwyth,* two Chandleresque crime novels, the author Malcolm Pryce, a native of the town now safely resident in the Far East, allows his fantasies free rein. There is an Aberystwyth Mafia made up of Druids who, having tired of organising the Eisteddfod in white sheets, have taken to organising crime 'in sharp Swansea suits'. The fantasies get wilder and wilder: there is a 24-hour whelk stall, and a town museum with a Combinations and Corsetry section.

The only thing is, as I walked the streets I came on such a museum: *it was holding an exhibition of women's underwear.* There is no need for fantasy in Aberystwyth, where in the High Street I came on two women in the full black burkha, the version you rarely see outside the Yemen, with a narrow strip for the eyes. They were disappearing at high speed into Dorothy Perkins.

I walked along the Promenade, where Ribbentrop may, or may not, have walked, past the Theological College from which my old headmaster, a student there, was expelled. He had let a piss-pot down on a string so that it clinked against the window of a professor who, putting his hand out, grasped it by the handle, at which point the string was released. Unfortunately the window could only open so far, so the reverend gentleman had to stand there, piss-pot in hand, watched by curious passers-by in the street beneath. Shortly afterwards my headmaster was encouraged to abandon all hopes of a career in the ministry.

Beyond this is one of the most curious buildings ever constructed. The old University College, with its towers and halls and stained glass, looks like an early Hollywood set incorporating all the architectural features known to man. Part Tudor palace, part station, part lunatic asylum, it should be on a moor, awaiting the arrival of Boris Karloff, or Laurel and Hardy, or anyone really: you could make any film here. Instead, like most of the public buildings in Aberystwyth, it started life as something else, being built as a hotel by a developer who dreamt of a chain of such hotels along Cardigan Bay and went into spectacular bankruptcy before it was even finished. The result was that it became the first Welsh university, helped through its birth pangs by collections among the Victorian poor. Education, and getting on, is an old Welsh concern.

But, though it was term time, the building looked empty. 'Why? They've all gone, that's why,' said the porter. 'All the departments have gone to the new university campus up the hill. Only the Welsh department is still here, they refused to move out.'

God knows what will become of it, with its huge bronze statues and its portraits in oil of the Victorian great and good. 'Just look at that sweet Welsh face.' A man had paused in front of a picture above an inscription recording someone's contribution to the county of Merionethshire. 'That bloke would hang you as soon as look at you.'

I looked in at what in my time had been the Senior Common Room. This can now be hired for the day, and the All-Wales Transport Forum had just adjourned for lunch. A stroke of genius that, to hold such a conference here, in the Welsh town most difficult to arrange transport for, or even get to.

A delegate, gathering up his papers, said in a voice full of awe, 'Just look at the furniture, I mean this is a public room now.' There were antique chests and settles, championship thrones from long-gone eisteddfodau, and a remarkable three-tiered sideboard, all in a dark oak which writhed with carvings; the fireplaces were made of alabaster. Here for a whole day men sat amidst this abandoned grandeur, discussing the lost buses and the closed railway lines of Wales.

But then this is the saddest thing about Aberystwyth, that, whatever was here once has moved on. The local gentry had their town houses, elegant Georgian buildings, but these are offices and flats now.

In Victorian times the great sweep of the Promenade was a sea-front of grand hotels, the poet Swinburne, not notorious for his interest in women, writing after a week on the tiles, 'Give my remembrances to my sailors.' But the hotels are DHSS refuges now, and in turn the university, the police and the county council have all moved inland, so Aberyswyth seems a paradigm for the evolution of life itself.

Like life, the town came in from the sea, and, again like life, moved on. The University buildings crowd the hill above it and may move over it into the hinterland, leaving its abandoned hostels on the Promenade to reluctant developers who appear not to have a clue as to what to do with them.

'I actually retired here, briefly,' said the steamy novelist Herbert Williams. 'I thought the sea would be enough. But it wasn't, so I moved.'

Beyond the Castle, the in-place in 1407, a line of cars was parked, their occupants staring out to sea as though awaiting something to happen. I paused beside a 1964 Austin Farina. 'If you could tell the blokes who bought these that they'd still be on the road in the 21st century they'd have a hell of a shock,' said its owner. 'I've got two.'

At the very top of the tower in the old College there was a door facing west, and seaward, there was a sign in large red capitals, 'Do Not Open This In High Weather', and it was like that door in the *Mabinogion* which, if opened, would mean an end to all good times. And it felt as though someone had.

The last thing I saw in Aberystwyth was the station. That too had become a pub.

When an earlier version of this essay was published, Aberystwyth town and Cyngor Sir Ceredigion councillor Carl Williams was quoted in the *Cambrian News* as saying that it had possibly done 'immense damage to the economy of the locality.'

18 PORTRAIT GALLERY (2)

CHRISTMAS

Eddie Evans, the licensee of the Drovers' Arms in Carmarthen, was recalling Christmas Eve, in his case...bleakly. At eight o'clock, as usual, he had had to lock his door against the mob baying to get in. 'Down here it's like that at Christmas,' he said. 'People go into a frenzy. We could hardly move in the pub, that's how it's always been in Carmarthen. Except this time it was a bit different.

'After we'd locked the door a girl came up to me and said that a man had passed out in the back bar. Nothing too unusual about that; I thought it would just be a matter of cuffing him round the ear and throwing him out into the street.

'But when I got to him and grabbed his collar, I found he was cold, very cold. And clammy. I couldn't find a pulse. I cleared a space because people were milling round us, not taking any notice of what was going on. He was a young man, barely in his twenties, and he was, quite literally, going blue. I turned him on his left side and gave him a good thump on his back.'

I shuddered, for Eddie was 20 stone or more. Being thumped by him was something a man would remember for the rest of his life. 'What happened?'

'Nothing. I did it again. At that moment, even in the crowd around us, with everyone drinking and singing and going to the lavatory, it was as though it was just the two of us, him and me. Then something happened. A pulse started, very faint, and his eyelids flickered. I thumped him again, and the pulse was stronger.

'I looked up and all I could see was people's backs, yet within a few feet of them something amazing had happened, a man had been brought back to life. I stared at my hands which had worked this miracle, then at his sleeping face, and I felt as close to him as I've been to anyone. But then there was a voice that seemed to come from a long way off. "*Bloody hell, he's not gone and done it again.*"

'It was someone I'd noticed in his company earlier. I heard myself ask what he meant. "It's him," he said. "He keeps dying."

'I didn't know whether he was mad, or I was, but he went on,

"He's got this asthma, so when he goes on a bender he dies. For a bit anyway. He's died all over town, he has."

'At that point the crowd parted, and there were two ambulance men with a stretcher. "Oh no," said one of them. "It *is* him, I thought it would be. The last time he died on us was a fortnight ago in the Red Lion."

'Anyway they took him off, and an hour went by. I was behind the bar when I heard someone shouting through the letter box. "Open up, there's a woman out here dying." My first inclination was to ignore this, I'd had enough dying for one night, but the voice came again, and there was real terror in it. "Honest, honest."

'She was in her twenties, covered with blood, but she could walk. Her husband had beaten her up, then dragged her down Water Street.'

Eddie Evans beamed. 'You've no idea how nice it was to get back to familiar things. It was just another domestic tiff in Carmarthen on Christmas Eve.'

Some days later, New Year's Eve in a village pub in Northamptonshire, there was a fancy-dress competition, as there always was at the time. This year the theme was the TV farce *'Allo, 'Allo*, which was a relief for it meant you could talk to people without having to lock your eyes with theirs. One year I had found myself in stunned conversation with a couple who had striven for realism when they came as Adam and Eve. Another time the theme was Vicars and Tarts, and the village postmaster gave the first prize to a girl who wasn't even competing, which prompted an awful row.

This time there was, of course, the odd mad blonde in an open tunic and black underwear, who kept hauling at her decolletage ('They wander, you know'), but most were decorous enough as French fishermen and RAF escapees. Oh, and Nazis; everywhere I looked there were peaked caps and Iron Crosses.

'Odd lot, the Nazis,' a tall man told me. 'Know what they did in 1943?'

'Retreated?'

'No, they legalised nudism.'

MICHAEL COMEY, CARMARTHEN PLUMBER

'There was this chap, he'd retired, he'd made a fortune during the War and he had us round, said he wanted a new bathroom suite. Money no object apparently.

' "But, boys, everything has to be as it was. Especially that power point."

' "Hang on, what power point?"

' "That one there, in the side of the bath."

' *"You've got a power point in the side of your bath?"*

' "Oh yes, it's essential, that is. You plug the electric fire in before you get out of the bath."

'When you think about it, there's an odd lot living round here. Remember that Big Freeze we had? When the thaw came we got called round to this house where the neighbours had seen water coming out under the front door. We couldn't get an answer, so we had to break in. And the mess, even I hadn't seen anything like it. The water must have been coming through the ceiling for days, the plaster was down. That's when we heard the singing.'

'What singing?' I said.

'It was coming from somewhere upstairs. We went up, and there was this old boy, surrounded by beer bottles, watching the racing on television. Know what he said?'

'I don't know. "Thank God, you've come."?'

'No, with his house falling around his ears, what he said was *What the fuck are you doing here?*" You don't half see life when you're a plumber in Carmarthen.'

RALPH SIGGERY, BUILDER, ON A CARMARTHEN WAR HERO

'There was this bloke, he was behind a wall in France when he and the bloke who was with him, they heard a tank in the lane. This other bloke, he was in charge of an anti-tank rifle, a PIAT or something they called it, great big thing. Anyway the Carmarthen boy said, "If we knock this one out, we'll get a medal." He'd already got the MM.

'But the other bloke, he was looking over the wall, and said, "You daft bugger, d'you know what kind of tank that is? It's a Tiger."

' "Oh, we'll get the VC for that. Bound to."
' "You have the fucking VC. You can have the fucking PIAT as well, I'm off."
'This boy from Carmarthen, he got the gun lined up. He could hear the tank now, it was in range. And then, looking over the wall, he saw the size of it. "Fuck it," he said. Very slowly, very quietly, he hid the PIAT in a bush, and two years later got the Freedom of the Borough of Carmarthen.'

A POLICE SERGEANT LOOKS BACK
What brought this up was a story that appeared in the local paper. A Mrs Y, found guilty of stabbing her husband, had been released from custody to look after him, he having become paralysed from the stabbing. It seems Mr Y had fallen asleep while watching television, and had murmured his secretary's name. Mrs Y said she could not remember anything after that, except that as he awoke he said he could not feel his legs, and asked for an orange juice. It was when she came back with this, she said, that she noticed the carving knife sticking out of his back. At that point she called an ambulance.

They have now moved to a bungalow specially adapted for his new wheelchair, and are hopeful he will recover. Which was when I remembered the sergeant. There came a point in a man's life, he had told me, when he realised nothing people did would ever surprise him again. It came to him in his twenties.

I had met him in the Queens Hotel in Carmarthen. It was lunch time, and we were the only two in the bar. The sergeant was retired then, and I knew him because I had been at school with his son Barry. But I had never talked to him before, and to my growing bewilderment this huge man, about six foot five inches tall, talked, in this order, about Welsh poetry, its metres, Welsh history, then, after his sixth pint of Bass (and my second), his own philosophy of life.

As a young man, he said, he had been stationed in the nearby industrial town of Llanelli. He was on night duty, it was quiet, and he was alone. He had lit the fire and was writing a report when he found his eyes wandering round the room, over unwashed tea-cups and full ashtrays. Wherever he looked there was mess, and after a while he could not stand it any longer. At one o'clock he was down on his hands and knees, sleeves rolled up, his collar off, with a bucket and scrubbing brush.

'I must have done half the floor when I became conscious a man was standing there. I'd been scrubbing so hard I hadn't heard him come in. He said, quite quietly, "I've killed the wife." He was so matter of fact I thought to myself, this one's had a few. Not only that, he is standing on my nice clean floor. "Out," I said. And he went, just like that.'

Just after two, the floor drying, the man was back. He had taken his cap off and was holding it in his hands. "Look, I'm sorry to be a nuisance, but, if I don't tell you, who do I tell?" At that time of morning the oddest people turned up in police stations, the sergeant said, spaced-out drifters from the night looking for someone to talk to, ready to confess to anything.

'It must have been raining for there was mud on the floor from his shoes. "Out," I said again, and I think I picked the brush up at that point. So now I've cleaned the floor, again, washed up, emptied the ashtrays, put some more coal on the fire, and made the cup of tea I'd been dreaming about. It was then the first little doubt came.

'The man had been quite well dressed; I'd not seen a drifter who looked like that. It was only a doubt, but I thought I'd better take a look to see what had become of him. It must have been about three in the morning then, but I didn't have to look far. He was sitting in the rain on a wall just outside the station, and didn't show any surprise at seeing me. "Come on," he said. And he took me to his house.'

The sergeant rattled his glass on the counter. 'Fancy another one?' But this was just automatic on his part, for he was staring into the middle distance.

'And he had,' the sergeant said.

ALAN JONES, A FUNERAL ADDRESS

Two weeks before he died, Al was given intensive radiotherapy.

'What was it like?' I asked.

'Terrible, awful. Wouldn't want to go through that again.'

'The pain, you mean?'

'No, the *music*.'

Throughout his time in theatre they had played him Dusty Springfield ('Dusty Springfield. I mean to say'); Tom Jones ('Be fair...Tom Jones'), the Beatles ('Nursery rhymes, mush'). Everything, he muttered, from the 1960s. Expletives have been deleted.

'They meant well, Al.'

'You think?'

Alan Jones, born Carmarthen 1943, died London 2006, a Civil Servant for most of his life, but this was a mere incidental detail, a winter afternoon. For this was a man with the best 1950s record collection in Europe: American rock 'n' roll, also Country, Rockabilly, Black rock 'n' roll, White rock 'n' roll, Blues, Hillbilly. But no Pop. No Pop ever. Consulted by record companies, his name is on their reissued CDs: this was a world authority. Which is ironic. For this was a man whose world had ended long before, on December 31, 1959.

The 1950s were for him a glorious decade, of the sort few, if any, of us ever experience. It started at the Model School, where in 1953 he was Victor Ludorum, having won every race in the school sports. Well, not quite every race.

'Didn't do too well in the sack race, did you?' I said.

'Course I didn't, I had the smallest sack. Monty Griffiths (who won), he had a sack so big, he could have won the high jump in it.'

Al, as you might expect, had perfect recall when it came to the 1950s. They ended with him in the grammar school, surrounded by adoring girls and a not-so-adoring headmaster, who, throughout his time there, waged relentless war over Al's interpretation of what was school uniform. Al was a Teddy Boy in a school blazer, but the infuriating thing was that he never quite broke the rules. He managed to arrange his hair so his cap was hidden in his Tony Curtis cut, from which, when challenged, he would produce it like a conjuror. But the man had his revenge. Stalin had his victims shot, then airbrushed out of history. Benjamin Howell, headmaster of the Queen Elizabeth Grammer School, Carmarthen, didn't bother to have Al shot, he just refused even to let him appear in the school photograph. In this way he hoped it would be as though Al had never been.

The Civil Service, in which Al worked, or lurked, for 30 years, must at times have had similar hopes. 'I don't think his heart is in his work,' reported a supervisor at the DTI. And of course it wasn't. Al's heart was in the little recording studios of the Deep South: everything else, apart from his own childhood, was unreal.

It was the last ten years of his life after retirement which were the most curious. He, who had never really been anywhere, became a full-time record dealer and, in the course of this, a world traveller. Record fairs in Utrecht, in Madrid, in Stockholm, Copenhagen: he and his friend Piers Chalmers racketed round Europe, sliding on glaciers, negotiating the alleys of Paris, in a van so full of records it was a diving bell from the 1950s. But, being Al, he bought more than he sold.

His collection, always large, now became enormous. 'Records behind me, records to the side of me, records everywhere,' said his mother after she stayed in his flat. He said once that he intended presenting his collection to the deaf.

'But they won't be able to hear it, Al,' said a friend.

'Then I shall sell it,' he said a bit huffily, 'and give the deaf the proceeds.'

But he never mentioned the deaf again.

We, each of us, hear a different drummer. Al heard many, and not just on records. He had friends who were record collectors. He had friends who were bird watchers. He had friends from his childhood. These, in their different categories, never met any of the others. And then there were those who, with him, knew every pub and Indian restaurant from Richmond to Islington (Al in his pomp ate nothing but the hottest of curries, which meant many never forgot the experience of eating with him). They never forgot Al either.

19 CRIME IN CARMARTHEN

In 1991, reading the national figures in the papers in which the overall total was described as an explosion in crime, those who were prepared, some of them eager, to rant happily about original sin found themselves stopped in their tracks. For the biggest rise of all, at 33.8 per cent, was not in Greater London or the Gorbals, it was in Dyfed. Over the cornflakes that morning mouths must have formed the question, 'Where's Dyfed?' Or, more to the point, 'What's Dyfed?'

Dyfed, once a Dark Age kingdom in west Wales, was in 1973 exhumed by Ted Heath and Peter Walker in their 'big is beautiful' reorganisation of local government. They forked in the counties of Cardigan, Carmarthen, and Pembroke, delighting many chief executive officers and signwriters, but, alas, like most Welsh Dark Age kingdoms, the latter day life of Dyfed was a brief one. Within two decades its three constituent parts had peeled away, delighting even more chief executive officers and signwriters, but for a moment in 1991 it stood in the world's eye: Dyfed's name led all the rest. Coming as I do from its administrative centre in Carmarthen, this was a source of pride to me, for each man likes to come from somewhere distinguished for something. But what crime?

Not murder. I could remember just three murders in 40 years, only one of which had been done by a local man, and the Welsh tend to lose interest when it is not one of their own ('Oh, an Englishman did it. From away.') An exception was the murder of one Polish farmer by another in the 1950s, when, despite there being no body, a guilty verdict was obtained. But it was the possibility that the dead man had been fed to the pigs which guaranteed local interest, especially among people who might in turn have eaten them.

Of commercial sex there was no sign, though the last two prostitutes in Carmarthen, Mary Ann Bogus and Fanny Cawl were not long dead. When I was a boy, Fanny was still gamely in business in her eighties, attending to the farmers on mart days, a shawl draped over a table lamp in her window to show she was occupied.

How different things were once, when in the 1840s a commercial traveller could alight from the Gloucester stage in Lammas Street, Carmarthen, politely ask a passing policeman for directions to the nearest brothel, and the policeman would just as politely *direct him*. We know this because the traveller said so in open court, having been robbed of his watch in the brothel.

It was a town of breathtaking humbug then, when little boys could be had up before the bench for playing marbles on a Sunday ('The Mayor severely but justly commented upon, and expressed his deep regret, at the immorality'). For at the same time, it was regular police practice to keep observation on the pubs at 7am again on a Sunday. *7am on a Sunday.* But then this was a frontier town of the sort the real American West never knew. Shoot-outs during elections were so regular that the entries in the town record were laconic ('1832, Charter Day Riots, the Star and Garter Inn attacked by mob, landlord defending himself with powder and shot. Treadwheel erected in Carmarthen Gaol'). Carmarthen had the highest annual death rate in Britain in 1873, only one inhabitant in six dying of what was described as old age.

But in 1991 what crime? The only headlines I remembered were prompted by the sporadic police raids on gentlemen's public lavatories, one of which netted the then MP. To such lavatories, built in the bleakest places, the dreamers came, almost all of them respectably married and prosperous local businessmen (the quality of the sports coats in the photographs was as impressive as those worn by leaders of the IRA when they discovered Donegal tweed was a more potent weapon than the Kalashnikov), most of them middle-aged, and all, like medieval barons embarking on rebellion, prepared to risk everything for this tumult in the cubicles. The next thing was, the luminaries of the golf clubs were running a gauntlet of cameramen outside the magistrates' courts, and there was the odd suicide, yet still the event recurred, as mysterious as corn circles. It got to the point at which, whenever I entired a public lavatory in west Wales, I called out, 'Anybody home?'

There were moments of the blackest comedy as when a local mayor hit top-C in the bleakest, most remote gents' lavatory of all, and promptly expired, leaving his entire wardrobe to a friend of mine who now props up bars in Carmarthen dressed in cashmere. All this is very mysterious because, growing up in a town where everybody knew everybody else, I can remember only one homosexual. Like Dr Livingstone, he was away a lot.

It was reported crime that didn't change, the roll-call of the drunk and the belligerent being more or less what it always was. Still the 1970s were the botanical years, when the ageing English flower children came. Pensioned off by their family trusts to hill farms which seemed to their relations as safely remote as Siberia, these began to gather in a harvest hitherto unknown to Welsh hill farmers or to the local police. I knew something was up when a young man I knew appeared in court, having been on drugs, he confessed, when he met the Archangel Gabriel in Furnace Terrace.

In Carmarthen, the crime capital of Britain.

part three

EXILE AND THE PAST

Caradog Prichard was for 34 years a Parliamentary sub on the *Daily Telegraph*. But in another country and another culture he was a poet, and the only man ever to win three crowns at the National Eisteddfod. Mrs Prichard kept these in a china cupboard in their house in St John's Wood where her daughter's school-friends would stare at them. In time she got used to fending off telephone calls from astonished parents who had been told, 'That girl Prichard, her father's some kind of king in exile.'

20 THE THIRD JOURNEY

Narrator: There is a third journey, one into what was, and into what might have been. This is a journey into the Welsh past, one that, the older he gets, the exile takes.

On a hill above a river two people talking. In the background there is a castle, its towers showing above the trees.

Dinefwr: My name is Richard Dynevor.

Byron: Come on, you can do better than that

Dinefwr: Well if you want the full thing, it's Richard Charles Urien Rhys, 9th baron Dynevor.

Byron: How long have your people been here?

Dinefwr: As far as my family's concerned, the first authentic documentary evidence dates to 1326. Why are you laughing?

Byron: Most of us don't have family trees. If we do, four generations and they've gone. You're going back to 1326.

Dinefwr: The genealogists tried to take it back further than that.

Byron: To the Knights of the Round Table, I gather.

Dinefwr: Indeed they did, to King Urien of Rheged, whose son had this bodyguard of ravens which were incorporated into our family coat of arms. Our first motto was, God feeds the ravens, something I've always loved. A pair of ravens still nests in the trees above this house.

Byron: If that's true, you go back to, what is it, the sixth and seventh centuries?

Dinefwr: Yes, but the historians are quite right to call it a day in 1326.

Byron: Sorry for laughing, but, you know, it's so extraordinary to have your ancestors pegged out to dry. The rest of us, we can invent ancestors, we can say they were nice people. You know yours weren't.

Narrator: I had already made one journey, when my parents moved from the Welsh-speaking countryside to the English-speaking town. But there was another journey, one that came to mean more and more to me. As R.S. Thomas had it:

> There is no present in Wales
> And no future;
> *There is only the past...*

Listen. A man is writing a letter.

'A siege has begun of my own castle and there is panic in those that are with me, for they have vowed to kill all those who are in it. Because of which I pray you give us warning very quickly whether we can expect help so that if not we can slip away to Brecon... Written at Dinefwr in haste and great dread.'

It is July 1403, and the writer, a Welshman called Jenkin Havard, is a member of the English Colonial Service. He is the constable of Dinefwr Castle overlooking the Tywi at Llandeilo, and he has just seen the most terrifying sight on earth; in the water meadows below his castle he has seen a human swarm pass. Once a guerilla leader, Owain Glyndŵr, with an army of 8,240 men, a curiously exact figure for the Middle Ages, has come like a prince out of exile.

You have to imagine such things, but the last journey is not just one in the imagination. Here the past is just a handshake away. His castle sold, the last lord of Dinefwr, he of the Ravens, is still here, living in a converted cowshed on the slopes of what was once his park.

Byron: Your people had control of, or owned, what was it 12 or 15 castles in West Wales?

Dinefwr: I didn't know that Gruffydd ap Nicholas or Rhys ap Thomas had got it up to quite that number, but it was a pretty long list.

Byron: One of them had put a king of England on the throne.

Dinefwr: Yes, yes, they played the game very cleverly. The effects of the Black Death and the Owain Glyndŵr rebellion had left Wales very weak. And with all the old medieval landholding systems going, it was a tremendous time for a new grasping young family to start up. There were quite a few families like that but I think Gruffydd ap Nicholas and his sons and his grandson...

Byron: Gruffydd having bounded on the stage out of nowhere.

Dinefwr: Oh, he did indeed, yes. He was pretty ruthless, they were hugely ambitious and pretty ruthless, terribly ruthless.

Byron: You told me once that your ancestors – the founding fathers of your noble house – were the most amazing thieves.

Dinefwr: Well they were when it came to land. The laws were pretty weak and they were up to every trick in the book, they cheated with the wardships and with leaseholds, with just about everything.

Byron: There's an amazing story about Rhys ap Thomas, Gruffydd's grandson, that nobody dared live within 20 miles of him, and certainly no one dared die within 20 miles of him because he inherited everything.

Dinefwr: There's a ghastly truth in that.

Byron: It's amazing how your people got away with it.

Dinefwr: There were pretty serious complaints but they always got round it somehow. It was a long way from London to Carmarthen and a lot could happen on the way, and a lot could happen in Carmarthen too.

Byron: Gruffydd ap Nicholas was a bugger. I mean, that story about the judicial duel...

Dinefwr: That's a terrible one, I've never really understood it. But it seems this man came to Gruffydd ap Nicholas and said someone had done something against him. Fine, said Gruffydd ap Nicholas.

Byron: Who ran the law in west Wales.

Dinefwr: Indeed he did, yes. So he said, right we'll have to sort this out. And he put them into armour, gave them weapons, and told them to fight it out. In other words, he got them to fight a judicial duel, something that had long gone from

135

English law. And one of them got killed. It was the old way of proving guilt, but Gruffydd ap Nicholas wouldn't have that, he cut the head off the man who'd won. He then went and charged his family £40 for the head.

Byron: That's an extraordinary amount of money

Dinefwr: It's enormous, it's a bad story, that.

Byron: Yes, the archers at Agincourt were paid fourpence a day. This maniac was selling a head for £40.

Dinefwr: And he certainly didn't need the money, this was sheer entertainment, his entertainment.

Byron: What do you feel? Someone like me can be quite romantic about this old family in the Tywi valley, but you've got the embarrassment of *knowing* what they were like.

Dinefwr: The fact it was 500 years ago does help slightly. I'd be a bit nervous if my grandfather had behaved like that.

Byron: When you walk in the streets of Llandeilo now, do people know you?

Dinefwr: Well some do. They certainly don't think I'm anything special if that's what you're getting at, and I wouldn't want them to. Damn it, things have changed, Byron.

Byron: Where once I'd have gone to war if you'd told me to, those three ravens stitched on my chest. When did you realise, not just who you were, but what Dinefwr was?

Dinefwr: I think pretty early on, when I had to start worrying about it because my grandfather had died, and my father was faced with these hefty death duties – which are a fair form of tax but too high then. And I think my father wondered whether he could keep going, but when he died six years later there was no question that I'd be able to keep this place on. That's when I thought of turning it into an arts centre. I knew I had to sell the place, so I was trying to find a use for the house and for the estate in some shape or form.

Byron: Shame the Prince of Wales couldn't have taken it on.

Dinefwr: I don't know really, I think a lot of Welsh people would rather it was kept either in Welsh hands or a Welsh institution had taken it on. I don't think that one really wants to have it taken over by this particular Prince of Wales. I'm not trying to get at him personally, I don't think one wants the UK royal family to take over.

Byron: Wasn't one of your ancestors done for treason?

Dinefwr: Yes, he was very young. He was 23, when Henry VIII had him executed.

Narrator: There were three places in the old Wales. One was Aberffraw, the seat of the Princes of Gwynedd, the second was Mathrafal, the seat of the Princes of Powys. The third was Dinefwr, the seat of the Princes of Deheubarth, of South Wales.

Of these, Aberffraw is under council houses now, Mathrafal a grassy mound beside a river, its location something even local people have forgotten. But Dinefwr survives, and because of this the past can come knocking.

Dinefwr: When I was very young, and on the stage, somebody said I was the rightful king of Wales. I was in *Macbeth* at the Gate Theatre in Dublin, and this story came out in the papers, saying that the king of Wales was playing the part of Seyton, Macbeth's servant.

Byron: That must have been a shock.

Dinefwr: Yes, a bit awkward really.

Byron: One knows how Welsh Rhys ap Thomas was, but how Welsh was the family after a certain point?

Dinefwr: My guess is that the last person who was able to speak Welsh was Henry Rice and he died in 1651.

Byron: Wasn't he the one who killed a man up in Bishop Auckland?

Dinefwr: No, that was his grandson. You're very good at picking up these violent acts, aren't you?

Byron: Then the slow English centuries came.

Dinefwr: Yes, all these families were keen on money, so they had to go in for marrying English heiresses, though a lot were Welsh heiresses. That was the game plan.

Byron: And then, education. As soon as public schools come, that completes the process.

Dinefwr: I think it does complete the process, but this business of going off to London had started as soon as Henry VII got onto the throne.

Byron: You've sold the estate, the National Trust has the house, the Welsh Office the castle, but you don't go away.

Dinefwr: I think I should have done. Once one sells the house then one goes off stage and should probably stay off stage, which I'm not very good at doing.

Byron: How much do you regret that you were the last lord of Dinefwr?

Dinefwr: Oh, I didn't like being the one who threw in the towel, I really didn't like that at all. I don't think many people would like to take on that role.

Byron: A silly question, but do you have to pay to go in now?

Dynefwr: No I don't; but then I'm also a member of the National Trust. But I do have special rights. When I sold them the deer park, there was a clause put in which said that I and my family could walk wherever we wanted, I think at any time of day and any time at night.

Byron: Do that at night, and you'd put the fear of God in people if they saw you among the oaks in moonlight. It'd be like a ghost walking.

Dinefwr laughs.

Byron: Especially now the wild cattle have returned. What was the story you told me about them during the War, that they'd been rounded up for the first time, and painted green?

Dinefwr: I've come to believe it did happen. My aunt Imogen died a couple of years ago in her nineties, she was the great family memory so what she could remember was very reliable. And she said it did happen. When there was the danger of the Germans bombing Swansea, which indeed they did, someone came to the conclusion that these white cattle in the Park could be seen from the air at night, they'd be luminous.

Byron: The cattle were white. And wild.

Dinefwr: Not that wild. But it was thought best to camouflage them with patches of green paint. I'd never really believed it, but apparently it did happen. At least it happened once, because it rains a lot in west Wales, and the green paint didn't last very long so they couldn't go on doing that. The cattle were quite difficult to round up, and there weren't many people left to round them up and paint them green.

Byron: They're one of only two surviving herds said to have been introduced by the Romans for sacrificial purposes.

Dinefwr: So they say. What is known is that in the old Welsh laws, if the lord of Dinefwr got taken prisoner, his ransom would have been a line of these cattle, each 20th animal a bull, stretching from Dinefwr to Argoel.

Byron: Where's Argoel?

Dinefwr: That's the point, the old laws didn't say where Argoel was. *Laughs.*

Byron: Hang on, had you been kidnapped, these cows with the long horns which, in the pens at Carmarthen Mart when you sold up, terrified the farmers, there'd have been a line of them stretching to infinity.

Dinefwr: Well, it's not as daft as that. People have had a few guesses at where Argoel was. I don't think it was that far away.

Byron: What will happen to this place? You're the last lord of Dinefwr. But you've got children: are they interested in their ancestry?

Dinefwr: Yes I think they've got a definite interest in the history of the place. There are four of them, my three daughters are married and have children, but I've no idea what will happen. I mean, this is just a converted cowshed, but I think Dinefwr will be special to them. It's not the place, it's the family history. Once you get dispossessed, as it were, you've got to rather rely on the history of your family. It's just sad that after 600 years history has been severed from this place.

Narrator: Below us the river flows, which was here before there were squires or princes, or even men on this hill. It flows on past Dryslwyn Castle where at midnight on New Year's Eve 1964, with no job and the future full of doubts, I held hands with the champion javelin thrower of Carmarthen Grammar School for Girls, who, 50 years on and a grandmother, reminded me that at the time she was also the champion javelin thrower of Wales. We could hear singing in the hills around us, and the sound of bells. And for a moment time stopped.

But it is 1994 now, and on a hot July afternoon from Dryslwyn bridge I am watching a young couple in a boat, the girl in a bikini rowing, and as they pass I can see in the sunlight the blonde down glinting on her back. Elizabeth and Essex beating oars. And then.

'Oy, can't 'ew read? *No Boatin'.*'

The girl's voice is small and startled. 'I'm sorry, is there a sign?'

'Course there's a sign. *No Swimmin'. No Boatin'.* Now get out of there.'

Welsh officialdom in a waistcoat, he stands on the bridge like the angel set with a flaming sword over Eden, as the two scuttle up the bank with their boat. 'If they got away with it, this place would be like bloody Blackpool,' he tells me.

'But why can't they row their boat?'

'Because the Electricity Board wouldn't like it, that's why not. They got the fishin' rights. Know what they charge per rod?'

The old order changes…

And now we are passing White Mill. See that farm in the meadows? Here, on July 28th, 1933, a man came running into the yard.

'You got a horse and cart?'

'Yes…'

'Thank God. Can I borrow it?'

'And what would you want with a horse and cart?'

'I've caught a fish.'

There is a photograph, taken later in the farmyard. The angler, a short man with a fag in his mouth, like all men photographed in the 1930s, is standing beside a trestle, but you only notice that later, much later. For on the trestle hangs a fish out of the dawn of things, towering over him by a good four feet. Alec Allen, a commercial traveller, has caught a 388-pound sturgeon with a rod and line.

When he dies, it will be a day of rain as his old friends, fishermen all, gather on the bank to commit his ashes to the river. No vicar, no minister of religion, has agreed to take part in the ceremony, for when a man who has taken its largest living thing from the river seeks to make amends in his own way, this suggests something older than the Christian faith.

The river is slow now. It slides by the town of Carmarthen, which is there only because of the river, that forgotten highway of the old world. Only, with a few exceptions, its inhabitants have forgotten this and the quay to which Roman galleys and medieval cogs came, and at which ships docked until the middle of the 20th century.

The exceptions are the few surviving coraclemen, whose ancestors were here before either. This is Dai Rees talking.

Dai: They'd start fishing at *cyflychwr*, at nightfall, and they'd go on until daylight forced them to stop because the fish could see the net.

Byron: What's it like in the darkness, out there drifting, the net between the two coracles?

Dai: You get used to the dark, it's as simple as that. The only time people got, what shall I say, apprehensive, was when that film *Jaws* came out. We had a body in the net once. I was all for letting it float on, but this bloke said, 'Come on, it could be your mother.' Turned out to be a dead pig.

Byron: Would you talk to each other, out there, or do you have to keep quiet?

Dai: You keep as quiet as you can, but obviously when you came together to sort the net or plan what you're going to do next, you'd talk then. Every bit of the river has its own name, has had it for ever. There's one called Banc yr Alma, after the battle in the Crimean War.

Byron: One thing has stayed with me from that story you told about that little boy who caught a salmon, then thought he'd won the pools when he was given a boiled egg. Dai, why didn't he eat the salmon?

Dai: Because they were going to sell it, that's why. I don't know any of the old families that would eat a salmon, that would have been sacrilege.

Byron: Things were that bad?

Dai: Yes, different attitudes, different times. My great-grandfather, Jack Stwmpy they called him, he'd lost his arm at eight years old working in the Priory iron foundry in Carmarthen. But it is the description of how he lost it...A steam hammer took the arm off, and the man working alongside him pushed him to the floor, put his foot on him, and they cauterised the arm, or what was left of it

Byron: How did they cauterise it?

Dai: Hot iron and tar. And then the last part of the story. 'Home to bed!' That's what struck me, he wasn't taken to the Infirmary. These were the lower orders you see, and they couldn't afford doctors. It's hard to imagine the pain the guy went through, a child of eight.

Byron: What did he do for the rest of his life, Stwmpy?

Dai: He became the champion swimmer of Wales. Yes, it's weird, isn't it? He got a bronze medal for saving 21 lives on the Quay. With one arm.

Byron: But that way of life in some form or other must have been there when the Romans came. There was a quay, they brought goods up, they brought booze. The Normans came, they had a quay. And it came to an end in our lifetime.

Dai: Just about. The last one was in 1956, a 250-ton coal steamer – that was the last one. It was the silting of the river that did it, but the railway was the big thing. 1850 – the railway came to Carmarthen and killed it, freight coming in on the railway. You had sailing ships until the 1930s, and you had ships after that, like the SS Merthyr, Captain Everett. He was steam and he'd tow a couple of barques up, that helped. But one boat lost the tide and it grounded, and these were the words the captain said to the pilot in Ferryside at the estuary, 'Goodbye pilot, thank you for your help. You'll never see me in Carmarthen again.' I think that sums it up.

Narrator: The river is like a great dying snake now, its coils twisting desperately in the mud, the woods in some places at the water's edge. Then, suddenly, everything clears, and before you, opening like a fan, there is the estuary.

See the ruined mansion to your left above Ferryside? That brick ruin is Iscoed, from which General Picton sailed out to Waterloo, booming, 'A peerage or Westminster Abbey.' Instead he got neither, he got death and St Paul's.

Now turn. Above you is Llansteffan Castle, from which another man sailed out, also to his death, at Agincourt. His name was Henry Gwynn, lord of the castle and lands of Llansteffan who had risen with Glyndŵr, and I was thinking of him when I wrote this poem after a London Welsh concert at the Albert Hall, when Princess Margaret was present. You will understand why I wrote it from the last line.

> What would they make of you,
> Henry Gwynn, this St David's Day,
> The stalls a blur
> Of middle-aged applause
> For the English Royal Box?
> What would they make of you,
> Who died at Agincourt?

No great death, nothing to
Nudge the chroniclers, and leave
You rampant in eternity.

The Tywi estuary was far
From that wet field, and your
High castle of Llansteffan.
And it is only
A lawyer's hand, a spikey brown,
Commends you to our notice,
Confiscating your estate,
Because you died,
Trampled with the thousands in the mud,
At Agincourt...on the French side.

Where we are was once the gateway to exile.

21 GRIFFS

At first you didn't notice it, it was just another small bookshop in
a line of small bookshops, and some of these were very strange
indeed. There was Meier's, which specialised in maps and had a
sideline in ornamental swords, one of which a customer used to kill
the manageress. Another, Watkins, specialised in the supernatural
and in spells, which must have come in handy when the black
magician Aleister Crowley made their entire stock disappear. But
not even one of these shops came close to Griffs. When you called
on this Welsh-language bookshop run by ex-miners in the West
End of London, it was, according to the novelist Emyr Humphreys,
like calling on Snow White and the Seven Dwarfs.

The shop, opened by William Griffiths in 1946, was after Will's
death in 1962 run by his three brothers, Jack, Jos and Arthur, and
by Jack's wife, Mary. I called first in the 1960s, being taken there
by my friend Teifion Griffiths, Arthur's son, whom I'd met at
university, and to me it was not so much straying into a fairy story

as stepping into Dr Who's police box. One minute there I was in Cecil Court, the walkway between the Charing Cross Road and St Martin's Lane, and the next, in the middle of London, I was back in the old unchanged Wales of my childhood.

Mary Griffiths sat upstairs among the new and the English books. She was a very good-looking woman, but encased in authority, and a rigid blue rinse, like those Welsh matrons I had looked down on from the gallery in chapel, women whose absolute authority, and blue rinses, I had not encountered anywhere else and thought I never should again. Mary sat beside the till with a large police truncheon hanging on a piece of string behind her, and at that moment I felt as though I had strayed even beyond childhood into one of the old Arthurian myths: Mary was Cei, the castle porter you had to talk your way past.

That way was clear. Beyond the book-shelves was a large sign, 'Welsh Department Downstairs', with an arrow pointing down, but Mary knew all too well to where those narrow stairs led. Like the Holy Grail, they led to time-wasting, also, unlike the Holy Grail, to tea, made with condensed milk. And to cake. And talk. The arrow pointed to where three goblins lurked, appropriately underground, for their working lives had been spent underground.

All three Griffs brothers, like their father and their brother Will, had been coal miners in the pits at Gilfach Goch in the Valleys, only magically the seams had become shelves full of Welsh verse, Welsh county histories, Biblical concordances, long uninterrupted runs of magazines, and the collected sermons of the long dead and the unread, mostly in Welsh. Given their heights (Jos and Jack were both five foot three, Arthur five foot seven), the seams would have been easier to work; it was the shelves, towering over them, which were the problem. And the talk. Down there time passed as it passes when the goblins get you, so when you did emerge, Mary staring at you through her upswept glasses, her accent more pointedly English than when you had come in, you found a whole afternoon had somehow been mislaid.

What did they talk about? Arthur, 'Y Sgwrsiwr Mawr', the Great Talker, talked to the writer Hafina Clwyd about the great, and therefore good, Welsh browsers all of whom had once called, or sometimes, I was assured, had just called and gone, a bit like the White Rabbit. In all the years I called I met none of them. But Arthur never lost faith in the great and good. Jack, less respectful, listened and interjected occasionally to run them down in the time-honoured Welsh way, as he chain-smoked and grimly hammered out final reminders to the recalcitrant county librarians of Wales. These were their main customers, for the good were not great book-buyers, even though their signed photographs lined the few bits of walls still available, photographs of tenors and actors, authors and politicians, the cultural Politburo of a small country. Hugh Griffith. Clifford Evans, my father's second cousin whom he did not much like. Paul Robeson, a sort of honorary Welshman. Jack Jones. T. Gwynn Jones. Dylan Thomas. Richard Burton. Goronwy Rees. All in time had called at what the historian Gwyn Alf Williams in *When Was Wales?* called 'an informal athenaeum off the Charing Cross Road'. So below ground the talk rolled on and on, the names getting grander and grander until you half expected to hear:

'Pity you didn't come earlier, you just missed him.'

'Who?'

'Owain Glyndŵr. Didn't buy anything. North Walian.'

Jos the third brother didn't talk much. He just wheezed, smoked his cigarillos, and dreamed of... holidays. He was always planning, or had just been, on some holiday or other despite his pacemaker, scurrying off to Egypt at the height of summer, a little detail that meant he could strike a deal with some tour operator.

'But Jos, it'll be 100 degrees or more.'

'They say.'

Or to Greece where he once went into a shop and asked if they had a statue of Zeus, helpfully repeating the name over and over, 'Zeus... Zeus', only to be directed across the road to a shop where they sold fruit juice. Jos lived in his own myths; his brothers in the bunker, the one exultantly, the other bleakly, lived in those of others. And all the time the unseen feet of the master race clattered on the gratings overhead, just as they had clattered on 600 years of Welsh history.

In the 1960s the Welsh experience of London took one of two forms. There were those who did not see it as exile, and severed all links with their past, being men who were making their way in the professions and, being usually called Jones, accountants and hospital consultants had hyphens materialise in their surnames like the black monoliths in the film *2001*. It was, after all, part of the Welsh way of getting on. In the 17th century John Aubrey, who knew his countrymen, could sneer at the Seisyllt family who had transformed themselves into the Cecils, and who, having got on with a vengeance, still own Cecil Court. One generation, that was all such a transformation took if their luck held, so in one generation the Berry brothers were Merthyr boys on the make in newspapers, and, in the next, vague English aristocrats. Their accents changed, the short 'a's being jettisoned first, one man I know talking about the film star 'Alan Laard', and there was the joy of hearing John Humphrys tell the time on the *Today* programme, five paarst, ten minutes paarst. I wrote a column about this in the *Daily Telegraph* and got a letter from Humphrys, telling me, reasonably enough, to thank my lucky stars that he was not still speaking with the accent of his native Splott. And, of course, ahead there was the water jump of 'situation', that terrible word into which the elaborately acquired accents of all Welshmen on the make, even that of Roy Jenkins, I was assured by the late Alan Watkins, sank without trace. But in the 1960s there were those who did none of this. It was then just possible to live in London in a lunar base of Welsh exile.

The godly still had their chapels, though attendances declined with each passing year, until now, of the 36 Welsh chapels in London, only five survive. The young had the London Welsh Club in the Grays Inn Road where on Saturday nights (the club having been denied a bar by its main sponsor, a cinema owner), male graduates staggered in from all the surrounding pubs to eye the female graduate talent which by then was rigid with small talk and boredom. 'Golden days,' said Hafina Clwyd. But there were also the former dairies, whose Welsh owners had once gratefully put wreaths each year at the statue of Sir Hugh Middleton, the first man to bring water to London. In my time these had become small dying grocers' shops, at one of which I once stopped, went in and heard a matron, leaning across the marble counter, solemnly tell another, 'He's just been drained', and I felt a rush of *hiraeth*.

And there was Griffs. I was then working on the *Times*, and it came to mean a lot to me when I called, usually after a Chinese meal, two pounds of cherries and a Nicaraguan cigar, to reassure Arthur I was getting on. As I scurried past the gaunt street-walkers, one of them whispered the enticement, 'Come on, it's good for your spots', and then, as I moved on, 'Don't squeeze them.' Griffs was a little synagogue in Babylon.

Its origins seemed to belong more to one of those family saga novels than to real life. It was such an adventure for a start, to have opened such a shop here, but it was even more curious than that. The shop's godfather was Al Jolson. In 1927, in *The Jazz Singer*, an otherwise silent film, he suddenly ad-libbed 'You ain't heard nothin' yet', and the Talkies were born. But in that one moment some 80,000 musicians in Britain were out of work virtually overnight, men who in cinemas had provided an accompaniment for the silents and played in the intermissions. Amongst these in Gilfach Goch were four miners, William Griffiths (violin) and his three brothers, Arthur and Jack on the violin and Jos on the piano, all of whom had managed to survive the Great Strike in this way.

William Griffiths was a remarkable man. Underground at 13, he had already been trapped in a flooded gallery and buried twice in rock falls, when at 29, after *The Jazz Singer*, he decided to seek his fortune in London. Having earlier graduated from the Guildhall School of Music, he was a full-time violinist before he discovered he had a talent for organisation and formed his own small orchestra, at one stage running six of these. Then in 1932 somehow (the word 'somehow' attaches itself to his career) he got himself a job as head of the Welsh department at Foyles bookshop. The fact that Foyles ever had a Welsh department is startling enough now, but under William Griffiths it was also a publishing house, bringing out, under the improbable imprint Gwasg Foyle, 50 books, among them a Welsh translation of *Macbeth* by the poet T. Gwynn Jones, and in the process launching the career of T. Rowland Hughes when it published his first novel *O Law i Law*. All this is so extraordinary you have to pinch yourself to be reminded it was all possible...once.

He was also instrumental in launching the careers of two best-selling authors in English. Richard Vaughan's *Moulded in Earth* came out after William, given his contacts, recommended it to the publisher John Murray, who, in a handwritten inscription, wrote 'To Mr Griffiths, its godfather.' And then there was *How Green Was My Valley*, the most famous novel ever written about Wales, and the most mysterious. It was said that Richard Llewellyn, the son of a London hotel manager, wrote it after working as a miner, and experiencing the dangers, in, of all places, Gilfach Goch. Llewellyn himself never did contradict this; what he did say, and often, was that in his book he always relied on first-hand knowledge. But there is no evidence that he worked as a miner in Gilfach or anywhere else. The only certainty is that in London he had met William Griffiths, who knew all there was to be known about flooded galleries and roof falls. William just happened to come from the Valley, and Llewellyn visited the Griffiths family there, to the point that, when the book came out, in a special collectors' edition of 200, one was signed and inscribed to William's father, 'To Joseph Griffiths, whom I am proud to call my friend.' Members of the Griffiths family were, and are, ambivalent about Richard Dafydd Vivian Llewellyn Lloyd of Wood Green. It did not help when they saw John Ford's film of the book in which miners are shown singing as they trudge uphill to the only coal pit ever sunk on top of a mountain, and heard Walter Pidgeon, with a Welsh accent never before heard in this world, play their father.

In 1946, William Griffiths left Foyles to set up his own bookshop, Griffs, and invited his three brothers up from Gilfach Goch. So there they were, four coal miners in a bunker in London, three of them, suddenly, improbable company directors, the fourth, William, being a man born to the boardroom. Under the imprint William Griffiths a'i Frodyr he went on publishing, books like Aneirin Talfan Davies's *Gwŷr Llen* and Geraint Dyfnallt Owen's *Dyddiau'r Gofid*, and, in

English, under the imprint William Griffiths and Co, Thomas Jones's *The Native Never Returns*, a title that must have seemed particularly wistful. He is said to have lost money on each one, so the publishing lapsed. In one of those long family sagas the shop becomes a chain of booksellers; in real life, when Griffs finally closed after 36 years, the two surviving brothers were still in the bunker.

There were some who thought the business itself would not survive Will's death, but somehow it did. Arthur became its rep, travelling with a suitcase of book jackets by bus and train across Wales from county library to county library, for this was how the brothers conducted a business that turned on personal contacts and small orders. Until, that is, 1974, and the Heath-Walker reorganisation of local government. Then, the counties having got bigger through amalgamation, their librarians began placing their orders with bigger companies who could allow bigger discounts and supply books with such fussy detail as plastic covers. The Griffs' main market vanished overnight.

'I was then working on Humberside,' said Iorwerth Davies, whose job as county librarian of Montgomeryshire had also vanished in the reorganisation. 'My boss, he was Director of Leisure Services or something, was a Welshman, Glyn Roberts. Anyway I'd just been reading in the paper that Arthur had got the MBE, and I was actually starting a letter to congratulate him when Glyn came into the room. He had never been to Griffs so I began telling him about the shop, and how nice it would be if we could put some business their way.

' "Do it," he said, he was one of these dynamic chaps. "Do it now, ring them up. Tell them I want £3,000 worth of Mills and Boon." So I rang them and got Arthur. "Good God, I can't do that," he said. Glyn was still marching up and down, so I couldn't let on what Arthur had said. I kept saying things like "You can? That's wonderful" when what Arthur was actually saying was "Me and Jack, we couldn't even pack that amount". In the end I couldn't resist it, I told him, "And we want them in a week. Fine, I'm so glad that won't be a problem." "WHAT?" Arthur said, so loudly I'm amazed Glyn Roberts didn't hear that in our office.

'Well as it happened Glyn was in London a couple of days later, so I told him to call on the Griffs where he would be guaranteed a cup of tea and, if he was lucky, some cake. So he called, they treated him like a lord and he, well he said, "You know that order? I want you to double it." Arthur, he told me, went white. At one point he was afraid he'd pass out, which he thought an odd sort of reaction in a man getting an order like that. I didn't say anything, but years later Arthur told me it had saved the firm, things were that delicate at the time.

'I always called on them when I was in London on business. One day, I was a county librarian by then, I spent the whole afternoon tidying the place up for them. They weren't like anybody else I dealt with, who'd take you out to a swish restaurant; the Griffs would take you round the corner to a pub and buy you a sausage. But they did take me to the theatre a few times, they used to get these free tickets. One night they took me to see a play in which Churchill was accused of murder. Most notorious play on the London stage at the time. Arthur fell asleep. Then they took me to see *Oh Calcutta*. Arthur managed to stay awake all through that. He was still in a state of shock years later.'

One of Arthur Griffiths's money-spinning schemes was to buy up all the early 19th-century topographical books he could get his hands on in country house and old bookshop sales, books like *The Beauties of South Wales,* for, though these had little value in themselves, they were bursting with engravings of castles and mountain landscapes. Arthur would remove these engravings, wrecking the books in the process, then send them to two old ladies in Ireland who, for half a crown a time, would colour them. As the human figures in the engravings were very small, the ladies were obliged to use the most vivid primary colours. So Arthur Griffiths, who then sold these framed, sold so many he became responsible for a widely held impression that 18th-century Wales bristled with men who looked like dance-band leaders, those who weren't in red coats being in blue. He was proud of his efforts as an art dealer.

Only time was passing. When Jos, whom Kenneth Williams on his one visit thought an aggressive little toad, died in 1978, his two brothers, both well into their seventies, decided it was time to close the shop. But if its origins seemed to belong more to a family saga than to real life, its closure was pure Hollywood. Arthur Griffiths wrote in his diary, 'Friday, 25 June, 1982. Our last day. Very busy. Mary had her ring stolen by a Welshman.'

A young man had come into the shop late in the afternoon, speaking in what Mary later described as 'perfect Welsh', a phrase much used by her generation in London, by then only too conscious of their own increasingly imperfect Welsh. This detail is important. Nobody there had met him before, but he sat and talked in Welsh to Mary until, noticing her diamond ring, asked her to hold this up to the light. He got even more charming then, there would have been many intakes of breath and lots of *ardderchog*s, and he asked if as a special favour she would let him take it out of the shop so he could see it really flash. This was not an Englishman, you must remember, or even a Welshman in Wales, things would have been very different then. But the clocks were ticking in the last hours of the last day, and Mary Griffiths had met in London a Welshman speaking perfect Welsh. She gave him the ring.

Mary died suddenly the next year, so Jack went back alone to Gilfach, something they had planned to do together; Arthur stayed on in his Dagenham council house until his death four years later. But in a film the last scene would already have been made. That would show a young man running, a youthful Richard Burton say, one arm held above him, a diamond flashing in the afternoon sun as he collides with the crowds in St Martin's Lane, and the dreams of three old people, dreams that had kept them going over five decades, collapse behind him. They did not see him or the ring, or hear his perfect Welsh, again.

It is moving and bleak at the same time, this parable of exile.

22 WELSH IN EXILE

FLETCHER WATKINS, CAERPHILLY,
ADVERTISING COPYWRITER AND TV DRAMATIST

We had been young together; we were both Welsh, and at the same Oxford college, so we had seen a lot of each other, yet it took him the best part of 40 years before he told me of the summer when, aged 20 and prompted by the Chatterley case, he decided it was time he lost his virginity. The problem, he paused, was the equipment, which, curiously enough, was the term Cherie Blair, in her delicate way, would use.

'Eh?'

'You know, French letters, condoms.'

'Hang on, all this was before the…uh, auditions?'

'Oh yes, it's like mountaineering. You have to have the right equipment. I mean, you never know when the weather's going to clear. The only thing was, every time I went into a pharmacy there was a woman my mother's age behind the counter, so I ended up buying Horlicks tablets. Remember Horlicks tablets? I ended up with a drawer full of the bloody things. Put on half a stone that summer.'

Then in the classified columns of a magazine he came on a mail order advertisement. Bingo. Except…except that the smallest order was for a gross. Still, as he put it, he was a young man, and by return of post the casket came. 144 condoms.

Unfortunately things never did get to the auditions, and by the end of term he still had the casket, unused, except for one he had blown up. To test, he said. And it occurred to him that, if he left them in his room, someone, either a college servant or a delegate to one of the conferences held in the holidays, would find them, and he would return to find himself a folk hero, either that or a figure of fun. That was when he decided to take them home with him in his laundry. He was hitchhiking.

'I don't know why, but there were lunatics loose that day on the A40, and with each lift I got more and more worried as to what would happen if I got killed.'

'And your mother had to identify you.'

'That's it, a corpse with 143 condoms in his luggage. Every time we overtook somebody I could see the headlines: "Sex Maniac in Car Crash." That was when I decided I had to get rid of the things.'

Between lifts, he dropped them in a rubbish bin in a lay-by, then retrieved them, for he was a responsible young man. What if a family stopped for a picnic and children found them? At one point he threw them into a field, but climbed over the gate when he saw sheep crowding round, and again could see the headlines 'Cotswold Sheep Found Dead, Full Of Condoms.'

'With every lift I'd just sit there, not saying a word, brooding. I don't know what the drivers thought.'

'Why didn't you give them to one of them?'

'How would you feel if you're giving some bugger a lift and he suddenly makes you a present of 143 condoms?'

'I hadn't thought of that.'

'Well I did, I couldn't think of anything else. You know it was years before I saw the Cotswolds in terms of anything except bloody condoms.'

A lorry driver, turning south at Gloucester, dropped him at the last roundabout, and, an accursed figure, he slunk westward, heavy with gloom and contraceptives, and paused, as such figures do in fiction, on a bridge. And it was there, almost without thinking, that he hurled the casket into the river.

'It was wonderful, I stood there in the sunlight, the tension rushing out of me as though someone had opened a stopcock. And then...then I heard this small voice far below. "Hoy." '

'You hadn't looked down?'

'Of course I hadn't, I'd just gone to the parapet and slung the damned things over. It hadn't occurred to me there could have been someone down there. He was in a boat, fat chap holding a very long fishing rod, only I remembered that afterwards, for he was up to his ankles in contraceptives. The box had burst, they were all over the boat.'

'Jesus, what did he say?'

'After that first shout, not a word. We just stared at each other, and he looked down, then up at me again. But I couldn't take any more of it, I was at the end of my tether, I just ran off into Wales. My last sight was of him, standing up, his mouth open, staring up at the sky out of which the things had come.'

'I wonder what he made of it.'

'It's not that, it's what other people would have made of it. Can you imagine his wife when he got home? *"Catch anything, dear?" "Well, in a way…"* When he spoke again his voice was very mild. 'It would have been the last time she believed anything he said.'

MARTYN HARRIS, SWANSEA, JOURNALIST

The last time I saw him he was on his deathbed to which he had summoned me by phone. 'There's this beautiful nurse on my ward, from Llansteffan. It'll be worth your coming to Barts, if only to see her.' I cycled down on what must have been the wettest afternoon of the year, only to find that the nurse from Llansteffan was on holiday. Martyn Harris from Swansea, the best writer among all the journalists I have ever met, was grinning as he told me that.

He had a black sense of humour. Of his final columns in the *Daily Telegraph,* written as he was dying of cancer and called 'On the Sick', he said, 'I am now writing to the ultimate deadline.' But he told me he had a whole series of columns, and one-liners, planned. In particular he was going to blast NHS cuts and anticipated the joy of seeing this in the pages of his Tory employer. 'They won't dare cut me now.'

At the end it was difficult knowing how to approach him, for there had never been anything in journalism quite like his last year. His cancer was a headland from which all his reports were exclusives, and, suddenly, aged 43, he was himself a public figure. 'You might just as well have married into the Royal Family,' I grumbled.

Of his final treatment, when he was given a bone-marrow transplant from his sister, he said, 'I don't know why I'm bothering. She smokes 50 a day.' With relish he told me that after her marrow was extracted, the imprint of a large red hand appeared like stigmata on his sister's bottom.

He was a greengrocer's son. His father, he wrote once, so loved his car that, had he been able, he would have driven upstairs to bed in it. Unlike Martyn, he could speak Welsh. 'If you spoke Welsh in Swansea, and wanted a cabbage, you came to our shop.' He himself, unlike other Welshmen making their way in England, had never bothered to iron out his accent, speaking, quietly, in broad Swansea.

We had much in common. We came from the same part of the world, were in the same trade, and were equally baffled as to how we had ended up in this. Despite his many fans, he thought of journalism as a wrong station at which he had somehow got off, and agonised over the novels he might have written, though he was dismissive of the two he had,

There was a touching naivety to him. Arranging to meet for the first time, he wrote me a note apologising for the fact that he had no London club. Because he knew so few journalists, even though one himself, he thought of them as figures of romance, even mystery, and assumed they would belong to clubs. We, of course, met in a pub.

For, though he was on the staff of the *Telegraph,* he had this curious arrangement with the paper by which he was not required to appear in its offices. He had been recruited after its editor read an article he had written in *New Society* on the merits of wet and electric shaving, and the only people he ever met were its commissioning editors. One of these once invited him to a dinner party where the other guests all knew, or knew of, each other; Martyn sat amongst them speechless as Banquo's ghost.

From time to time, he told me, misgivings were voiced about the quantity of his output (nobody ever questioned its quality), and attempts were made to get him to go freelance. These he resisted. 'It's an advantage being on the staff if you get cancer,' he told me. In a column he once gave details of his salary, something no other journalist has ever done. It was not large.

He would probably have killed you had you mislaid one of his commas, but he had no ego. He told me his sister was a fan of mine, and that, when he had told her that he, Martyn, had a bigger by-line in the paper, she had said, 'Yes, but he's got class.' Don't get me wrong. I hope I would have told the story, had it been the other way round, but I doubt it. The point is, Martyn did tell it.

He wrote like an angel, but there was also an honesty and a recklessness to his profiles that made these unique. When he wrote about a National Front councillor, about as open a target as you can get, he tried to explain the man, showing him as a figure in an East End landscape, so a sadness fell like rain on the outrage.

When I saw him, a week before his death, he looked well and strong, and had been writing so vividly, especially in his account of sloping off for a smoke in the hospital linen cupboard that had become his equivalent of the school bicycle shed. Here he had found a neat pile of shrouds, an item of laundry, he wrote, he had previously encountered only in metaphor.

There was disagreement about those last columns. Some found them ghoulish, but I thought them the best things he had done, these frontline dispatches from a war in which, in time, no one is a spectator.

He told me one story that wet September afternoon. A friend of his, an Englishman visiting him in Swansea, had gone bounding into a pub on a hot day, and asked, in the elaborate English middle-class way, if he might, please, have two pints of bitter beer?

'No,' said the landlord.

This is how I shall always think of Martyn, his head made bald by chemotherapy, but grinning. 'No,' a Swansea landlord said.

JOHN JAMES, PORT TALBOT, HISTORICAL NOVELIST
When John James died, aged 69, in Cambridge in 1993, I wrote his obituary. It was the only one to him in the national press, yet this was a man who was not only the greatest historical novelist of my time, he was also, perhaps, the only genuinely historical novelist of any time.

In the 1960s he wrote three novels *Votan, Not For All The Gold*

In Ireland, and *Men Went to Cattraeth*, set in periods ranging from second-century Germany to sixth-century Britain. Once I owned all three, but the second was stolen from me by Michael Wharton who was the columnist Peter Simple, for, though all three are long out of print, there are forms of recommendation that transcend literary reviews and book reviews.

John understood the past because he was able to live in it. He knew what Rome meant to a man living beyond its frontiers, to whom this was not just the Eternal City, it was the Eternal Harrods bursting with consumer goods and booze. But then he knew how such a man would have dressed and what he would have eaten, and, which is far more important, he knew what went on in his head. He was the only writer I know who, when he conjured up the past, had a man from the past as his hero.

All other historical novelists cheat. Some cheat blithely, like the Hollywood scriptwriter who had Virginia Mayo, leaning over the battlements, tell the departing Lionheart, played by George Sanders, 'War, war, war, that's all you think about, Dickie Plantagenet.' It is when they aspire to art that the cheating becomes insidious.

The most famous work of historical fiction in living memory is Robert Bolt's *A Man For All Seasons*, probably the most misleading title ever invented, for its hero, Sir Thomas More, is nowhere allowed to be a man for his own season. Bolt shows us the family man and the statesman, a man of honour, but there is one curtain he dares not lift. Had he done so there would have been no play, and certainly no film. For what modern audience would have sympathised with a man who had his own private gaol in which he kept those he considered heretics, and who, had his king been happily married, might have introduced the Inquisition into England? You have only to look at the grim face staring out of the Holbein portrait to realise this is not the face of a man for all seasons. But Bolt did what all writers of historical fiction do: he sent a liberal democrat into the past, a decent modern man among the horrors.

Lytton Strachey's biographical work *Elizabeth and Essex*, declared Max Beerbohm, was at best 'guesswork', dealing as it did with 'beings whose actions and motives are to me as mysterious as those of wild animals in an impenetrable jungle.' There is however a key to most of those actions and motives. It is just that no one dares turn it, but John James did.

The novelist J.L. Carr put his finger on the problem in *The Harpole Report* when he has a character say, 'The Middle Ages were not *us* in fancy dress. *Their* minds did nor rattle along the same lines as our Broiler House Society. They believed in Hellfire and the Everlasting Pit.' The door which has closed between us and our ancestors is religion.

It is not a matter of belief, it is a matter of the intensity of that belief. As John James once said in a lecture, 'If, in writing fictional conversation for educated people up to the beginning of this century, you gave to religion the bulk it really occupied, you would bore your readers to death.' For the lives of our ancestors were threaded on religion. Religion was politics, the fixtures and fittings of a church a war zone, when in Christian times religion allowed our ancestors to watch as a living man's skin became crackling in fires lit for his own and their spiritual good.

John James's achievement was that in his books religion was centre stage, so even his main character, the Greek businessman (and con artist) Photinus, talks to Apollo, with the result that the god had his first walk-on part in millennia (he was later to appear in *Star Trek)*. This was done without sensationalism, but with the matter-of-factness of the old pagan world, where the miraculous dropped in with the regularity of a Jehovah's Witness.

John James also attempted something just as startling; he has Photinus walk beyond the limit of the known world into the dawn of religion, for, to the German tribesmen who met him, a sophisticated figure like his hero is himself a god. Photinus becomes Votan or Odin.

James could think himself into the past where his throwaway remarks could stop you in your tracks. 'Roman religion is about giving the god his dinner on time, with all the proper words and ceremonial, in case he starts an earthquake. Greek religion is about saying, "This place feels creepy, there must be a god about. Let's think up a story as to why this should be."'

Other remarks I found maddening, as when he claimed to know to within 30 feet where King Arthur's body is buried ('very easy to someone who knows a little mild Egyptology'). He never said where, though I did press him once on why he had said of Camelot that it was no point seeking this, and he at last admitted that it was because this was the field headquarters of a cavalry general. Camelot had been wherever Arthur was, just as Rome in its last centuries had been wherever the emperor was. John James loved his mysteries.

Before he died he told me he had planned his last resting place in the ruined abbey of Strata Florida, where the princes of his people had been buried. Whether he managed this, I don't know, but like his heroes, John James had a disturbingly practical bent.

RICHARD TURNER, CAERNARFON, SEA-CAPTAIN AND AVENGER OF OLD WRONGS

He was 72 when he died in 1996, the son, grandson and great-grandson of seafarers. Richard Turner was also the only human being who, because of something I had written, was moved to action. *Did some words of mine send out / Certain men the English shot?* Nobody shot the Captain, but, like Yeats, I found the experience unnerving.

It all began when I wrote a newspaper article about Gwenllian, the only child of the last Prince of Wales, stolen in her cradle by English troopers to live out her days as a nun at Sempringham Priory in Lincolnshire. It was a sad little story, and I thought it might make people pause over their cornflakes. But I hadn't met the Captain then. Nor had the Bishop of Grantham.

Bill Ind was at Sempringham to dedicate a plaque in memory of St Gilbert, the Priory's founder, when, in the pulpit and presiding over an ecumenical assembly of several hundred dignitaries, he saw a sturdy old gentleman come up the path that leads to the little church which is all that remains of the great monastic buildings. The old gentleman was staggering under the weight of something large, wrapped in brown paper.

The Bishop was a bit preoccupied that day, for dozens of portaloos ordered for Sempringham had been delivered to a presumably bewildered Royal Family at Sandringham, and the last thing he expected, or wanted, to see was a man delivering a stone to a Welsh princess dead these seven centuries. The Captain, having ordered a memorial for Gwenllian, had come to put it in place.

He had not asked permission of the Crown, which owns the land; he had not even approached the diocesan authorities. The Captain had just ordered the stone ('Chap called Jones did it for me'), put it in the boot of his car, then driven 300 miles with it to Sempringham.

There was some consternation in the Church over his idea of an epitaph ('Died at Sempringham 7.6.1337, having been held prisoner for 54 years'). Some people might think she had had a vocation as a nun, said the Bishop mildly. But in the end they allowed him to have his stone on the old road leading to the Priory. A local mason put it in place and it became a little shrine, with flowers put there each month by the Captain's cousin, a commercial traveller from Halifax, his beat mysteriously extended, unknown to his employers.

The Captain had little, or no, interest in modern practical politics. He was not a member of the Welsh Nationalist Party, and was bitterly opposed to the Welsh Assembly, which he thought would come to be dominated by the majority southern Wales. It was just that on long nightwatches at sea he had taken to brooding on what had been done to his nation centuries ago. Scotland had the Stone of Scone, it had its crown jewels and royal tombs: Wales had nothing. Its tombs plundered, its regalia stolen, its little princes and princesses made to disappear, it had been subject to a house clearance on a national scale. To the Captain, Edward I was not a figure out of history: he was a contemporary politician whom he hated.

So it was a bit of a mistake on my part when I wrote about that lost regalia, in particular the piece of the True Cross that had belonged to the Last Prince but became part of the inventory taken by Edward. The final reference to this was in 1548, when its gold backing was sold, but the tradition persisted that the wooden fragment had been built into the roof of St George's Chapel in Windsor. And so the inevitable phone-call came. The Captain had of course been to Windsor. 'Why? To nick it of course.'

He had this odd telephone manner. He never introduced himself but launched into a conversation he assumed had already started but had been interrupted. And it didn't help that he sounded like Bluto, Popeye's enemy, at his most gravel-voiced. But that day he was rueful.

'Couldn't get near the damn thing. Roof's a hundred feet up, I hadn't read that in the guide. It was too high, and I'm too old.'

Bishop Ind, who after his first encounter with the Captain must have thought little in this world would surprise him again, was rung up and asked abruptly whether he had any influence over the Dean of Windsor. The Bishop thought he had once sat next to him at dinner, and the Captain did not pursue the matter.

He phoned many people in his time. He harangued Welsh bishops when that romantic organisation Welsh Water turned a medieval friary, where two Princesses of Wales were buried, into a sewage farm. But it wasn't just history. His other great love was opera, and he wrote to Norma Major, amongst others, suggesting that pressure be put on the BBC to broadcast an evening of Gigli. He had, he explained to the then Prime Minister's wife, 44 lost years at sea to make up. Mrs Major replied with a polite puzzled letter.

A Roman Catholic, though he had been married three times, the Captain lived alone at the end, cooked for by local nuns who in return he allowed to watch soccer on his television. 'He was like a character out of one of G.K. Chesterton's novels, in one sense dotty, in another, quite wonderful,' said Bishop Ind.

Like me, he had found it impossible to forget the Captain.

BARTHOLOMEW ROBERTS, PIRATE

It is a small white stone on the village green at Casnewydd Bach, Little Newcastle, in the foothills of the Preseli. It does not look like a memorial so you might not even stop, thinking it a milestone, which in its way it is. In North Pembrokeshire a small white stone points to the Spanish Main. But it is the intimacy of the inscription that is striking, for there are no dates, not even a man's full name, just a nickname and his choice of profession, 'Barti Ddu, Môr-leidr Enwog', Black Bart, Famous Pirate. One of ours, *who got on.*

Getting on has always been important for the Welsh, and it doesn't much matter how one goes about it. When a boy I had known at school got a job at Porton Down, then the germ warfare place, and went happily off to bottle the Black Death for the Government, the *Carmarthen Journal* carried the news on its front page under the headline, Local Man's Success. Had it not been for the accident of time, it might have done the same for Bartholomew Roberts, who, in just two crowded years, claimed to have plundered 400 ships. But then he was a late developer.

A farmer's son whose first language was Welsh, he was 37 in 1720 and still only second mate on a Bristol slaver when the ship was taken by Howel Davies, a Carmarthen pirate, piracy being then for the Welsh what the London headmastership would become. There was even the Abergavenny labourer turned pirate Henry Morgan, who made so much money from massacre and torture that the English class structure in its old cynical way felt obliged to include him. *Sir* Henry Morgan. Morgan, a nasty bit of work whatever the many film versions, had managed to subcontract himself into a colonial war between Spain and England, and in the process had re-invented himself as a gentleman. Poor Bart in 1720 had no war to fall back on.

Howel Davies forcibly enlisted him, but when Davies was killed just six weeks later, the crew elected Bart as captain in his place. Odd that, that piracy should turn on democracy and the Royal Navy on the absolute tyranny of his officers, but, like a Roman general elected emperor by his troops, he probably had little choice, though he remarked equably in a letter (he was a great letter-writer) that having dipped his hands in muddy waters it was better to be a commander than a common man. Only the farmer's son then had himself a ball.

He was the only pirate captain who could have strolled onto

any Hollywood set without bothering the costume department, for he dressed the part, in red damask (the French called him *Le Joli Rouge*) with plumes and lace, and recruited an orchestra, an African in full warpaint on the drums, which played whenever his ship went into action, though not on Sundays. There were to be no battles, or music, on Sundays.

Uniquely among the pirate captains, he established a code by which all who sailed with him had to abide: no gambling, no women (unlike Sir Henry Morgan, he drew the line at rape, and posted a guard on female captives), bed by eight, and, like the chapel boy he had been, the observance of Sundays. He seems to have established a welfare system for his crews, with a rising scale of pensions, even though few pirates managed to retire, and was a good host to his victims, taking tea with them. Politely, he wrote to an English colonial governor whose shipping had been captured under his great shore batteries, 'Sir, This comes expressly from me to let you know that had you come off...and drunk a glass of wine with me...I should not have harmed the least vessel in your harbour.' This was pure bravado.

But there were things about him that nobody doubted. The first was that he could put the fear of God into those he encountered. When he entered a harbour in Newfoundland, the crews of 30 fishing vessels there, also that of a 26-gun French ship, promptly rowed for shore, and when a slaver refused to pay a ransom he burned it 'with a full cargo of negroes on board.' Whatever his feelings about Sunday, Roberts was still a man of his times, and negroes were just that, cargo.

The second thing that nobody doubted was his seamanship. He could, and did, plot a course from the Americas to Africa in just 28 days, so it was ironic that it was here, just off the African coast, that his nemesis caught up with him. Nemesis was Ogle, Captain Chaloner Ogle RN.

Roberts was in a 40-gun frigate, Ogle in HMS Swallow had 60 guns, and the outcome was inevitable. The band played on, but Bart was killed and thrown overboard in his red damask. Of his crew, 52 were hanged, 19 died, and 77, who probably had also been forcibly enlisted, were acquitted. There were 75 negro slaves who were then sold.

And it is what happened next that provides a rare moment of stocktaking in the stories of fabulous pirate wealth. Slaves, together with the money on board and the ship itself, fetched £3,000, and we know this because there was a row. Ogle, who had been knighted for this exploit, refused to share any of the prize money with his crew, saying he needed the lot to support his new dignity.

So for once we know exactly what a pirate's credit rating was. Though the £3,000 may not sound much to you, it would have been a fortune to his old friends in Casnewydd Bach, for it would have taken a clergyman of the time 60 years to earn that.

> He left a name, at which the world grew pale
> To point a moral or adorn a tale.

But it was two-and-a-half centuries before it adorned a roadside stone.

OLIVER WILLIAMS, ALIAS CROMWELL, HEAD OF STATE

'Oh God,' said the painter Rigby Graham, so sharply I turned to look at him.

We were driving through the town of Stamford in Lincolnshire on the trail of the poet John Clare, every building connected with whom Rigby had painted, with the exception of the odd earth closet. Only we weren't talking about Clare. I had just mentioned the old story that in the Second World War the Soviet Marshal Timoshenko's real name hadn't been Timoshenko at all, but Timothy Jenkins. His people had come from the Rhondda.

'Has anyone come into this world who wasn't Welsh?' said Rigby.

An English patriot, he was a man who bought drinks for Morris dancers in pubs, though the last time he did this it had cost him £52.30. So he hadn't taken too well to what I had just told him. And then I told him about the astonishing letter.

Introducing herself as a Miss Martin, the writer said she was 88 years old, and that Timoshenko's people hadn't come from the Rhondda at all but from Dowlais. She herself came from three generations of Dowlais ironmasters, one of whom, her father Stanley, had in 1890 been invited to the Ukraine by the industrialist John Hughes, to the town named after him, Hughesovska. Stanley Martin was to build blast furnaces there, but with industrialisation coming virtually overnight to Tsarist Russia, he had had to take his own foremen out with him, amongst them a young man called Timothy Jenkins. Jenkins did not return to Wales but stayed on, marrying a Russian girl.

'Martin? Good God, yes, they were ironmasters in the town,' said the historian Professor Gwyn A. Williams, himself a Dowlais man. 'But that Timoshenko business, I thought that was a joke. Mind you, I'd heard of a Dowlais family going native over there.' He had tried to trace this family when he did a TV documentary about Hughesovska, but two world wars had rolled over the Ukraine in the interval.

Miss Martin took up the story. 'My mother opened a paper one day and said. "Oh look, there's Timothy Jenkins's boy. He seems to be a marshal now, but he's the image of his father, he's even got the same upper lip." My parents always took a great interest in their workmen. And everything fitted, the date of birth in 1895 and all. My mother kept the photograph for the rest of her life, I've still got it somewhere.'

Timoshenko made no mention of his Welsh ancestry, but then any man holding high military rank would under Stalin have kept his head down, for any hint of Western contagion would have guaranteed him a one-way trip to Siberia.

'You don't say,' said Rigby Graham.

We were through Stamford and on our right a wall seemed to stretch to infinity. Beyond this were the minarets of Burghley, a house the size of a town centre, which looked as though it floated above the trees like something out of the *Arabian Nights*.

'I don't know whether you know this, but the family which owned that, the Cecils, they were Welsh too,' I said. 'Only their name wasn't Cecil at all, it was Seisyllt, only of course that wasn't suitable for anyone on the make in England. You all right?'

Rigby was making a strange noise in his throat, but didn't

appear to be ill, so I continued, 'To get on, you had to conceal such origins, even under the Tudors, whose real name should have been Meredith. Robert Cecil, the son of the chap who built that place, he used to throw a fit whenever anyone reminded him he was Welsh. I wonder if that's why Oliver Cromwell...'

'Oh ****,' said Rigby.

'Yes, his real name was...'

'Did I ever tell you about the time I buried my dog?' said Rigby. It was a very big dog, weighing eleven-and-a-half stone, and he was still telling the story when we found ourselves in the village of Northborough.

We were about to leave the main road to see Clare's cottage when we saw something very odd indeed, a small medieval gatehouse on the corner of a road. Beyond this, in a courtyard, were the long windows of what was clearly a great hall, all this, not in some grand park, but at the roadside... in a village street.

We parked the car and walked over to where a man was mowing a thin strip of grass in front of the house. He, it turned out, was the owner ('It was a restaurant, only the diners froze in the great hall'), and much of the house, he went on, was 14th century, having been built for one of Edward III's bishops. It was not open to the public, but he offered to show us round.

'I suppose you know Oliver Cromwell's widow died here,' he said as we crossed the courtyard. 'It had been her daughter's house, Cromwell's favourite, Elizabeth Claypole.'

And I remembered the portrait. It was that of a good-natured flighty face over whose spiritual development her father had agonised, and who, by one joke, probably changed English constitutional history.

There was a party at which she had been one of the few women present when someone asked where all the generals' wives were, and she answered that they were at home washing up. This actually happened, and the little joke, the new military regime being very touchy about its origins, was not forgotten. It is said the wives intervened decisively when the question of crowning Cromwell came up, as this meant she would have become the princess Elizabeth.

You can forgive her much for that laugh in a bleak time, just as her father forgave her, and went on to pardon royalist prisoners at her intercession. She was only 29 when she died, and the old Protector nursed her in her last illness, surviving her by only a few weeks. That she was everyone's favourite is shown by the fact that, unlike him, she was allowed to remain in her grave in Westminster Abbey.

But it is fitting that her mother should lie just down the road in the churchyard at Northborough, that uncrowned queen of England who loathed all palaces and greatness, and about whom little else is known except this one fact.

We were standing in the great hall, looking up at the armour and at portraits of the Cromwell family, when I asked if there was such a thing as a family tree. Our host pointed to the wall where this hung, and I approached it nervously.

For, whatever their feelings about Cromwell, the English have always found it next to impossible to accept anything but his English origin. When Lloyd George brought the matter up at a dinner party, H. G. Wells giggled and said, 'You'll be talking about Williams the Conqueror next.' To them the blunt squire from the shires is the very epitome of Englishness, so when Christopher Hill wrote his biography he called this *God's Own Englishman*. And he wasn't, he came from a Glamorgan family.

His great great grandfather was an archer called William ap Ieuan, who, like so many others, came to London with the Tudors. Here he prospered, and his son Morgan changed his name to Williams, dropping the patronymic, again as so many Welshmen on the make did. Only this Morgan Williams then went on to marry the sister of the great Thomas Cromwell, Henry VIII's minister, and it was their son Richard, Oliver Cromwell's grandfather, who took his uncle's name, Cromwell. Generations on, the family was still uneasy about this, for even in his own marriage contract Oliver was referred to as Cromwell alias Williams, and at the Restoration one branch, given what had happened in the meantime, pointedly and quietly changed the name back to Williams.

It is hard to get one's mind round all this, but on the family tree at Northborough I followed the names back and there, just two generations back, was the name I had been looking for, that of Oliver's paternal grandfather Richard...Richard WILLIAMS.

'Oh, Rigby.'

23 A HISTORICAL GAZETEER

The poetry of history lies in the quasi-miraculous fact that once, on this earth, on this familiar spot of ground, walked other men and women, as actual as we are today, thinking their own thoughts, swayed by their own passions, but now all gone, one generation vanishing after another, gone as utterly as we shall be gone, like ghosts at cock-crow.

> G.M. Trevelyan in *Autobiography of a Historian.*

MAEN MADOC

It is the most extraordinary thing I have ever seen. Picture moorland, the horizon a long way off and the sky huge. Now imagine a sunrise up there, as the drums in Strauss's *Thus Spake Zarathustra* give way to a single, unearthly trumpet. Rising in front of you, ringed with light, is the great black monolith out of the classic science-fiction film *2001: A Space Odyssey.*

It stands at the edge of a road not known to the AA, and there are no signs as to where it goes, but then there would have been no need of a sign, for when that was built men knew exactly where it went. That road went to Rome.

Get an Ordnance Survey Map, sheet 160. On this find Glynneath on the A465, the Heads of the Valley road from Abergavenny to Neath. Now trace the yellow mountain road that goes north from Glynneath to Ystradfellte, noting as you do so how the green shading falls away until there is just white space and contour lines, the blank moorland of Fforest Fawr. Here, two-and-a-half miles north of Ystradfellte, on your left, you will see on the map the dotted lines of the old Roman road.

Now the map dissolves. In front of you there is a gate opening on something that is still a metalled road, just, some stones probably put there by a local farmer, but these give way to older, much older stones, and a point comes, a quarter of a mile along, when, before a second gate, you see the monolith start to rise. And rise, until there are 11 feet of this against the sky. On the Ordnance Survey map, it is marked as Maen Madoc, but that is just the name given it in much later centuries when men had long forgotten what this was. In front of you is a gravestone.

And the drums are beating again.

If the light hits the stone at the right angle, you can still make out the letters. DERVACI FILIUS JUSTHIC IACIT. Dervacus, son of Justus, here he lies. The inscription is badly cut, the letters jumbled and close together, the 'A's upside down, as though the mason was cutting an inscription he barely understood, as he did his best to follow a tradition, perhaps literacy itself, which by then would have been only dimly remembered. No one knows who Dervacus was, or Justus, and no one will ever know. But the artist Alan Sorrell has painted an imaginative reconstruction of the raising of this stone, a little group of men and riders on the moor with the shadows lengthening as the sun starts to go down. Which is how it would have seemed to them. The stone was set up in a world in ruins.

> For the end of the world was long ago,
> And all we dwell today
> As children of some second birth,
> Like a strange people left on earth
> After a judgement day.

G.K. Chesterton in his great poem *The Ballad of the White Horse* was writing about the fall of the Roman Empire, the scale of which we still find it hard to acknowledge. For this was the nearest thing to a world state this planet has known, a state with a standing army and a civil service, its public buildings grander than ours, and far more beautiful, and, for the rich, villas with comforts we can only dream of today. The Roman Room recreated in the Museum of London, with its couches and sideboards and its underfloor central heating, is one in which we would all like to live (unlike the recreated medieval room next to it, which, crouched and crowded, is like a large pigsty). The men who knew such things would have thought all this would last forever, but it ended with an abruptness that is terrifying even now, when all that was left, to quote Chesterton again, was 'the plunging of the nations in the night.'

Still, if the Roman world bears comparison to our own, being as highly organised, it is the differences, its otherness, that makes it so startling. Not that far away in Caerleon, where a Legionary fortress of 60 acres still dwarfs the modern town, you glimpse their indifference to human suffering in the great amphitheatre where, if the sponsors could afford it, men fought to the death. And in the town museum you find things that today would have respectable Welsh matrons screaming blue murder, except these would have been household ornaments to their equally respectable ancestors. The carvings of an erect penis, a much-loved family symbol of fertility, would have been their equivalent of a Royal Doulton Balloon Lady. Now you try telling a Methodist that.

But then in the porch of the village church at Caerwent you will find an altar that is not to a Christian God at all. It is to Mars. An inscription records that a junior Roman officer had 'paid his vow willingly and duly', as though his HP payments were now complete. A Roman, and our ancestors with him, would have been more business-like in his dealings with his god than William Williams Pantycelyn.

Unlike us, they buried their dead, not in towns, but beside the roads that led out of these. At High Rochester, north of Hadrian's Wall, four tombs have been found, and they are very strange, being big things, taller than a man, and more alien in their appearance than any other surviving Roman structures, for while we have copied their public buildings, these we have not. One of these is circular and conical, like a large ice-cream cornet; the other three are miniature pyramids. But all were put up when the Empire still ruled Britain. The one on the moors above Neath was not.

When the archaeologist Sir Cyril Fox excavated it in 1940, he found that it had been put up, not beside the road, but in it, for someone had dug through the metalling of the road itself. So while the road may still have been in use it must by then have been overgrown. Fox thought the burial took place in the early fifth century, perhaps two generations after the end of the Empire in Britain. The towns were ominously deserted by then, the warbands of the first English immigrants picking their way through the countryside, when his mourners, perhaps for reasons of their own safety, decided to bury Dervacus up here in the old Imperial way. They must have been conservative people, deeply conscious of what had been lost, yet still rich enough to have afforded this burial. Only Fox found no body.

He found a pit eight feet square and two feet deep some ten feet from the stone, which was probably the grave, but this was empty. What he did find was evidence that the site had at some point been disturbed, which, he concluded, together with the acid soil in such a high place, would have destroyed the human remains. But it was what he did next which is so wonderful.

That stone had fallen and was lying beside the road, but instead of carting it off to some museum, the fate of so many Roman and Dark Age memorials, Fox, in 1940, the darkest time of the Second World War, took what is probably the most imaginative decision ever taken by an archaeologist. He put the stone up again. For while it would have been one thing to see it indoors in a museum gallery, tastefully lit, it is quite another to see it in the wind and rain where it has been for 1500 years.

Where once the last Roman lay.

THE FORD AT MONTGOMERY

We slowed where the road had begun to narrow and there was a long bend. On one side a lane led to a rail crossing, and on the other there was a gap in the hedge through which it was possible to drive into a small wood of willow trees. The place looked as you would expect it to look in our time, there were the inevitable dumped sacks of black polythene, and, further off among the trees, an abandoned car. Beyond, there was the Severn.

Two cars were already parked in the wood, one of them a Stoke-on-Trent taxi, and I could see two men, presumably their owners, fishing. There was the smell of wild garlic as my guide pointed to the river. 'That's where it was,' he said. There was no plaque, apart from a crumbled notice about fishing rights, but then, even on maps, there had not been one of those odd little symbols to indicate what had happened here.

'The Prince would have been on the far side,' said my guide. 'The King would have been here.'

The Ford at Montgomery.

It is a name that recurs in history books and in old manuscripts, and it can still make quiet men in libraries, who may have never been here, look up, dizzy with speculation, from their footnotes, all because of what took place at this spot on September 29, 1267. A Welsh nation state might have dated its beginnings to a meeting in the middle of a river, the water swirling around the horses, as in the presence of a cardinal, the Pope's personal representative (which would have been the equivalent of the United Nations), Henry III met Llywelyn.

Did they meet in the river? Most probably. The men of the Middle Ages were hot on political symbolism, and centuries later it was how two emperors at Tilsit, Napoleon and Alexander, would stage their meeting, in their case on a raft. On each occasion the terms would already have been agreed down to the last political and financial detail, but something of this magnitude required a meeting, not on territory that would have given one or the other an advantage, but on neutral ground. So it was here, in the Ford at Montgomery, that for the first and last time England recognised a Welshman as Prince of Wales.

It was a ford long before that, and a ford after, but for that one moment the history of two countries turned about it, men swarming around a gap in a wood half a mile along the B4385 just after it leaves the B4386 (though they would not have known these names), three miles from the English castle at Montgomery. Long before newspapers, this was yesterday's dateline.

Such places have always fascinated me, places where nothing at all survives of a moment which became part of the bagwash of memories that a nation calls history. The irregular grass lumps in a field are all that remains of the house where a young man from hunting saw a young widow for the first time. Because of this the dynastic marriage arranged for him collapsed amid recriminations, and the Wars of the Roses went on and on. At Grafton Regis, a hamlet in Northamptonshire, Edward IV met Elizabeth Woodville, and the trail of blood began that would end with the murders of the Princes in the Tower. Six miles away, by a freakish coincidence, another house is still there in a street in Stony Stratford, once a pub, latterly a DIY shop, where Richard III got his hands on his nephew, the little Edward V, the child of that marriage.

Other places. The crossroads at Pencader where an old man answered an English king back. The six ash trees on the skyline at Bridgnorth which might have become a national frontier, when Owain Glyndŵr and his allies sought to divide England between them. Events lead up to such places, events lead away, but the ash trees are long gone, the crossroads widened out of recognition.

I have in front of me Thomas Cook's International Railway Timetables, and I am looking at the stopping times of a train that every night, at 9.20, leaves Hanoi, and 70 hours later arrives in Saigon. On the second day, at 3.16am, it leaves Hue; at 8.22 it leaves Da Nang. The terror and the tragedy of the Vietnam War have been resolved into a timetable.

At 10.34am the 8 o'clock from Bangkok stops at a bridge crossing the Kwai river. The Bridge on the River Kwai. Half an hour earlier the Yukon train has pulled out of Skagway, following the route on which men died of frostbite in the Gold Rush. A train stops at Sarajevo. Human history, could it be filmed from space and then speeded up, would be a series of frantic swarms around one place after another. And then the swarm has gone.

So a taxi driver from Stoke-on-Trent fishes on and knows nothing of the excitement once focused on the water meadows in which he stands. He does not even look up to see the two men who have come so far just to stare.

A POSTCARD FROM DEGANWY

When I had climbed to a certain height I found myself quite suddenly not among rocks but looking out across a great flat field 300 yards across, a field in the sky that could be a playground of the gods halfway between earth and heaven. From here the drop was so sheer that far below me, like pieces of dolls' house furniture, I looked down on the roofs of houses and, beyond them, the sea. And the climb was not over.

Above me, ringed by the setting sun, were the broken teeth of masonry, and I knew then where I was, for a letter written up there had been racketing around in my imagination for years. No one knows the name of the writer, except he was an English knight here on campaign with Henry III in his disastrous invasion of North Wales. So not only is it one of the earliest letters to survive in these islands, it is the first postcard, if you like. The knight wrote it in French, on September 24, 1245, from a tent at Deganwy, and, as in many postcards sent subsequently from North Wales, it was raining.

Find a road map and trace the outline westwards of the small peninsula that ends in Llandudno, to where, depending on the scale of the map, you will see the name Deganwy. If you have been on holiday here you may remember it as nothing more than a line of houses trickling into Llandudno. That is, if you have never stopped and looked up. When Llandudno was a cluster of fishing huts there were already ruins on the crag above Deganwy, a reminder of a time when this was a war zone, out of which a postcard got written.

It is September 1245 and Henry III is frantically building a castle on that crag. 'We live round it in our tents in watching, fasting and praying, in cold and want of clothing.' Now if you know anything about the formal phrases men used when they wrote anything in the Middle Ages you will appreciate that the tone of this is very odd indeed. A contemporary human voice is speaking to you.

Below him, across the river Conwy, is enemy country, the start of the Welsh principality of Gwynedd, from which they are under attack most of the time. They have no winter clothing, the price of a loaf has rocketed from a farthing to fivepence; a hen costs eightpence. What makes it worse is that there is no chivalry about this war, it is a matter of ambushes, from one of which, he boasts, they brought a hundred severed Welsh heads. But there is no feeling of satisfaction, or even hope of victory; there is just famine in the ten weeks he is here. And rain. Yet for us the clouds have rolled back across eight centuries.

And at Deganwy they roll back on almost seven centuries before that again, to the most mysterious period in our whole history. It is the sixth century, and the lights which went down on Roman Britain are not risen on Saxon England, and the one thing written in all that time is a denunciation of the Kings of the Britons, or the Welsh as the English would come to call them. Foremost among these is the king who lived on this crag. His name is Maelgwn, and they call him the Tall.

The infuriating thing about the writer is that he could have settled one of our oldest mysteries, but Gildas does not even mention Arthur, choosing instead to hurl abuse at Maelgwn. For here the Tall One sits, 24 bards, a precise number, bawling his praises, a king who was formerly a monk, then a devil who has murdered his wife and his nephew. And still the bards sing, until, that is, around the year 550, Maelgwn comes running down the crag to take refuge in a church below it. The Yellow Plague has come to Deganwy.

There is still a church where Maelgwn may have knelt, and, putting his eye to a crack in the door, sees loping towards him (the use of that verb in the old myths is still terrifying) what he dreads most, a thing with yellow eyes, yellow teeth and yellow hair, and the long sleep of Maelgwn in the court at Rhos has begun.

I climbed the crag down which he ran, noting the pit out of which Henry III's men in the rain dug stones for their castle. I stood there, as they and Maelgwn must have done, watching the sun slide into the puckered sea beyond Anglesey.

Y Pwll Melyn, THE YELLOW POOL

I do not know his name. All I know, and this from a Scottish abbot writing 40 years after the event, is that he was a priest, a friar, and on a May morning, six centuries ago, he stood in front of a small army, assuring the soldiers that those who died that day would that evening sup in Paradise. *Ym Mharadwys*, for that would have been the language he used, here in the town of Usk, and this the last war, virtually the last battle, between the English and the Welsh.

But the day, as usual, turning against the Welsh, the priest was seen slipping away by soldiers who taunted him, asking why he was not waiting with them to share the celestial banquet. And this remarkable man said that, alas, it was one of his fasting days. It is a moment of such black humour, you know something like this must have happened: men shouting, horses screaming as the arrows came out of the sky, and a man delivering his grim one-liner.

Which is why on a hot September afternoon I am climbing the steep hill behind the castle at Usk in search of someone who had his 15 minutes of fame on the battlefield of the Yellow Pool on May 5th, 1405, the date according to Sir John Lloyd. This defeat was a turning point in the rising of Owain Glyndŵr, and little is known about it, except that according to local tradition, which often turns out to be right, the Welsh were besieging the castle when its defenders rushed out and overwhelmed them in some kind of running battle. In the course of this Glyndŵr's brother Tudor was killed, which raised English hopes for he bore a startling resemblance to the Prince, whose son Gruffydd was taken prisoner.

Some place-names survive, such as Monkswood on the outskirts of the town, where Gruffydd is said to have been taken, but where is, or was, the Yellow Pool? Sir John Lloyd in a footnote, which is where historians usually admit to uncertainty, said he did not know. But the castle is the clue. If there was a counter attack and the besiegers fell back, where would they have gone? To the nearest strongpoint, the hill behind the castle itself...

It is a beautiful afternoon, Usk falling away beneath us as we start to climb, my wife, my small daughter, our Jack Russell dog, and me: the castle in the trees, the town square a mass of flowers, and, beyond these, the bleak outline of the Victorian gaol that is still a gaol.

We come to the old farm on top of the hill, where the lady renting the farmhouse says she has never heard of a Yellow Pool. So we walk on for some 30 yards and stand, looking at the hills behind this hill. On our left is a thicket of trees, so dense at first I do not notice the dark hollow in their midst, but when I walk round I see this patch of mud in shadow, at the centre of which is a small pond. My daughter picks up a stone and throws it into the pond, and there is more of a slapping sound than a splash.

'Grab her,' I shout, but it is too late, for my daughter has forgotten that there is one amongst us who would follow a thrown stone into the mouth of Hell. The Jack Russell is already in the mud. 'Shit,' I say, 'we've got nothing to clean her with.' The dog is covered in mud, an odd mud very light in colour.

But my wife says nothing, she merely points to the dog. And at that moment we both know where we are.

Nobody in Usk had known anything about the Yellow Pool, not even in the town museum, and it was only a chance meeting with a passing postwoman that had me calling on the town ironmonger, for, yes, Usk still had an ironmonger, who, so she assured me, had lived all his life in the town. If he were me, the ironmonger said, he would call at the castle.

The castle? I had been walking round Usk for two hours, I said, and I had seen no sign of a castle. Castles had brown signs pointing to them, which said 'Castle'. Ah, said the ironmonger, but this castle was like no other. It was hidden in trees, and a family still lived in it. In the castle? Oh yes. So it wasn't open to the public then? Yes, there was a handbell at the gate which you had to ring very loudly.

I rang very loudly indeed on account of the fact that the chatelaine was usually in the garden. After a few minutes a young woman appeared, secateurs in hand.

Usk castle has latterly been owned by three generations of a local family. They were farmers, sitting tenants of the farmland attached to it, and when an old estate was wound up they bought the land and they found the castle went with it, and, remarkably, moved in. They lived in the gatehouse, said the lady of the castle. It was possible to get used to anything in time, she went on, even to walls 11 feet thick. Would it be all right to walk round? Yes, of course.

As I climbed the steps to the inner bailey, I remembered there had been no talk of an admission fee. It was an extraordinary place, a half-wild garden with roses and hydrangeas, and lawns among the remains of towers and arches and bits of wall. In the ruined chapel the family had set up its own memorial stones, and on one of these a child had laid a plastic sword. Chickens and geese wandered about, and an old sheep lay chewing in the middle of the bailey. But under all this an old terror lingered.

On one side I peered over the battlements, then drew back for the line of stone was so sheer I could see the castle ditch far below me, that ditch where after the battle, the lady of the castle had told me, they massacred the Welsh prisoners. Adam of Usk, who came from this town, was buried in its church, and is the main contemporary source for these events, wrote that 300 were killed.

And so it comes about that on a September afternoon I am watching a Jack Russell crawl guiltily out of a pond, a dog covered in a mud of a colour I have not seen before, being almost reddish-yellow. 'Don't you see,' says my wife, 'this *is* the Yellow Pool.'

Across 600 years a man is laughing.

NARBERTH

'Pwyll, Prince of Dyfed, was lord of the seven Cantrefs of Dyfed; and once upon a time he was at Narberth, his chief place...' *Yn Arberth,* in Narberth where adventures start. And end. 'Give me Narberth on a wet Saturday afternoon,' muttered a 19th-century squire bored with the splendours of Imperial Rome. It now has a Spanish restaurant, a bonded warehouse, and a crematorium, so it is a place where the Welsh of west Wales can get paellas, 100 proof Guyana rum, and get burnt. Nothing has changed.

Another wet Saturday afternoon, and I was in Narberth with my family when I fell back on an old way of passing the time and tried to find the castle, which wasn't easy. No signs direct you there, and the castle itself is set back on its mound among the trees; you can live in the town and not even know it is there, it is that ruined. Or rather, it was ruined once. What follows is the strangest story I have stumbled on.

A short drive led to the castle, only stretched across this was a plastic chain, a *plastic* chain, with the notice 'PRIVATE'. Beyond this was what looked like an abandoned car, its tyres flat. And that was the first surprise.

Although the weeds and grass on the mound had grown high, someone had been doing a lot of building work on the castle. The masonry was newly pointed, a roof had been built over one chamber and iron grilles set into its windows as though that someone had started to build himself a small gaol.

As I climbed higher, I came on a cleared plateau on which there was a rusting cement mixer. *And a caravan.* Whoever he was, the builder had moved into Narberth Castle. And had had water and electricity laid on, for there was a tap and an overhead electric cable.

About nine years earlier, seven by some accounts, an elderly stranger some said had been an Australian sheep farmer, others a retired P & O liner steward, had turned up in the town. His name, he said, was Perrot.

This may not mean much to you, but in Narberth it was as though someone called Caesar or Plantagenet had come. The Perrots had been the great lords of South Pembrokeshire until the most famous of them, Sir John Perrot, a giant said to have been the illegitmate son of Henry VIII, died in the Tower, accused of high treason by Henry's daughter Elizabeth. And now they were back.

The castle then belonged to the local doctor, for it is a little known fact that most castles actually do belong to someone. They may not be able to do anything with them, the laws on ancient monuments are precise and severe; all you can do with one is own it. Anyway this doctor was so impressed with the man's story that he sold him the ruin for, so it is said, £5. And if that wasn't sufficiently odd in itself, what happened next took everyone aback. The old chap moved in.

The first thing he did was remove the entire top soil from the plateau, a plot of land some 40 yards long. This, you must remember, was done by a man well into his seventies, who would start work at daybreak and continue until the light went. Few people in the town saw him for he rarely came down from his mound.

But a man living in the terrace at the foot of this said his wife had become so concerned she often took cakes up to him. He rarely went himself. 'He'd start talking about his family, and you'd be up there for hours.'

He remembered tons of stones being delivered, and gravel. The old gentleman, having rid himself of the top soil, dug down around the castle, two, three, even four feet down, to reveal the curve of towers hidden for centuries. This work was meticulously done. But in the mysterious roofed chamber he used new stone, cut new sandstone at that, building a porch with this, an offence not only against all planning laws but against every law on ancient monuments ever drafted. *And nobody intervened.*

Nobody in a local council which would throw the book at you if you decided to build yourself a conservatory without planning permission. Nobody in CADW, for whom this would have been something out of all their worst nightmares. Yet this was a man in the middle of a Welsh town rebuilding a castle, for whom, presumably, the respective boards had laid on water and electricity. So far as I know no single person in authority even knew what the lost heir was up to on his mound.

It ended only when the lady with the cakes, having missed the sound of the cement mixer, went up and found there would be no need for cakes ever again. Time had stopped again for Narberth Castle, and Robert Perrot, aged 77, was dead in his caravan.

Everything was just as he had left it, the car, the cement mixer and the tools, and quite possibly this might have been as he wanted it for the last of the Perrots had achieved his heart's desire: he had died in the castle of his ancestors.

But if it was an embarrassment for the authorities, for the bureaucrats and the archaeologists, think what it must have been like for a young dentist in Chelmsford. Perrot's sister's grandson, he was left a ruined castle in West Wales in the old man's will. *Yn Arberth.*

'And thus ends this portion of the *Mabinogion*.'

A TALE OF TWO CASTLES

I grew up near the first of them, as a boy climbing the mound on which it stands, at Dryslwyn, near Carmarthen. The second castle is not a climbing frame or a picturesque ruin, it has no romantic associations of any kind: it stands for nightmare. That is Norwich.

It stands on a hill above a city or what was once a city. Below it are the disasters of modern planning, the pedestrianized precincts, the one-way traffic systems and the shopping malls, but the castle has changed hardly at all. It is as windowless and massive as it always was, so it still reeks of power and oppression. Until the late 19th century, it was the county gaol.

Do not go in. It is a museum now, and the little china collections and wildlife displays would be a distraction. Go, as I did, in the early evening when the museum is closed but they have not yet closed the gates of the park in which it stands. Now pause at the castle door and read the plaque put up by the people of Norwich to say sorry for what was done here, 400 years ago, to the rebel Robert Kett.

They hung him here, but not by the neck. In the unique punishment for treason reserved by Henry VIII for those who had really scared him, Kett was hung, a living man, in chains, swaying and turning for days above the city, his body its highest point, as, by infinitesimal degrees, life ebbed. The novelist H.F.M. Prescott in *Man On a Donkey* attempted to convey the agonies of another Tudor rebel, Robert Aske, after five days in chains, 'That which dangled from top of the Keep at York, moving only as the wind swung it, knew neither day nor night, nor that it had been Robert Aske, nor even that it had been a man...'

But it was not that which had brought me to Norwich, it was a fact I had found among footnotes and had been unable to forget. On October 16, 1340, a man disappeared here, or at least disappeared from the columns of a medieval household account recording the cost of keeping him alive: thereafter, nothing. His name was Rhys, and his ancestors had been kings in South Wales. His father was Rhys ap Maredudd, lord of Dryslwyn, where he himself had been brought up, but we know nothing about him, no scrap of recorded speech survives, not even a letter written in his name; all we know is that since childhood he was in gaol, he who had committed no offence except that of being his father's son, living on and on in Norwich Castle.

He would have been a boy when in 1287 the English brought up their equivalent of a V2, the biggest siege engine in their history, to destroy Dryslwyn. A trebuchet, it required 40 oxen to draw it over smooth ground, 60 when the going got rough; 20 horsemen guarded it, and a screen of 480 footmen was thrown around it. It hurled round stones weighing 500 pounds each, some of which survive in a shed at Carmarthen Museum, and the walls of Dryslwyn fell outwards, ironically on its besiegers.

Rhys ap Maredudd is not a pin-up boy in Welsh history. He had practised *realpolitik,* fighting for the English against the Last Prince, Llywelyn, and only rose against them when the rewards he expected did not materialize. Men of his own race handed him over, and the English half-hanged him, before castrating, then pulling his entrails out before his eyes, another novel punishment they had choreographed for their frighteners, which left his son the last heir to a centuries old royal dynasty.

That humbug, Edward I, made great show of his leniency towards the royal children of Wales, 'that the innocent may not seem to atone for the iniquity and ill-doing of the wicked'. Stalin just put his victims' children into orphanages, from which eventually they re-emerged. These never re-emerged. Edward simply made them disappear, the little girls into nunneries, the little boys into perpetual imprisonment. And with that they disappeared out of history, apart from the odd passing reference in footnotes, for there was nothing for historians to write once the doors had closed on childhood. But Edward did not forget, directing in his old age, 30 years on, that a wooden cage bound with iron be built in Bristol Castle for Owain, nephew of the Last Prince of Wales, who was thereafter kept inside it.

But then something very odd happened. Edward I was long dead when out of that cage a petition was presented to his son's Council, and it is the only time one of the lost children speaks, albeit in French. The Council is so startled to get something that seemed to be out of time altogether that you can see where a hand has scrawled, this time in Latin, across the document, 'Let it be enquired who sues this petition.'

In it Owain reveals he has been kept in gaol since he was seven years old, and the petition itself reads as though it has been written by a small boy. 'He prays the King that he may go and play within the walls of the Castle.' But it is a middle-aged man who is pleading to be allowed some form of exercise.

It was not granted him, for the Latin hand writes, 'It has been testified that he has enough in victuals and clothing, therefore nothing.' Darkness and damp, and time passing. Owain was known to have been alive eight years later, in 1320, for another bureaucratic hand records a change of castle constable; not afterwards.

But in Norwich that other footnote lived on and on. He too had been in Bristol in 1297, briefly, being transferred to Norwich two months later, where 43 years on the Calendar of Close Rolls noted the cost of his keep on the ridge above the city. His grave is unknown, as are those of all the lost children. And even the people of Norwich, anxious to make amends for the local farmer Kett, have forgotten this descendant of kings.

Remember him, who died here like a rabbit in a hutch.

THE SKULL OF ST TEILO

Who was there? Well, for a start, a sixth-century Welsh saint, or at least his skull, with its herditary keeper, a gentleman from Hong Kong, also, as might be expected, the chairman of a brewery. All were at Llandaff Cathedral in 1994, at a Sung Eucharist held by the Bishop in open defiance of the 22nd Article of the Anglican

Church ('The Romish Doctrine concerning…the worshipping and adoration as well of images as of relics, and also invocation of saints, is a fond thing vainly invented…'). But then, after five-and-a-half centuries on its travels, the skull of St Teilo, long thought to have been lost, had come home.

The most remarkable feature of this story is the way it defies time. Relics and hereditary keepers are things of the Middle Ages; when they stray beyond this it is as objects of black comedy, as when in the late 17th century the last Hereditary Keeper of the Book of Armagh pawned this to pay for his passage to England, and a new, industrious, career in perjury. But the story of the skull of Teilo evades this, just as it evades the cycles of history. The Reformation came and went, Welsh Nonconformity rose, roared and fell, but in living memory men still believed in the power of the skull.

All that is known about Teilo is that in sixth-century Wales, he founded monasteries which survive only as place-names like Llandeilo, the church of Teilo. There were others like him in the Age of Saints, all cheerfully canonized and, with one exception, David, not one of them recognised subsequently as a saint outside this island and this nation; between the few facts and the names on a road map, legends gathered like summer flies. It was said that in death Teilo politely became three corpses to accomodate the claims of three competing churches. However, only one tomb survived, that in Llandaff Cathedral, of which, by the Middle Ages, a local family, Matthew, had become hereditary keepers.

One of them, Sir David Matthew, having restored the tomb after the sack of the Cathedral by Owain Glyndŵr, was in 1450 given the saint's skull by the Bishop. This descended through seven generations of the family until a William Matthew, dying childless in 1658, left it to the Melchior family of Llandeilo Isaf on the slopes of the Preseli in Pembrokeshire. It is not known why he did this, but the surname argues for an interest in religious matters on the part of the Melchiors, the name of one of the Wise Men; families then often adopted the names of the roles taken by their ancestors in long-ago Mystery Plays. But the switch westwards had an extraordinary effect.

There was already a holy well at Llandeilo Isaf, dedicated to St Teilo, which, like all such wells, was a survival from a time before Christianity. But when skull and well came together, it was like plugging into the National Grid of religious faith, this in an area too remote for the authorities, both civil and religious, to interfere. At Llandeilo Isaf a ritual was evolved, so detailed that the Royal Commission on Ancient Monuments felt obliged to record it: 'To ensure the full benefit of the water the skull must be completely filled, and the vessel offered to the pilgrim only by the senior living member of the Melchior family.'

It is at this point that Major Kemmis Buckley, chairman of Buckley's Brewery, enters the story. Buckley's interest was in holy wells, so to Llandeilo Isaf he duly came: he found a tiny ruined church, he found the well, but where was the skull? All he knew was that in 1906 a man had been alive who could remember a carriage full of invalids from Gower calling, who had gone away dissatisfied until it was pointed out that they had not followed the ritual and drunk the water from the skull. They made the journey again, did so, and returned to Gower in perfect health.

But this, whatever else it suggested, meant the scent was not long cold. Buckley switched his search to the Llandaff archives, where he found a remarkable twist: in the 19th century another branch of the Matthew family, having migrated to Australia, reappeared, intent on getting the skull back. For was there not a curse that ill luck would dog the family until the skull was restored to the last male of the line?

In 1927 a Gregory Matthew bought the skull for 50 pounds from a Miss Dinah Melchior, and had it set in a silver reliquary. This he left to his son, a second-hand bookseller in Bournemouth, whose only recorded pronouncement on his strange inheritance was that it was safe in a bank. And with that the trail faded out again, Buckley's inquiries revealing only that the bookseller was dead, with his nearest relative an Australian cousin born in 1907.

And that seemed that. Half-forgotten wells, a relic the Cathedral clergy knew nothing about, a disappeared skull with its keeper, they were settling to the back of Buckley's mind for he had assumed they had gone forever. Then one night in Ferryside his phone rang: it was the Dean of Llandaff, a puzzled man. 'I'm not sure what to make of this, but I think you should know a chap's just turned up from Hong Kong. Says his name's Matthew, and that he's the last male of his line, though I don't know what that's got to do with it. Oh yes, and he's got this human skull.'

A thousand years ago a man would have sunk to the floor, reaching for the nearest holy relic. In 1994, in Ferryside, Buckley reached for the Gordon's.

24 CLOSE ENCOUNTERS OF THE THIRD KIND

i *And then the visitors came*

I cannot remember getting such pleasure from a book as I did from Glyn Tegai Hughes's anthology *The Romantics in Wales* (Gwasg Gregynog, £775). It is not just its beauty, the hand-made paper, the quarter leather, the engraving of the Rhaeadr Falls cut in purple into the cover cloth of something the size of an atlas. These are accidental details (as, I note bemusedly, is the fact that it costs £300 more than the current value of my car). This, quite simply, is the funniest book I have read in years.

Its inspiration seems to have been to have been Napoleon, whose wars sealed Europe off to the English Romantic poets. In other words, he deprived them of their fixes of the Sublime and the Picturesque, things that brought the Prospects of Infinity; the Emperor deprived them of mountains.

So where were they to go? 'Scotland,' Dr Tegai Hughes observes drily in his introduction, 'might be more familiar and enticing, but Wales was a good deal more accessible...' Accessibility mattered, for, being broke, they came on foot, and there was something else, something which mattered almost as much. In Wales walking was socially acceptable (there was, wrote De Quincey, 'no sort of disgrace attached in Wales, as too generally upon the great roads of England, to the pedestrian style of travelling'). And Wales was cheap. Its inns cost a third of what one would have cost in England, though Welsh landlords soon caught up as over the Border came the most bizarre invaders the old Principality had ever known, Wordsworth, Coleridge, Southey, Shelley, with assorted wives, sisters, friends, their own radical politics, and, of course, notebooks.

Until then, the only travellers in Wales had been drovers, itinerant preachers, and the odd English king at the head of an army (though James II, frantic for a male heir, did come to Holywell to soak his testicles in the holy well which duly did the trick). The men of the 18th century took a distant interest, for there was a lot to be interested in, like druids and bards and castle ruins. Luckily 'the ruins came equipped with dimly understood historical associations,' murmurs Dr Hughes. For this allowed Gray to write about Edward I's massacre of the bards, something which had never happened, and Blake to declare that Adam and Noah had both been druids. But the Romantics were different: they *bounded* into Wales, the way the training SAS now bounds into the Brecon Beacons.

Creatures of quite extraordinary physical fitness, the writers climbed the mountains, Wordsworth up Snowdon at midnight, and the popular poet Mrs Felicia Hemans to spend a whole night on Cader Idris in the hope of seeing visions, which she duly achieved. 'I *felt* their dim presence – but knew not their forms.' She came on her own, Mr Hemans, not unexpectedly, having earlier done a runner. As for the rest, they paced the moorlands, got rained on, got lost (Coleridge on the way to Tintern Abbey) and misspelt the place names, thereby ensuring gainful employment in the years to come as Eng lit. scholars puzzled over where they had actually been.

But they all faced one problem. The old Welsh heroes were romantic figures, so they could agonise excitedly over Caractacus and Llywelyn and Glyndŵr, for these were all safely dead. It was the Welsh people they met, still very much alive, who were the problem. 'The society in Wales is very stupid,' wrote Shelley. 'They are all Aristocrats and Christians, but that as I tell you I do not mind in the least; the unpleasant part of the business is that they hunt people to Death who are not so likewise.' Dr Hughes records, in parentheses, 'Shelley had been briefly arrested in Caernarfon for debt.' He had also, he claimed, been shot at in Tremadoc by a burglar, and hollered in a letter, 'I have just escaped an atrocious assassination. Oh, send me 20 pounds if you have it.'

The curious thing is that the burglar, at whom Shelley fired in return, had also done his share of hollering, 'By God, I will be revenged! I will murder your wife. I will ravish your sister.' The poet seems to have encountered the only English-speaking burglar in North Wales. Almost everyone else he, and the others, encountered was monoglot Welsh, so the Romantics would not have understood a word they said. This, however, did not stop Coleridge airily pronouncing that to the peasants of North Wales 'the ancient mountains, with all their terrors, are pictures to the blind, and music to the deaf.' Or Southey, encountering those of South Wales, to say, 'These creatures were somewhat between me and the animals, and were as useful to the landscape as masses of weed or stranded boats.' As human beings, the Romantics do not come well out of this book, being revealed as racists, prigs and hysterics, and it would have been fascinating had it been possible to include some Welsh reactions to them. As it was, one Welsh vicar was so irritated by Wordsworth, and in particular by his talk, he took a knife to him.

But the greatest ordeal the Welsh had to face since Edward I was to come: they had still to be talked at by George Borrow. His appearance was bad enough, this white-haired giant with an umbrella, but Borrow had also taught himself to speak Welsh, which he did every chance he got but with an accent so peculiar that, sixty years on, an old lady could still remember her terror as a child on hearing it. Dr Hughes, stretching his definition of Romantic, includes an extract from Borrow in full linguistic cry after a Welsh lady who until then had been peacefully knitting ('the general occupation of Welsh females').

This book is a classic of comedy.

ii *Some visitors stayed*

In a 300-acre wood at the end of Wales there is a white tower, white because, like most towers and castles were once, it was lime-washed against the rain, and the moment I saw it I felt I had come home. For 60 years the endpapers of *Rupert* annuals have shown such a tower above the trees, inhabited by the Professor and the Dwarf, his servant, the former dressed in a suit, the latter in the black velvet and floppy shoes of the late Middle Ages. It is just that in middle age and real life no one expects to find himself in Nutwood.

I had followed the directions I had been given and driven into the wood, but then something happened. I had reached a fork and braked, not sure which way to go, when there was a light whirr of wings and a small bird was perching on my wing mirror. It was a yellow wagtail, a sighting of which is rare in itself, but this bird seemed to be completely without fear. It stayed on the wing mirror as I wound the window down, the two of us looking at each other just a foot apart, and it moved only when the car did, transferring its perch to the windscreen wipers from which it carried on looking at me. And so the three of us, the bird, my wife and I, drove together the long mile to the Tower, in shadow all the way because of the trees which shut out the sun. But then there was sunlight, as suddenly as though someone had switched stage lights on, and the bird was gone.

We were on a plateau, in the middle of which was something the size of a Saturn Five rocket, dazzling white with battlements. Two large dogs came running, and as I got out of the car one of them, an Alsatian, reared up and put paws the width of hands on my shoulders. I froze. But the dog, its head held back, was just inspecting me as the little bird had done.

'Down, down,' said a small, tough lady. 'I keep telling her not to do that.' She has died since I first wrote about the Tower, and her son now lives there, but I promised her then I would not reveal its whereabouts, and I will not do so now.

As we stood there I noticed on the terrace below us what seemed to be a labyrinth, ring upon ring of what she said were discarded kerbstones. This, she went on, a magazine dedicated to the paranormal had recently had photographed. But the accompanying article had much irritated her, and she had written to the magazine to complain, for it contained the description of a column of light which hovered over the labyrinth at night, accompanied by balls of orange fire. It was not the column of light that had exercised her; her neighbours, she said briskly, had seen that. It was the balls of fire, they were a complete invention.

As we, my wife and I and the dogs, followed her through the small door into the Tower, I noticed the stonework which must have been all of ten feet thick. Inside, on a table in a small, very high room, were maps and a computer. She was, she said, trying to find a small plane that had disappeared into the Irish Sea. For this she used a prism dangling from a cord, and, as she passed the prism over one map it did begin to move. Police forces, she said chattily, sometimes asked her to trace dead bodies.

We had only been in the Tower for a few minutes, and we just stared, my wife and I. As she wrote later in her diary, 'I seemed to hear all sorts of bells ringing, echoes of all the fairy stories I had ever read. The lady with supernatural powers in the tower in the wood; the two attendants in the shape of huge dogs; the little bird which flies and hops in front of visitors, and stares at them. And then the labyrinth, the centre of which you sometimes cannot reach, but at other times you can reach without effort...'

Not that this would have surprised earlier travellers. On December 22, 1693, a local man wrote about the Tower to the Oxford scholar Edward Lhuyd, then Keeper of the Ashmolean Museum. 'Formerly said to be haunted, upon which account seldom visited, where they said the Devil would often appear in the shape of a black mastiff dog, and sometimes lie by the fire, but mostly in a vault or cellar, to guard some hidden treasure there...'

Not that this again would have deterred its lady owner. 'When we first moved in 40 years ago there was a heavy fall of snow two days before Christmas, and we were going to bed just before midnight when we heard the sound of hooves. My husband said, 'Oh God, there go my lawns.' But the next morning there were no hoofmarks in the snow. I have heard that horse three times now.'

Castles were last lived in during the late Middle Ages, for they were uncomfortable (the White Tower has just one fireplace), they were draughty, they supported a way of life that would now only attract Boy Scouts and ageing rugby supporters, being communal and raucous, conducted in a smoky great hall where there was no privacy. So their owners moved out and into houses that had windows with glass in them, also chimneys. They popped back briefly during the Civil War, as the owners of the White Tower did when Cromwell's cannon came trundling through the wood.

It was then the lost centuries began, when the castle became the local quarry, where, if you wanted to extend your cowshed you turned up quietly at night and, as here, by morning the barbican was a few stone courses lower. But then in the 19th century their owners began to see castles as play pens, and made additions, for, before CADW and English Heritage, no one would or could stop them. At Llandeilo the Lords Dinefwr built a tea-house on top of their ruined keep, at Pembroke Castle Sir Thomas Phillips put all the battlements back, and at Manorbier a solicitor called Cobb went even further, he built a house within the castle and moved in.

All this stopped abruptly in 1922, when Goodrich Castle, near Monmouth, in which an old gentleman was living quietly in a shed, became the first castle in Britain to be taken into care. For the first time since the Civil Wars the authorities had become interested in castles again. 'Would I buy a castle? Not in a million years,' said Dr Glyn Coppach of English Heritage. 'The sites are worth nothing, and the buildings are scheduled ancient monuments. Owners can do nothing with them.'

But say there was a castle which time, and the authorities, had forgotten, a castle within a 300-acre wood at the end of Wales. So it was in the 1930s that there came to the White Tower a remarkable man called Ernest Pegge.

His real name was Pigge, and his ancestors had owned the Briton Ferry Lunatic Asylum. Alas, I am not making any of this up. Pegge, né Pigge, bought the White Tower from its owners, the Scourfield family, who were as remarkable as he was. The writer Herbert Vaughan recorded his meeting with Sir Owen Scourfield, the last baronet, at the turn of the century. 'By way of saying something, I asked him for the tonnage of the annual output of coal in Pembrokeshire. Thereupon, as though I had touched on some secret spring in his mental apparatus, he proceeded to give me the tonnage for Pembrokeshire, then for Carmarthenshire, then for Wales, then for all Britain. Nor did this voluminous reply end here, *for he launched forth into the tonnage produced in America, China, Japan, Australia, the whole world...*'

Pegge, 'the genial hermit Ernest Pegge' as the writer H.M. Lockley called him, disappeared off the maps as, alone in the wood, he set out to restore something that had been a ruin for 300 years. He reassembled its fallen stones, fitted beams he found in shipbreakers' yards, and, while Europe slithered into the Second World War, the White Tower rose again. Lockley, visiting Pegge on his building site, found him 'a surprising but sane man.' The restoration, according to the architectural historian Tom Lloyd, who has had access to Pegge's plans, was done 'with extreme skill'.

And the irony is that he may have been a man in advance of his time, for the authorities, after decades of conserving ruins as found, are now experimenting with rebuilding as a means of conservation, and have re-roofed the Great Hall at Caerphilly Castle.

By the 1950s Pegge was dead, and his nephew, a doctor, who did not share his enthusiasm for castle life, put the White Tower on the market, to the bemusement of local estate agents. It was at a time when the lady and her husband, a retired Army officer, had just moved into the area and were living in rented accomodation.

'Life was fun, the fishing was good, but then the rains came. We had 40 buckets in the bedroom alone, and spent every weekend that first autumn looking at houses. And then the phone rang. My husband put the receiver down, turned to me and said, 'Chap's trying to sell a castle.' We just stared at each other. We went to see it more out of curiosity than anything. There were potholes in the road, no mains electricity, the water came through an old gas-pipe, a ladder led to the second floor. We...' She smiled. 'We fell for it.'

That had been 40 years before, but then the work started. 'In the Army you just rang up the quartermaster, and somebody came.

Now nobody came. I had no painters in, I just got a trade-book and got on with it. Pegge had done a wonderful job, but I made this place liveable.'

Their main problem was to find an use for the tiny rooms which simply occurred off the spiral stair like ledges in a dovecot. Pegge, who had just had trapdoors between the storeys, had left most of these empty. Now they became bedrooms, a library, a study. 'And if we found a hole in the wall we put a lavatory in it.' One of these was so deep in the wall you felt all that was required was some problem with the door-bolt for you to be entombed forever like a high priest accompanying his Pharaoh into the next world.

When they finally went onto the mains, the electricity board was so intrigued they sent a photographer along. There were other visitors. One day a whole gang of people turned up, and, when they were told it was a private house, said a small boy was selling tickets at the edge of the wood. Their younger son, then seven, who now lives in the tower, had always been enthusiastic at the prospect, and a drawing done by him is in the family scrapbook under the caption 'LOOK WHAT WE'VE BOUGHT'. Their elder son, who would become a general, was too embarrassed to admit at boarding school that his father had bought a castle and gave the authorities such a vague address his school bill only arrived on the eve of a new term.

We were now climbing the stairs. 'See those steps? Feller fell off 'em, not having turned and come down backwards as he was told. You never heard such a fuss, he was screaming before he even hit the ground. Claimed £10,000 off my house insurance.'

As she and her husband were both from military and colonial families, the interior decoration was appropriate, with three swords on one wall. 'All from Trafalgar, all *used.*' In a cabinet on the fifth, or sixth, floor, I was beginning to lose count, there was a crumpled book with the Eagle and the Swastika on the cover. 'That? Martin Bormann's phone directory. But see that?' It was a round brass knob. 'Hitler's lavatory pull. My husband was one of the first British officers into the Bunker. Bought them off a Russian guard.'

I nodded. By that stage I was beginning to feel that nothing would surprise me again. And still the relentless inventory went on. 'That piece of metal there, it's been round the moon. Part of Apollo 8.'

We started up the final steps to where a bolted door opened onto the turret. As we did so, I noticed, hanging up, the longest coil of rope I had ever seen, and asked its length. Sixty feet. I asked what it was for, but then the door opened and we stepped out into the wind and vertigo, not that I noticed either for I was still reeling from her reply.

'Fire escape,' she said.

iii *And stayed*

Anyone who can speak Welsh is going to get a lot of fun from *The Garden in the Clouds* by Antony Woodward (Harper Press, £16.99). The author buys a six-acre smallholding 1200 feet up a mountain near Crickhowell in Wales where he sets about trying to fulfil his dream of creating what may be the highest garden in Britain. The smallholding is called Tair Ffynnon, which, he informs his readers, means Four Wells. Ooops. For this is where the Welsh start to snigger.

Part of his mad project on the mountain is the creation of a pond, which involves diverting water from his four wells into this. Only he has, of course, first to locate them, which proves difficult. Very difficult. And even now an increasingly frantic Mr Woodward may be up there in the clouds trying to locate his lost fourth well. For Tair Ffynnon does not mean Four Wells. Close, mind. Tair Ffynnon means Three Wells.

Sad really. For this is the funniest thing about a book which is in itself funny and rather nice, and neither the author nor his editors knew, or know, anything about it. To be blunt, what it means is that yet another Englishman, in his case with a partner called Vez and two children called Maya and Storm, has moved into the place of his dreams and written 70,000 words about it. It is just that in the process not only has he not bothered to find out anything about the people who were there before him, or how they managed to make a living out of these thin acres (like all such books, this is vague on economics, his own included), he has not even bothered to translate the name of his new home. It would not happen in Provence or Tuscany, but it happens in Wales, and it is the last act in an old black comedy.

When they conquered Wales the English practised ethnic cleansing, pushing the Welsh up into the poor country of hills and moorland to make way for their own people, the new colonial settlers, so the Welsh became a species you encountered at 600 feet. Now, and it is almost beyond belief, the Welsh have come down, and the English have gone up. Looking up at a line of cottages high in the mountains of Llŷn, I asked an old Welsh farmer, who lived up there? 'The English, they need the *view*,' he said, and might have been talking about a new strain of goat. It is not only the last act in an old black comedy, it is the last twitch in the English colonial experience.

Once they sought fat fields and profit, now they seek a contour where they can really be themselves, and at some point the two races must again have passed each other, the dressers and the Bible chests coming down by tractor to the fat fields and the profit, the fitted Magnet kitchens going up by van to the dreams. Fair enough. If it were not for the English, there would be even more ruins on the hillside; but by taking little or no interest in the history and the people among whom they now find themselves, they could just as well be living on the moon. This is how their Empire staggers to its end.

You will have gathered from this rant that I set out determined to dislike the book, *and I completely failed to do so.* There can be no higher praise than that. Mr Woodward writes well and is at his best when he describes a process, a technique or a craft, which he has set out to learn or in which he has played a part.

Thus he sets out to re-introduce sheep on the Three Wells. Only he brings in Welsh Mountain sheep, a breed he has been warned against ('If they get in anywhere, they destroy everything.'). But he ignores the warnings. The next thing is that he sees a sheep, which has eaten its way steadily through the wreckage of his garden, peering in at him as he sits drinking his morning coffee. The sheep eat everything, 'hay, straw, silage, horse and cattle feed, chicken feed, bird seed, cat food, grass cuttings'; they even eat, and are none the worse for eating, ivy, and, incredibly, yew, both of which, he reports bemusedly, he had always been told were poisonous. And they can jump.

One day a lone long-distance walker staggers in, feeling he must tell someone, anyone, what he has just seen against the sky; from his footpath he has seen sheep run at a hedge, then clear this in a pole vaulter's hop. There is some fine comedy in Mr Woodward's war on the sheep as they get more and more smug and he, by now deranged, orders ten-foot gates, the previous owners having taken the old ones with them along with the dressers and the Bible chests.

Then there is the coming of the 20-foot-long, 20-ton railway carriage ('The Perfect Country Room'), which it takes two tractors and a bulldozer to bring up the lane, breaking gateposts and stone walls. And the coming of the bees. And the bottling of the honey, which leaves the kitchen a padded cell of stickiness. As I say, he makes such things readable, which is a great gift.

Structure is provided by his ambition to get his garden in the clouds into the Yellow Book, the National Gardens Scheme's prestigious roster of gardens open to the public for charity; he succeeds in this. There is little in the way of autobiography except when grief intrudes, and he has to come down to include his mother's slow death after a riding accident. But even that is part of the old world, and, quoting Proust, he returns to his mountain, driving 'with the usual feeling of self-satisfaction into the murk.'

I wish him well. I read his book through in one sitting, at first from malice, then for enjoyment.

25 HOLIDAY HOME

And then there was that most melancholy of all new developments in Wales, the Holiday Home.

ABERFFRAW OF THE PRINCES, IN AUGUST

The house overlooked a bay so beautiful it was not until the third day, finding myself alone in it, the French windows open to the west, that it occurred to me that nothing like the house had ever existed in human history before. Purpose-built for holidaymakers, it was there to be rented by the week, as I was doing. The house had never been, never would be, anybody's home.

No man would ever leave it for work, no children to go to school, for no family would ever be brought up here, no one could die, even though in a year the population of a small village would pass through its rooms. It would forever be Year Zero, one field from the sea.

Most holiday houses, holiday homes, call them what you will, have something, a collection of knick-knacks, a book by Dick Francis or Maeve Binchey, to remind this was, or had been, someone's home. Here there was nothing, and that was when the weirdness of it broke on me.

I did not meet any human being connected with the house. Rented through an agency, its keys had come by post, and when my week's tenure was done, I would, as instructed, put these through the letter box and leave. By that evening someone else would be there, puzzling over the smoke alarms, the security fittings on all doors and windows, the dishwasher, the washing machine, the central-heating boiler, the microwave, the wall oven, the latest model of television set, and the immaculately cleaned barbecue with charcoal and firelighters. But no books. My predecessors had left nothing behind them. In front of me there was the sunset, and I felt as though I had plunged off the edge of the world, as Columbus's sailors had feared they might.

It was just like the last scene of *2001: A Space Odyssey,* when the one surviving astronaut, protected by an unseen force, had crossed a myriad galaxies to find himself in a room assembled by alien hands to make him feel at home, with sofas and chairs and a telephone. But when he lifted the receiver, the silence was absolute.

I too had a phone, but its coin box was the sort that precludes one from ringing Enquiries or even the Operator, and there was no local directory. Geography, and the human race, were elsewhere. And it didn't help that the instructions to the state of the art kitchen equipment at the end of Wales were all in German. Not only that, there was no relationship between the house and its surroundings: for all practical purposes it could have been a station hanging in deep space.

But there was another house.

It was about a mile away, where through binoculars I had seen some roofs huddled in a pleat of land. I had made enquiries about this in the village and they told me that it had been a smallholding until its last owner gave up his unequal struggle with gales and loneliness. This, you must remember, in a place where in summer strangers came to stare at beauty.

Some of these must have also stared at this whitewashed cottage, some 200 years old or more, for it was the stuff of holiday snapshots. But what their photographs would not have revealed was a way of life already old when that came to an end here.

I walked through nettles and ragwort to get to the first barn. He must have been a formidable bodger, its last occupant, for somehow he had managed to fit an up-and-over metal door, scrounged from some scrapyard, which made this barn look like a suburban garage. But the hay on the floor showed he had kept animals here. There were also four dozen spark plugs in a heap, I counted them, so whatever cars he had driven must have been on their last legs. And everywhere I looked there were tins of linseed putty, enough to glaze the Palace of Versailles.

But then he must have been house-proud for, as I pushed open the front door, the lock on which had been smashed, I came on neatness. This was incongrous, given its context, but the wallpaper, expertly fitted, hung on the walls, and there was a boxed-in bath and a fitted cupboard. It was the abandoned things that were most poignant, a cologne stick ('A Present from the Yorkshire Dales'), and the last delivery of coal still in the outdoor barn. Desolation had not quite come, for the windows were intact, as they ought to have been with all that putty.

I stood there, trying to imagine the long silence of the winter months and then the bizarre summers that brought the world and his brother to the beach beyond the sagging gate, their feet, innocent but relentless, pressing down the life which had endured here. In the house I had rented there was an idyllic painting of country life, a farmer following his sheep down a lane. But there can have been no idyll here.

I fiddled with the door-lock until this seemed to hold, and walked slowly away. Time had stopped forever in the little cottage. In the house of strangers it had not even started, even though five digital clocks, flickering on various pieces of machinery, awaited me.

THE BATH TOWER, CAERNARFON

One night there was a wind. Opening the window on the west, that one thing in the old Welsh legend men are warned not to do, I saw beneath me the white of the wild sea. And for that moment in the Bath Tower in Caernarfon it was as though those lines of Keats were being spoken through a megaphone.

> magic casements, opening on the foam
> Of perilous seas, in faery lands forlorn.

Other times I watched the little fishing boats pass beneath me, and through binoculars counted their catches of whelks. Sitting there, Sir Ralph Payne-Galloway's Victorian masterwork *The Crossbow* open on my knee, it was as though the 21st century had been set adrift far below me.

But what about when it rained; it always rains in the north of Wales, does it not? Ah yes, I was coming to that. When it rained there was the fascination of seeing how a 13th-century military fortification, its walls six feet thick, had been plumbed and wired into being a four-storey dwelling, the donjon a reception hall and French windows opening onto the battlements.

And of course there was always the Tower Log to fall back on, volumes of it, for the people who stay in Landmark Trust properties, of which the Tower is one, in follies, forts, lighthouses and a converted pigsty, are as garrulous as seafarers in captains' logs in Hollywood films (though not in life). There is a wonderful comedy in these books that deserves to be published, for while most entries are rhapsodic, there is always, at some time, the high true lunacy of dissent.

He was an American teenager of 14 staying here with his parents, and had clearly woken early in a 700 year-old building without the life support system of a television set.

> 7.15. Bored to tears.
> 7.16. Bored to tears.

Time was passing slowly in the tower at the end of the world.

> 8.00. Still boring.
> 9.00. Still boring.
> 10.00. Still boring.

At that point his father must have intervened, for an adult hand records that the water heating had broken down. 'We are Californians who left 70 degree temperatures to bask in the 40 degrees of the Welsh climate.'

Then there was the honeymooner who, with his Colombian bride, did not notice from the battlements that the Tower was being burgled beneath them. A Tower, never taken by storm, *burgled*.

And the lady who went to pick up a friend from Manchester, and returned to find the donjon door she had locked ajar in the darkness, as were the casements on the floor above which she had shut, curtains blowing into the room. Dawn was a long time coming, though not the explanation, which was just that an absent-minded window-cleaner had called.

But best of all was a beautifully done spoof of the Landmark Trust's own catalogue. The Trust, you will probably not need reminding, allows you to stay in the oddest places from the past, ingeniously converted, so that in the Bath Tower 'a medieval atmosphere has been achieved without all the discomforts of the period.' That is, without war, famine, pestilence and violent death calling on you like Jehovah's Witnesses.

Some joker had inserted in the Tower Log a typeface catching the style and the photography of the real thing, an entry showing St Willda's, a 14th-century sanctuary, now a public lavatory ('to this day the visitor may still find charming remnants of this former usage in unsuspected corners'). Later still, it had been used as a storage facility by the local nuclear power station just before the Trust acquired it. This was so perfect I was taken in until I read below this an entry recording that April Fool's Day seemed to have come early.

But then for a Welshman to stay in the Bath Tower of Caernarfon's town wall is such an odd experience, he is prepared to believe anything. For the first 200 years of its existence I should have been hanged for this alone, when for anyone of my race being found overnight in the town was a capital offence. Caernarfon, like almost all old towns in Wales, was an English colonial foundation from which the Welsh were excluded.

But Caernarfon was always a bit different, being the showpiece of the English Conquest. Edward I built a castle here, only he built this so big (its walls were modelled on those of Constantinople) there were only ten acres left within the town walls for people. Yet here, crowded into the ten acres of its narrow streets, was all the imperial panoply of his principality of Wales. *And its shadowy detail is still there.* The offices of the local county council, the law courts, and the police, a whole administrative structure, sit hunched together in the centre of the town. Caernarfon is worth visiting just to see this alone.

But the sands ran out for the English settlers, who in their time were the most extreme racists of all the colonials, resisting intermarriage and trying to hold on to their old privileges. The Welsh had quietly slipped into the other towns, but in Caernarfon, these nutters, like an SS battalion left high and dry by history, were still bawling for their total exclusion, this at a time when the King of England, Henry VII, was a Welshman.

And now this is the most Welsh of all Welsh towns. It was the last to have Sunday closing, and is a place where you get such thoughtful reflections as this chalked up on a wall, 'F*** the English, they steal our shops.' Alas, whoever was responsible seems to have got his races mixed up, it is not the old enemy but a very new one which is doing this.

Within ten miles of the town I found three closed pubs with large signs, 'Soon to re-open as an Indian restaurant'. It is the vindaloo they have to fear now, not the knight service of England. In the street market on the town square I heard two Welshmen teasing an Indian trader in Welsh, and he, fluently and cheerfully, was giving as good as he got in the same language.

But the most enduring comedy has to do with history, or what men think of as history. Edward I meant Caernarfon to be an imperial palace, only nobody came. After him, only one English king turned up here, until, that is, 1911, when Lloyd George conned the whole Royal Family into coming to enact the all-singing, all-dancing Prince of Wales show he had dreamt up. A statue of Lloyd George stands above the public lavatory in the town square.

So this whole place, castle and town, is one of the most expensive follies ever built. The castle is immaculate because its deputy constable, a chap called Turner, *rebuilt* it in the late 19th century. Then there are the town walls and towers, which the local council began trying to reclaim from the local residents who had quietly extended their gardens during the lost centuries. The process is still not complete. Some have built walkways up to them, territorial dogs patrol the parapets, there are TV aerials and sheds, even the odd brick boundary. A yacht club has moved into Edward I's Golden Gate.

And this is the most fascinating thing of all about Caernarfon. Here the past is not fenced off, or destroyed, but adapted and used by the present. All towns were like this once, before the Heritage people and the developers came.

The Bath Tower, when the tumult and the shouting died, became a public bath house, hence the name. Later it was taken over by a Church training college to be used partly as a pantry, partly as a chapel, the leaded lights from which survive. And now of course it is there for anyone who wants to dabble a toe in the Middle Ages, which can have alarming results.

Having seen the whelk boats pass, I followed them to their wharf, thinking to vary my diet. 'Hello, sailor boys,' I said brightly, assuming the right tone for anyone who had just popped out of a tower to trade. This was a mistake.

26 SOME DAY MY PRINCE WILL COME

What did he look like? He looked as I had hoped he might, as a warlord of the Middle Ages should look. The man was huge. Cradling a battle axe, he would not have seemed out of place in the great hall of any castle. The shock was seeing him in shorts, framed in the doorway of a bungalow in a seaside resort at the end of Wales.

'How would you have reacted had I gone down on one knee?' I asked him later.

'I was wondering whether you would,' said a maths master gloomily.

But then Evan Vaughan Anwyl B.Sc. of Tywyn is not just a maths master. He has only to switch on Google to be reminded of this. Here, on page after page, website after geneaological website, men he has never met are excitedly discussing the fact he and his family are 'a surviving fragment of medieval Welsh royalty.' Another website goes even further. 'He, his son, and two cousins are the ONLY people who can prove a direct male ancestry to any reigning Welsh prince.' Or, as somebody, preferring longer words, put it, 'the only known direct patrilinear descendant of Rhodri the Great.' Dear God, Rhodri the Great ruled in Wales in the ninth century. Mr Anwyl has been identified as the head of the House of Aberffraw, the last Royal Family of Wales.

And then it begins, the long wistful inventory of the titles to which he might lay claim. King of Gwynedd, Prince of Aberffraw,

EXILE AND THE PAST

Lord of Snowdon. But these are titles in the safe past, for inevitably the inventory ends in the real minefield of Prince of Wales, a title once held by a member of his family. On at least one site he has been identified as the Pretender of Wales, the old way of describing the claimant to a title held by someone else. Only Mr Anwyl has never laid claim to anything.

All he has ever wanted to be is a maths master in a bungalow, a private man in middle age, playing golf in his retirement. Until very recently that other identity had been unknown, for while others proudly lay claim to descent from minor princes in Wales, nobody thought that anyone existed with a descent from the grandest dynasty of all. The very possibility was the stuff of daydream. Except it wasn't to one man. The only thing is, Mr Anwyl couldn't give a damn.

What follows would make a wonderful film, as the stuff of daydream becomes the stuff of black comedy. For while the BBC programme *Who Do You Think You Are?* introduces people to their long-dead ancestors, provoking moments of wonder and poignance, a man in Wales, who might be the subject of the most startling programme of all, wants nothing to do with any of it.

Yet out of a BBC blog-site comes the call, 'From my perspective I would invite Evan Vaughan Anwyl to become Prince of Wales.' No Welshman for 600 years, not since Owain Glyndŵr, has claimed the title, and, unlike Mr Anwyl, even Glyndŵr was not of the old dynasty. In response to that call, there was this: 'Wouldn't that be historic justice on an epic scale, restoring the family that had fought so valiantly for Welsh independence but were disinherited by the Edwardian Conquest?' Another contributor: 'Hopefully Charles will be the last English Prince of Wales.'

Amidst the excitement there is just one doubting, and very puzzled, voice. 'Do you really think the Welsh will go for it? They have only just got the Welsh Assembly, and that took some doing.'

Yet in spite of a hullabaloo that has been going on for something like two years now, nobody has ever approached Mr Anwyl, let alone asked him whether he wants to become King of Gwynedd, Prince of Aberffraw, Lord of Snowdon, or Prince of Wales.

'History was never a favourite subject of mine,' he said. 'We've always been humble farmers in our family, that is, until my two sisters and I became teachers. Yes, we've always been proud of our family tree, but only amongst ourselves. Beyond that, no.'

The family tree hangs in the passageway of his bungalow, just as photocopies of it hang in the passageways of his two sisters' houses, and once hung in the family farm. It is an enormous framed thing, this family tree, over three foot by two foot six, with the abbreviations of most family trees, b for born, m for married, but this one also has sln for slain. There are many slns.

The tree starts with the 11th-century king Gruffydd ap Cynan of North Wales, and after him his son, King Owain Gwynedd, whose coat of arms, the three eagles' heads, and whose motto *Eryr Eryrod Eryri,* Eagle of the Eagles of Snowdonia, the family still bears.

The centuries move like windscreen wipers. The kings become princes, the princes lords, the lords constables of castles. Then the killing stops and the farming centuries begin. The constables become squires, the squires farmers, the farmers tenant farmers, and there are no more slns.

'Where are you?' There were so many columns, so many names.

A huge forefinger stabbed the glass. 'That's me.' At the very bottom, Evan Vaughan Anwyl, the latest in seven Evan Anwyls, for like any Royal Family they have kept the name in generation after generation. Mr Anwyl's son, called the Edling, the Heir, in some sites, Dafydd V in others, is a Manchester businessman.

'Is Dafydd V interested in any of this?' I asked.

'Even less than me. Mind you, if it had been anything to do with cricket...'

Who were the Welsh? English historians in the Middle Ages thought they knew, albeit uncomfortably. 'The Welsh, formerly called the Britons, were once noble, crowned over the whole realm of England. But they were expelled by the Saxons and lost both the name and the kingdom. The fertile plains went to the Saxons, but the sterile and mountainous districts to the Welsh. But from the sayings of the prophet Merlin they still hope to recover England.'

Their main hope was that one day a Messiah might come, the

one they called *Y Mab Darogan,* the Son of Prophecy. But as time passed, and he didn't come, the Welsh occupied their time by fighting each other in the dreary intervals between the seed-times and the harvests. And so it might have gone on, except that the English, or at least their Norman overlords, were better at fighting. A series of piece-meal invasions began which, on the eve of the late 13th century, had left just one formidable native Welsh dynasty. In control of North and Mid Wales was the House of Aberffraw under Llywelyn, the first and only Welsh Prince of Wales to be recognised by the English State.

The full-scale English invasion in 1282 under Edward I destroyed him, his dynasty and what might well have become a nation state in its shaky beginnings. But it is what happened next that is so horrible.

The children of that dynasty were hunted down, the little girls put into nunneries, the boys into wooden cages where they spent the rest of their lives. These are not details you will have found in any school history, but the English took the threat they represented so seriously that almost a century later a man in English pay was sent into France to murder the one they had forgotten about, Llywelyn's great-nephew. They were taking no chances.

But say one branch of the family had survived, a branch they had also forgotten, which kept its head down, living on its estates in the countryside. This is the branch from which the Anwyl family, a name they adopted in the 16th century, is said to be descended, still in Merionethshire, as they have always been.

On the Internet they have no doubts. And on the Anwyl family tree there are no doubts, with name after name moving relentlessly back into the Middle Ages. But at the National Library of Wales I was told, 'The registration of births only dates from the early 19th century. Before that it's church registers and of course this is long, long before church registers. People turn up here claiming to be descended from Owain Glyndŵr, a few from King Arthur, I think we've even had one who claimed to be descended from Merlin. So we are sceptical about such claims, but in genealogy anything's possible.'

Professor Prys Morgan of the University of Swansea echoed this. 'It is possible.'

And what tethers it even more closely to possibility is the complete lack of interest on the part of the Anwyl family. If there had been enthusiasm of any kind, but no, to them it is just matter of fact. As Janet Mostert, Vaughan Anwyl's sister, said, 'I look at all this with a mixture of pride and embarrassment, we don't like fuss.' Or as his other sister Margaret Williams said, 'To be honest, our family tree was just something that was there, hanging on the wall. If it had been my husband, that would have been very different. He's fascinated by history.

'Only in his case he can only go back to 1700.'

But there may have been a clue to their survival among the slns in what she said next. 'We're just a family that loves to pootle along quietly.'

There are probably no political implications, though Plaid Cymru, the Welsh Nationalist Party, has in the past flirted with constitutional monarchy. But things have changed a lot since then. Representatives of the National Eisteddfod and the Gorsedd attended the Investiture of Prince Charles as Prince of Wales in 1969. In 2010, the new Archdruid said that they would not do so again. But then it has been a feature of both Investitures, the only ones ever held in Wales, that those who took part later showed a marked eagerness to distance themselves. The Duke of Windsor wrote of his 'preposterous rig', the knee breeches and coronet in which he appeared, and had to deliver one line of Welsh, *Mor o gân yw Cymru i gyd*. Anyone obliged to materialise in knee breeches in a medieval tower and inform the crowds beneath him that all Wales was a sea of song might have thought he was just one step ahead of the men in the white coats. And the Duke had his revenge: when he abdicated and went into exile he took the coronet with him, which meant another had to be commissioned for the 1969 ceremony.

Of this the Earl of Snowdon has said that the ceremony was 'bogus as Hell', and that his own costume had made him look like 'a cinema usherette from the 1950s or the panto character Buttons', overlooking the fact that he designed the costume himself.

But more to the point, Lord Elis-Thomas, Presiding Officer of the Welsh Assembly, has gone on record to say there should never again be an Investiture. Only he went further. He said the title of Prince of Wales was 'no longer relevant in the constitutional development long shifted to Wales's own institutions.' But that was before a home-grown candidate had been identified.

'Know what that king did?' I was trying to interest Vaughan Anwyl in his family. 'He put out the eyes of one of his nephews, then castrated him. He wouldn't have been a threat to the succession then.'

'Really?' said Mr Anwyl distantly.

It would make a wonderful black comedy, with Sir Anthony Hopkins as the head of the House of Aberffraw who, when a wanderer called to pay homage, did not offer him a cup of tea. I have talked about this to anyone who would listen.

> *Poni welwch-chwi hynt y gwynt a'r glaw?*
> *Poni welwch-chwi'r deri'n ymdaraw?*
>
> Don't you see the way of the wind and rain?
> Don't you see the oaks buffet together?

EPILOGUE

ALUN EVANS OF AMMANFORD, REMEMBRANCER

The bomber came down 13 years before he was born, crashing into the Black Mountain above the valley where he was raised, so a little boy grew up with the story. It is what happens with such events, but little boys forget: Alun Evans of Ammanford did not forget.

In another time Alun Evans would have been of the company of Aneirin and Lewys Glyn Cothi. This is the last remembrancer.

> *The Air Historical Branch,*
> *Ministry of Defence*
> *November 15, 1991.*

Dear Mr Evans,

Thank you for your letter enquiring about the circumstances in which Lancaster W 4929 was lost on September 5, 1943. From our records I have been able to find the following information:

The crew were engaged on a night navigational exercise over Wales when the aircraft crashed. The weather conditions were very bad, a heavy storm taking place...It can only be assumed that the loss was due to the storm...

Alun Evans found the wreckage in 1978. He had known something was up there, at around 1800 feet, ever since he heard the story that a party of hill walkers had come down and talked of seeing craters with twisted pieces of metal in them, also scattered ammunition. That they were still there was due to one fact: the Black Mountain, where Carmarthenshire meets the old county of Brecon, is a place where souvenir hunters dare not go.

Stray from its sheep tracks outside the brief window of summer and you face the very real possibility that you may not get down through the bogs and the sink holes. Up there the weather can change abruptly over what in parts is a vast trampoline, where, if you jump up and down, a companion 15 feet away can be thrown into the air. Men die on the Black Mountain, a man who crashed there later in the War being found dead on Christmas Day a mile from a village, having crawled down towards the lights which by then had come on again, the elbows and knees of his flying suit worn away. For the terrifying thing is that there is a sort of frontier up there which people know nothing about.

A small, unclassified road crosses its lower slopes, beside which in summer families picnic, not realising that if they went more than a hundred yards beyond this they would do so at their peril. Even now Alun Evans never goes up the mountain without leaving a route on a large-scale map for his wife, with detailed instructions as to when she should phone the police.

The map is in their parlour, a small room which, as he says, his wife was obliged long ago to forget had ever been part of their house. This is something which in west Wales is without precedent, for here there are no china cabinets of wedding presents, no photographs of small children, no balloon ladies on the mantelpiece. A huge wooden propeller stands behind the door, there are models of planes, bits of metal, and a whole wall given over to books and files; landing wheels collected from crashed planes are outside in a garden shed. 'A nice man,' said my cousin Gareth, a farmer in the hills, 'but you have to forget the rest of the day if you get him talking about the Second World War.'

When I met him, Alun Evans was the pest control officer, 'rat-catcher, if you like', of what was once the small mining town of Ammanford. Here, in the valley, he had always been fascinated by flight, and, in particular, by the end of flight, something he would have found it difficult to avoid: on the mountain to the north-east the planes came down, six of them within a radius of five miles.

The first thing he saw when he found the site of the crash was a long ditch torn into the side of the mountain and, in front of this, four deep gouges. It was an awesome sight, for there had clearly been such a fireball there that nothing had subsequently been able to grow in these. The gouges indicated to him that this had been a four-engined bomber, and as he searched among the pieces of metal he noted the shape of a casting, a squashed piece of exhaust stub and part of an inlet manifold which together spelt out Rolls-

Royce Merlin engines. Four Merlins equalled a Lancaster bomber. But was it a wartime crash?

There were no markings to indicate a squadron, but the flakes of matt black paint indicated the wartime night camouflage of Bomber Command. Then on the bullets scattered around he came on dates of manufacture, 1941, 1942, 1943, but no bullets after that. He realised everything was coming together: a Lancaster of Bomber Command had crashed here at some point in 1943.

Then, by chance, he found a book, *The Lancaster File*, published by Air Britain, in which three crashes in Wales were indexed for 1943, for this was a time when young men were being let loose on the skies just as now they are being let loose on the roads in Ford Transits (almost every one of the 350 wartime crashes in Wales was a training flight, though in folklore they have become those of German bombers). One crash was near the town of Haverfordwest, a second near Llanwrtyd Wells, but the third was in an area he had never heard of, listed simply as 'Brecon Firth.'

'It had to be the one, I could imagine some man with Home Counties vowels shouting down a phone on a rainy night back in 1943, trying to make sense of Welsh place-names. Later I found that the brothers of one of those on board had given up their attempt to locate the crash when they found this listed as Rhydwenfach. They thought it a town in Wales, which they couldn't find on any map. They were not to know that it was just a hill on a large-scale Ordnance Survey.'

But from *The Lancaster File* he had a number now, W4929, and a date, September 5, 1943: he wrote the first of what were to be many letters to the Ministry, and the reply on November 15, 1991 changed the whole nature of his quest.

> *The crew were as follows: Pilot Officer N.T. Duxbury, pilot; Sgt. J.G. Curran, air gunner; Sgt. E. Buckby, Royal Australian Air Force, air gunner; Pilot Officer V.R. Volkerson (sic), Royal Canadian Air Force, navigator; Sgt. L. Holding, flight engineer; Pilot Officer T.F.E. Johnson Distinguished Flying Medal, bomb aimer; Sgt. F.W. Pratt, air gunner; Sgt. B. Wilson, bomb aimer.*

So suddenly it was not the Lancaster 4929 which had crashed on the mountain, it was eight young men. And it was this that changed the whole nature of his quest.

'My children were small, and I wondered whether these men had had children, whether they had been married, and it was then I decided to trace their families.

'It seemed to me that if any of these were still alive all these years later, then they must often have wondered where it took place, this event that had changed their lives. I was up there when I thought this, and I looked at that desolate place and there was nothing at all around me to say what had happened there. And it came to me: I would see to it that these men were remembered.'

When he looks back now it is on years of letters, writing these 'night after night, letter after letter.' A letter to the Commonwealth War Graves Commission: this brought the location of their burial places, also the names of their next of kin. Only of course half a century had passed; the next of kin had died or moved, names had been misspelt. The air-mail letters began.

> *Department of Defence,*
> *Canberra.*
>
> *Dear Mr Evans,*
> *Re: Flight Sergeant Ernest Middleton Bucky (sic). Enlisted: July 18,*
> *1942. Mustering: air gunner. Overseas Service: United Kingdom,*
> *from March 5, 1943, to September 5, 1943. Deceased: killed as a*
> *result of a flying accident on 5 September, 1943.*

There were other misspellings. The War Graves Commission said they had no details of a Canadian called 'Volkerson', but the Canadian authorities confirmed the navigator's name as Folkersen, and, remarkably, it emerged that Folkersen Lake in Saskatchewan had been named after him.

Alun Evans was by now assembling details of the Lancaster's last flight. It had taken off from RAF Winthorpe near Newark with a trainee crew of seven, plus Pilot Officer T.F.E. Johnson, a veteran bomb aimer of 30 operations. It had been a Sunday when, just after tea, they had headed north to practise bombing runs off the Scottish coast. They were returning when at night over Wales they ran into the storm and then into the mountain rising abruptly out of the fields of Carmarthenshire. The time of the crash was 11.40 pm, 20 minutes to midnight, an exact time for in the nearby village of Llanddeusant, people had felt the explosion and seen a fireball light up the sky. Yet in the awful weather the local Home Guard were unable to find the crashed plane that night.

At this stage Alun Evans was still among facts as recorded by a remote bureaucracy: names, ages, squadrons. For anything else he knew he would have to contact the families. But how? The War Graves Commission, having provided him with the names of the next of kin and those of the towns where they then lived, had said it was not its policy to give addresses as well. It added gently that by now these would be of little use anyway.

That was when Alun Evans, getting the names of local papers from his reference library, began to advertise in these, and, having started to think of some kind of memorial on the mountain, had had a brief announcement to that effect read out on BBC radio on, of all things, the Charlie Chester Show, a rambling assembly of records and chat by the old comedian. Alun Evans used to listen to the Charlie Chester Show, and it is one of the lovely little details in the story.

It was after this that it came, the letter he had waited so long for, half dreading its coming.

July 12, 1993.

Dear Mr Evans,
I am the youngest brother of Sgt. Frank William Pratt 1271536, who was killed in Lancaster W4929 on 5.9.43 in Wales...

For how would the families react to him, an outsider intruding on an old grief? He replied immediately, telling Les Pratt on the phone of how he intended to erect some kind of memorial stone, and within a week the second letter came, a very different kind of letter.

July 19, 1993.

Dear Alun,
Thank you for your phone-call. My brother Ron and I thank you
for all the kind work that you have done to commemorate Frank
and the crew...

No formality now, a family was opening to receive him as though he were an old friend they had just met again. Eventually he got used to such letters; what he did not get used to was the poignancy that was in all their first paragraphs.

August 19, 1993.

Dear Mr Evans,
I am Nan Wareham, formerly Johnson...My husband, Pilot Officer
T.F.E. Johnson DFM, was the navigator on the training flight...

Nan Wareham, now widowed again, recalled how she had felt when, having been traced by the Pratt brothers, she had heard of Alun Evans's quest. 'It was almost unbelievable: I'd not known where the crash was, except I'd read on the death certificate that it had been somewhere on what was called the Van Foel hills. So I'd known the general area, and for years I hadn't wanted to go anywhere near, but in time that goes to the back of your mind. I'd shed all my tears long ago, and life had gone on, though it had been a different life from the one I thought it would be...'

Through Mrs Wareham, Alun Evans glimpsed the bleakness of that moment when it arrives, what the writer Jack Trevor Story called 'the receipt', the official telegram. 'Deeply regret to inform you that your husband 145822...' Then the letters. 'Madam, I am commanded by the Air Council to express to you their great regret...' And then perhaps the bleakest of all, the stocktaking. 'Dear Mrs Johnson, I wish to advise you that the personal effects of your late husband have been forwarded to the Central Depository, Slough...I have on hand at this station one BSA ladies' cycle and I shall be obliged if you will let me know whether you wish this to be forwarded to your home address.' Nan Wareham, who received each of these in turn, was 20 years old.

There was a glimpse of the man in a talk given on BBC radio by a Mrs Brodie, an attendant at a swimming pool in Lincoln much frequented by the bomber crews. 'Nan is Johnny's wife, and he used to talk to me about her. He had told her that if he didn't come home he wanted her to carry on as if it was just one of those things. And if she found another fellow – well, he wanted her to be happy.'

Photographs, some a little faded, had started coming through the post, and Alun Evans saw neat young men smiling under the planes. People wrote, who had been at school with them or had known their families. 'My own letters went out, and sometimes there was nothing, sometimes there was a blitz.' He wrote to the mayors of small Australian and Canadian towns, wondering as he did so what sort of landscapes those who received them would be looking out on as they opened his letters. Newspapers thousands of miles away heard of his quest, and letters began coming from Swift Current and Brisbane, so suddenly Flight Sergeant Buckby was 'Ernie', and Pilot Officer Folkersen 'Vic'.

And there were other glimpses, this time of the world the eight young men had so briefly shared a half century ago. In a tattered copy of *The Air Gunner's Lament*, Alun Evans came on their forced cynicism.

> A young aviator lay dying
> At the close of a bright summer's day.
> All his comrades were gathered about him
> To carry his fragments away.
> 'Take the sparking plugs out of my elbows,
> Take the aerial out of my brain.
> If you look near my furthest appendix
> There's the rest of the old aeroplane.
> Slip the battery plates out of my elbows.
> Take the butterfly valves off my neck,
> Take the lead off my feet, get busy.
> There's a lot of good parts in the wreck.

There was a terrible irony to all this for when the coffins were sent on to the relatives these came with instructions that on no account were they to be opened. But one father did, saying he had to see his son for the last time. He went into the parlour alone, and when he came out he did not say anything but took his cap and coat and went down the pub, something no one in his family could remember him doing. He never talked about what he had seen.

At first Alun Evans had thought of paying the cost of a memorial himself, but then he met Seimon Pugh-Jones, a fellow flight enthusiast in the Ministry of Defence's research establishment at Pendine, who told his colleagues there about the quest. They made a small memorial in concrete, and attached a brass plate on which they wrote the names of the crew, also a line from a Welsh hymn, *A bu tawelwch ar ôl y ddrycin faith.* And there was peace after the lengthy storm.

It was also through Pugh-Jones that the Search and Rescue helicopter squadron based at Brawdy became involved. If there was to be a ceremony Alun Evans wanted the families present, and, half a century having passed, some means had to be found of getting them up there, also of transporting the stone. From Brawdy the languid letter came.

> *…September 5th this year is a Sunday, and would thus be a good day for us to venture into the hills, since the fast jet fraternity only work part-time and will be on their golf courses.*

But then things began to go wrong. That August, a month before the ceremony, grief came to a man who had sifted through the griefs of so many others, when his own father died suddenly. Whether because of this or because of the responsibility of co-ordinating the travel plans of so many old people, he found as summer became autumn on the mountain he could no longer find the crash site. He had gone down with a chest infection but, refusing anti-biotics so as to keep his mind clear, he tried once again, going up the mountain with a member of the local walking club. That was the Tuesday before the Sunday morning of the ceremony, and he looked, as he put it, like something out of a Passion play. On his back he had two seven-foot marker boards, which he intended to use so the helicopter could find a landing site. The two men were also carrying shovels, cement and chippings, so a base could be built for the memorial stone.

Alun Evans was near to despair, for, in spite of all his compass readings, he still could not find the site. 'There was a point when I couldn't tell what was sky and which was mountain. My throat was as rough as a cuttlefish bone, and I thought all my work had come to nothing, when I heard my companion, Wyn Jenkins, shout from what seemed to be miles away. He had come on some torn metal.'

They mixed cement to make the footing, and pinned down the boards so the descending helicopter would not send the pieces of metal into the air. Everything was ready.

The relatives were coming, Pilot Officer Johnson's widow, the Pratt brothers and their families, Sergeant Holding's cousin; 15 of them in all. The Canadian and Australian families could not make the trip, neither could Sergeant Curran's cousin or Sergeant Wilson's widow, whom Alun Evans had managed to trace too late. He had been unable to find any relatives of Duxbury, the pilot, though some friends had written.

Then, on Thursday night, RAF St Athans phoned to say that their chaplain, who had agreed to conduct the service, would be unable to attend. Where in west Wales, at two days' notice, would Alun Evans find a priest free on a Sunday morning? It was then he remembered a story in his local paper that a retired RAF chaplain, a group captain, had come to live in the area. At 10.20 pm the group captain returned his call to say that in other circumstances he would have been honoured, but that he now found walking difficult, let alone the ascent of a mountain. There was no problem, said Alun Evans airily; he had a helicopter.

It came out of the morning, a huge yellow thing, and Alun Evans, who had staggered up the mountain with even more cement and chippings, watched as its rotors flattened the grass. Then, with difficulty, for they were old now, and one was in a wheelchair, they climbed out, the people he had waited so long to meet. It was an end.

And a beginning.